Label-Prefixes

Label-Prefix	Function
' (apostrophe)	Left-aligned (program default unless changed)
^ (circumflex)	Centered
" (double quote)	Right-aligned (like values)
\ (backslash)	Repeats character typed after it across entire cell width.
¦ (broken vertical)	Instructs 1-2-3 not to print the row it precedes.

Arithmetic and Logical Operators

Operator	Meaning	Operator	Meaning
^	Exponentiation	<	Less than
+	Addition	>	Greater than
−	Subtraction	< >	Not equal to
*	Multiplication	#AND#	Logical AND
/	Division	#OR#	Logical OR
+ , −	Positive, Negative		

The ABC's of 1-2-3®
Release 2.2

Chris Gilbert

Laurie Williams

SYBEX®

SAN FRANCISCO · PARIS · DÜSSELDORF · LONDON

Acquisitions Editor: Dianne King
Supervising Editor: Joanne Cuthbertson
Copy Editor: Alan Hislop
Technical Editor: Aziz Khatri
Word Processors: Chris Mockel and Scott Campbell
Book Designer: Jeffrey James Giese
Part Art: Helen Bruno
Screen Graphics: Sonja Schenk
Typesetter: Winnie Kelly
Proofreader: Ami Knox
Indexer: Ted Laux
Cover Designer: Thomas Ingalls + Associates
Cover Photographer: David Bishop
Screen reproductions produced by XenoFont

dBASE is a trademark of Ashton-Tate.
DIF is a trademark of Lotus Development Corporation.
DisplayWrite and IBM are trademarks of International Business Machines Corporation.
Epson is a trademark of Epson America, Inc.
HP LaserJet is a trademark of Hewlett-Packard Corporation.
Lotus, 1-2-3, and Symphony are trademarks of Lotus Development Corporation.
Multiplan is a trademark of Microsoft Corporation.
VisiCalc is a trademark of VisiCorp., Inc.
XenoFont is a trademark of XenoSoft.

SYBEX is a registered trademark of SYBEX, Inc.

SYBEX is not affiliated with any manufacturer.

Every effort has been made to supply complete and accurate information. However, SYBEX assumes no responsibility for its use, nor for any infringements of patents or other rights of third parties which would result.

Library of Congress Card Number: 89-62753
ISBN 0-89588-623-5
Manufactured in the United States of America
10 9 8 7 6 5

To R.J.L.

—L.W.

To Mom for the computer.

—C.G.

Acknowledgments

Thanks to Janos Gereben, without whom *The ABC's of 1-2-3* would have been only another "good idea," Rick Nielsen whose timely appearance and positive thinking were crucial, and Professor Fred Friedman, who was so generous with his time and educational expertise.

Contents at a Glance

Table of Contents

Part Two
Building a Worksheet

Part Three

Using a Worksheet

Part Four

Graphing the Worksheet

Part Five

Database Management

Part Six

Macros

Part Seven

Functions

Part Eight

The Allways Spreadsheet Publisher

Introduction

If you've never used Lotus 1-2-3 before and want to learn how, this book is for you. Written in nontechnical, everyday English, it introduces 1-2-3 simply and practically in a series of 67 lessons. The product of two authors—one with the technical background to teach corporate users, the other a novice who had never before used the program—the book is a readable, easy-to-follow set of explanations and instructions that anyone can follow, including those who have never operated a computer.

This book is written for use with IBM and IBM-compatible personal computers. The keyboard will vary slightly from model to model. For example, depending on the computer, the key that instructs 1-2-3 to perform an operation may be labeled with a symbol, such as an arrow, or by a word, such as Return or Enter. If you don't know which keys on your keyboard correspond to the keys in the book's instructions, refer to your computer manual.

This book is written especially for use with Release 2.2 of 1-2-3. If you are using a version of the program earlier than Release 2.2, bypass the initialization procedure in Part 1, Lesson 2. You will notice some discrepancies between releases but they are minor. (For a detailed list of the differences between versions, refer to 1-2-3 documentation, *Upgraders Handbook*.)

The book is designed so that you can begin working immediately. The first part, "Getting Started," consists of five lessons. If you just purchased 1-2-3 and have never used it on your computer, follow the instructions that fit your computer's disk system, floppy or hard. This will take approximately one-half to one hour, and it is recommended that it be done in one sitting.

For floppy-disk computers, if 1-2-3 has already been set up to operate on your computer, but you do not have an extra, specially prepared disk on which to save your work, read the introductory explanations for each of the five lessons but follow *only* the instructions in Lesson 1, "Starting Your Computer," and Lesson 3, "Preparing Blank Disks and Making Backup Copies of 1-2-3: For Floppy-Disk Systems Only."

If 1-2-3 is set up to work on your computer and you have disks already prepared on which to store your work, do Lesson 1, skim the next four lessons, without completing the instructions, then continue with Lesson 6, "Displaying a Blank Worksheet."

Does the Following Sound Familiar?

You're working on a report, and you need to compile a lot of numbers. Your employer just purchased the Lotus 1-2-3 software program, and you can't wait to start calculating your figures, forecasting profits, and creating fancy graphs. You've never operated a computer and, although they do sound familiar, you have to admit you don't know what disks, drives, and database management really are.

"No problem," you tell yourself, "with the manual, I'll be able to do it in no time."

Two hours later, you're still trying to figure out how to get the program to run.

"And I thought all I had to do was slip in the program, turn on the machine, and start entering . . . ," you mumble under your breath.

If this sounds familiar, you're not alone. You're in the company of other somewhat confused first-time computer users, among whom are small business owners who need to keep track of inventory, college administrators who need an effective means of presenting budgets to the board, division sales managers who need to forecast sales over the next six months, shop owners who want to determine which items are most profitable, teachers who want to analyze test scores to evaluate innovative programs, accounts-receivable clerks who need to mail hundreds of bills every month, and the entrepreneur who wants to open a chain of stores but first must gather information about particular neighborhoods. In fact, anyone who is even vaguely aware of what 1-2-3 can do will be eager to see immediate results.

What Can 1-2-3 Do?

On its own, nothing. But with your data input and instructions, you have at your fingertips a powerful, integrated program that combines three programs in one: a worksheet (or spreadsheet) program, a graphics program, and a database management program. A closer look at each of these three components best illustrates how you can conveniently put several capabilities to work without having to use a new program or a new set of instructions.

The first and most sophisticated of the three, the *worksheet,* electronically duplicates an accountant's or bookkeeper's tools: a ledger pad, a pencil, an eraser, and a calculator. With the worksheet, however, you enter and correct figures by typing on a keyboard, rather than writing with a pencil, and you view the figures on a computer screen, or monitor, rather than read a ledger pad.

Once you enter data on the worksheet, you can apply a variety of calculations—from simple addition, subtraction, multiplication, and division to trigonometric, statistical, and business calculations. With the worksheet you can prepare such things as

- Budgets
- Annual reports
- Portfolio analyses
- Accounts payable and receivable
- Production schedules
- Invoices
- Income statements
- Loan analyses
- Tax statements

In addition to entering and calculating numbers, the worksheet responds to "what if" scenarios. For example, let's assume you own a retail business and you want to know how a holiday sale will affect your profit. You start by entering the current prices of the items you are selling, the number of items for sale, and the cost of each item.

After entering a formula to calculate your projected profit without the sale, you can recalculate to answer the question: If I put several items on sale for 30 percent less, how will this affect profit? As you enter each new figure, 1-2-3 automatically recalculates profit and displays the answer on the screen.

But that's only the beginning. By expanding this particular worksheet to include overhead and salaries, you can ask more questions, such as: How will a drop in overhead or an increase in salaries affect profit? And, if you want to discuss the results with others in the office, you can print copies of each version of the worksheet.

The second component, *graphics,* enables you to create various kinds of graphs, such as a bar or line graph, from the information on the worksheet. To continue with the previous example, the retail profits before and after the sale can be charted on a bar graph, where they can be compared visually. The visual impact of the graph makes it an effective communication tool since it is simpler to interpret a graph than it is to interpret columns of numbers—and not so boring.

Although you may not realize it, you probably have in your possession several examples of *database management,* 1-2-3's third component. Do you keep an address book in your briefcase? What about a notebook where you tally up your work-related car mileage and bridge tolls? Do you keep your paycheck stubs in order? Each is a source of information, as well as a means of managing it; hence, each is a database. Other examples are personnel files, inventory lists, customer records, and "to do" lists. The major difference between managing any of these examples and using database management to do it for you is that 1-2-3 can instantly retrieve and reorganize all the information without consuming time by turning pages or searching through files.

Another advantage of 1-2-3's database management is that it can retrieve and organize by using any one piece of the database. For example, consider a traditional phone book as a database. You can find the phone number of a friend only if you know your friend's last name. With 1-2-3, however, you could find his phone number by entering his address or the first three numbers of his phone number. 1-2-3 can index every category of information: first name, last name, address, and phone number. Plugging in any one piece brings up the entire entry.

In addition to the three main components, 1-2-3 offers a fourth, more complex feature: *keyboard macros,* which simplify tasks that you find yourself doing over and over again, such as typing the twelve months of the year across the top of every budget you prepare. Rather than retype the headings each time, you can program your computer to do this for you automatically with two keystrokes. The set of instructions included in the keystrokes is called a macro. Keyboard macros are especially helpful on forms such as invoices that require you to type the same information hundreds or thousands of times.

A note of warning, though. Macros are considered an advanced use of 1-2-3. While there are some simple macros that a beginner can quickly put to use, it helps to be familiar with programming procedures.

Now let's take a closer look at how the four features interact. To do so, assume you are an accountant for a firm that manufactures industrial equipment for fertilizer plants. It's October, and you are conscientiously preparing some figures for your annual report, which you will present at the January board meeting. An early draft should save time, you think to yourself.

You start by finding the dollar values of your assets and liabilities. 1-2-3 calculates your total inventory value from a list in the data base, which includes the number of items on hand and their value at cost. From several other worksheets, you transfer more figures, such as cash on hand, accounts payable and receivable, fixed assets, and outstanding loans. Once you've calculated net worth, you want to see what percentage of total assets is represented by inventory. With a few keystrokes, a pie chart represents the unsold inventory as a large part of assets. (So far, everything you've done has required only a few keystrokes because you've speeded up this annual task by using macros.)

But it's only October. What will happen to net worth if half of the inventory is shipped C.O.D. before the end of the year? 1-2-3 recalculates the figures, and you view the graph again. The results are more positive. But how do the results compare to figures for the past five years? From previous budgets you transfer the end-of-year figures for all five years to a line graph, and again the results are impressive. After adding some last-minute labels, you print several copies and show them to the sales department managers to see if they agree with your projections.

What Can This Book Do for You?

Because 1-2-3 is a powerful business tool, it can be complex. If you've never used a computer before, just learning how to get started will take time. The program manual and its accompanying on-screen lessons are excellent reference tools, but each requires several hours of reading before you can begin to take advantage of 1-2-3's capabilities. The manual does not help the novice make use of the program from the very start, and the on-screen lessons do not leave room for experimentation. Each explains how to operate the program, but not how to apply it.

This book does both. In a sense, this book, like the program, is integrated. It provides step-by-step instructions that get you started immediately while it explains each step. As a hands-on introduction for the novice, it is meant to be read while you operate the computer. You will produce results while you learn, and, since you will learn how as well as why, you will be able to apply what you learn to your own work. Part 8, "The Allways Spreadsheet Publisher," will enable you to produce a sophisticated, professional-looking printed version of your worksheet, enhanced by graphics and printed in different colors (if you have a color printer).

Since each step builds on preceding steps, it is necessary to follow them in order. However, after you complete the lessons once, you can use this book as a reference guide. By the time you finish reading it, you will have built a worksheet, displayed the worksheet as a graph, built a database, and simplified several operations using some simple macros. Along the way, you will accomplish many more related tasks, such as calculating data within the worksheet and printing reports.

Never Used a Computer Before?

No problem. Everything is explained, step-by-step, throughout the book. A quick overview of how your computer works, though, will set you straight from the very start.

What is normally referred to as a computer is actually a computer system that consists of microprocessors (which include the brains and memory), a display screen, a printer, a keyboard, and storage devices such as disks. These, and any other pieces of equipment you might add to your system, are called *hardware*.

In order for the entire system to operate, it needs instructions, or *software programs.* The basic set of instructions needed to run the computer is referred to as *DOS,* for disk operating system. Another example of a software program is 1-2-3 itself.

Programs are generally stored on floppy disks (also called diskettes) or hard disks. 1-2-3 can be used on both floppy-disk and hard-disk systems. Floppy disks are thin, circular sheets of plastic like the ones your 1-2-3 program came on. Looking like undersized 45 rpm records, they are enclosed in square jackets to protect them from damage. The plastic is coated with a substance that the computer encodes with magnetic impulses, much as a stereo tape deck encodes music on a tape cassette. Hard disks operate similarly, but instead of being thin and soft, they are rigid.

1-2-3 comes on either 5-1/4-inch or 3-1/2-inch floppy disks, each of which can store about 180 or 360 pages of double-spaced text, respectively. In contrast, a hard disk can store at least 5,000 pages of text.

Unless your computer can find its DOS operating instructions on a floppy or hard disk and place them in its memory (or RAM, for *random access memory*), the computer is useless for programs such as 1-2-3. One of the disk drives must *read* a disk on which DOS resides. Depending on the kind of disk drives you have, DOS may be stored on a floppy disk that you insert in one of the two floppy-disk drives or it may be stored on a hard disk that is permanently sealed in a hard-disk drive.

Computers that use 1-2-3 have either two floppy-disk drives or one or two floppy drives paired with a hard-disk drive. Each drive has a one-letter name to identify it. The floppy-disk drives are called drive A and drive B. The hard-disk drive is normally drive C.

Because the computer's memory is short-term, it forgets everything as soon as you turn it off, including how to operate. Therefore DOS must be read from disk to memory every time you want to operate your computer. This is commonly referred to as *bootstrapping* or *booting* the computer because the machine pulls itself up by its bootstraps.

A

C

B

1

3

1

2

2

Part One

Getting Started

LESSON

1

Starting Your Computer

FEATURING

The Enter key
The Backspace key
The Shift key
The Ctrl key
The Break key

You are seated at your computer, ready to begin using 1-2-3. The manuals are neatly stacked on your right; the disks on your left. Where to begin?

First, start your computer. Follow the instructions below that fit your computer's disk system: floppy or hard. Then continue to the next four lessons in Part 1, "Getting Started," if you are putting 1-2-3 onto your computer for the first time. If 1-2-3 is already set up for your computer, after this lesson skip to Part 2, "Building a Worksheet."

In this first lesson you will use five keys in addition to letters and numbers on your keyboard: the Enter, Backspace, Shift, Control, and Break keys shown in Figure 1.1. When you press Enter, 1-2-3 is instructed to perform any instructions you have typed and to proceed to the next step. When you press Backspace, you erase what you have just typed, one character at a time to the left. The Shift key, pressed in conjunction with another key, types uppercase letters and makes available all the punctuation and symbols on the top halves of the keys.

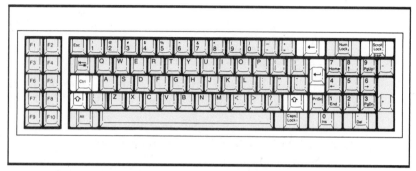

Figure 1.1: *The Enter, Backspace, Shift, Ctrl, and Break Keys*

The Ctrl and Break keys are used together to interrupt a procedure. If necessary, you can interrupt initialization and cancel your entries by pressing these two keys.

How to Start Your Computer

If You Have a Floppy-Disk System

1. Place the operating system (DOS) disk for your computer in drive A (the one on the left if the drives are side by side, or the one on top if the drives are one above the other). To ensure that you don't erase the DOS disk, use a copy if you have one. Do not touch any of the disk's exposed areas, and be sure that the long, oval slot is toward the back of the computer. The label should face up if the disk is inserted horizontally or to the left if the disk is inserted vertically.

2. Close the drive door.

3. Turn on the computer. Wait a few moments. As the DOS programs are read into the computer, a whirring sound is emitted.

4. Enter the date and time if necessary. (Some computers automatically display the date and time since they contain internal clocks. If your computer does, you do not need to type them in.) Although various ways of typing the date are acceptable, one is recommended for simplicity's sake. If it were July 3,

1990, you would enter:

7-3-90

If you make a mistake, use the Backspace key to correct it.

5. Press Enter. If the word **Invalid** appears, you've made an error. Repeat step four and press Enter.

6. Type in the current time. Again, one way is recommended. If it were 8:20 in the morning, you would enter:

8:20

If you prefer, you can add seconds after another colon; however, seconds, as well as minutes, are optional. When it is after 12 noon, hours are entered the way they are referred to in the military: 1:00 PM is 13:00, 4:15 PM is 16:15, and so on.

7. Press Enter. The **A>** prompt will appear on the screen. It means you are using drive A.

If you made a mistake typing the date or time, you may reenter them by typing DATE and pressing Enter or TIME and pressing Enter and then retyping the correct date or time.

If You Have a Hard-Disk System

1. Turn on the computer. Wait a few moments. As the DOS programs are read into the computer, a whirring sound is emitted.

2. Enter the date and time if necessary. (Some computers automatically display the date and time since they contain internal clocks. If your computer does, you do not need to type them in.) Although various ways of typing the date are acceptable, one is recommended for simplicity's sake. If it were July 3, 1990, you would enter:

7-3-90

If you make a mistake, use the Backspace key to correct it.

3. Press Enter. If the word **Invalid** appears, you've made an error. Repeat step two and press Enter.

4. Type in the current time. Again, one way is recommended. If it were 8:20 in the morning, you would enter:

8:20

If you prefer, you can add seconds after another colon; however, seconds, as well as minutes, are optional. When it is after 12 noon, hours are entered the way they are referred to in the military: 1:00 PM is 13:00, 4:15 PM is 16:15, and so on.

5. Press Enter. The **C>** prompt will appear on the screen.

If you made a mistake typing the date or time, you may reenter them by typing DATE and pressing Enter or TIME and pressing Enter and then retyping the correct date or time.

2

Initializing 1-2-3 (Release 2.2)

FEATURING

Recording your name and company name

If you are using Release 2.2, you must initialize 1-2-3. Initializing records your name and company name as the licensee on the original system disk. The procedure is necessary to start 1-2-3, and it is done once only; thereafter, your initials and company name will appear on the first screen displayed when you start 1-2-3.

Only users of 1-2-3 Release 2.2 must complete the following steps. If you have a prior version of 1-2-3, skip ahead to Lesson 3.

How to Initialize 1-2-3 (Release 2.2)— Floppy- and Hard-Disk Systems

1. With your computer on, insert the System disk into one of the floppy drives of your computer.

2. Change to the floppy drive. For example, if the System disk is in drive A, type **A:** and press Enter.

3. Type: **INIT**.

4. Press Enter. The copyright screen appears.

5. To continue, press Enter again. A screen describing the initialization process is displayed.

6. Read the screen and press Enter when you are ready to start the process. (To stop at this point without initializing 1-2-3, hold down the Ctrl key and tap the Break key. This will end the process. To start again type **INIT** at the DOS prompt.)

7. At the name prompt, type your first and last name. If you make a mistake, use the Backspace key to correct it.

8. When you finish typing your name, press Enter.

9. To confirm that your name is correct, type **Y** and press Enter.

(If it is not correct, type **N**, press Enter, and correct it using the Backspace key.)

10. Type your company's name or type your name again.

11. Press Enter.

12. Confirm that your entry is correct. Type **Y** and press Enter.

(Again, if it is not, type **N**, press Enter, and correct it as described previously.)

A screen displays your entries. Once you press Enter to confirm that the entries are correct, you will not be able to change this information. It will be permanently encoded on your 1-2-3 System disk. Each time you start 1-2-3, this information will flash on the screen prior to the worksheet.

13. To confirm that the entries are correct, press Enter. To cancel and start over, hold down the Ctrl key and press the Break key.

14. Press Enter to exit.

LESSON

3

Preparing Blank Disks and Making Backup Copies of 1-2-3: For Floppy-Disk Systems Only

FEATURING

DOS format
DOS copy

Imagine how frustrated you would feel if you had just spilled a cup of hot tea on the 1-2-3 System disk. To be sure that you don't risk losing your disks and your investment, it is always advisable to make copies of the original 1-2-3 disks. Then if you destroy or lose one of your copies, you will still have the original.

Before you can copy the 1-2-3 disks, you must first prepare or *format* additional diskettes. When a disk is formatted, it is divided into sectors, much like slices of a pie, and tracks, which are like grooves in a record. These sectors and tracks store information in *files*. A *directory* of file names is created from all the files stored on a particular disk.

For 1-2-3, Release 2.2, you will be making copies of all of the 1-2-3 disks, except the Allways diskettes. For older versions of 1-2-3 (1A, 2.0, and 2.01), the System disk and its backup copy are copy-protected; these two disks cannot be copied. (However, for Releases 2.0 and 2.01, Lotus Development Corporation makes a special program to unlock the copy protection. Contact Lotus Development Corporation for the program.) Check your manual to determine which release of 1-2-3 you have.

For each 1-2-3 disk that you plan to copy, you will need one formatted disk. In addition, you will need a formatted disk to store your work. For Release 2.2, if you are using 5-1/4" disks you will format eight disks; if you are using 3-1/2" disks you will format four disks.

You will format these disks only once. Never format a disk that contains valuable data; it will all be erased. You can use disks with data that you no longer need, however.

Have a sufficient number of diskettes on hand before you begin. Be sure you have an extra one on which to store your work.

If you have a hard-disk computer, skip to Lesson 4.

How to Format a Diskette

Do not use the 1-2-3 Program disks for the next steps on formatting disks.

1. As explained in Lesson 1, start your computer and be sure that the **A >** is displayed. Type:

   FORMAT B:

   (You may use either uppercase or lowercase letters.)

2. Press Enter.

3. Place the disk to be formatted in drive B.

4. Press any key. When the red light(s) on the disk drive(s) goes off, indicating that formatting has finished, remove the newly formatted diskette and set it aside.

5. After the Format another (Y,N)? prompt appears, type:

   Y

6. Insert the second diskette to be formatted in the appropriate drive and repeat the same process until the remaining blank diskettes are all formatted.

7. When you have finished formatting and the *Format another (Y,N)?* message appears, type:

   N

   The **A>** appears on the screen.

8. Put blank labels on the diskettes and proceed to make copies of the program diskettes.

How to Copy Your 1-2-3 Program Disks

1. Have on hand all 1-2-3 disks except the Allways disks for Release 2.2. We recommend that you place a gummed write-protect tab over the small rectangular slot cut in on the right side of each diskette. This tab protects the disk from being erased accidentally, but it allows you to copy information from the diskette. To store new information on the diskette, you would have to remove the tab. Write-protect tabs come with your 1-2-3 disks and are included in boxes of new blank diskettes.

2. Place any one of the 1-2-3 diskettes in drive A. (For releases of 1-2-3 prior to 2.2, you cannot copy the System disks.)

3. Place a formatted diskette in drive B.

4. At the **A>**, type:

   COPY A:*.* B:

5. Press Enter. This command tells your computer to copy all of the files on the diskette in drive A to the diskette in drive B. As the files are copied, their names appear on the screen.

6. When the screen tells you copying is complete, remove both disks. Write the name of the disk on the label, being sure not to use a metal-tipped writing tool like a ball point pen, which can harm the diskette. Use a plastic- or felt-tipped pen or soft pencil.

7. Repeat steps 2 through 6 until all 1-2-3 disks have been copied.

8. Place the DOS disk in drive A. Place the System disk copy in drive B. (For releases prior to 1-2-3, Release 2.2, use the original System disk if copy-protected.)

9. After the **A>**, type:

   COPY A:COMMAND.COM B:

10. Press Enter. This command copies the command.com file from the DOS disk to the System disk. This file will enable you to perform DOS-level tasks, such as erasing and renaming files, from within 1-2-3, rather than having to exit to the operating system.

11. Repeat the previous three steps for the copies of the Print-Graph and Install disks. When you are finished, the **A>** appears on the screen.

Floppy-disk system users should skip the next lesson and proceed to Lesson 5, "Installing 1-2-3 on Floppy-Disk and Hard-Disk Systems."

4

Storing 1-2-3 on a Hard Disk

FEATURING

Running 1-2-3 from a hard disk

The fastest way to run 1-2-3 is from a hard disk. Once the steps in this lesson are completed, you will be able to run 1-2-3 from your hard disk.

In order to keep your hard disk organized, it is best to store the 1-2-3 program files in a separate area of the hard disk called a *sub-directory.* This will separate the files from other programs, such as word processing files.

Have on hand all diskettes that came with 1-2-3. If you are using Release 2.2, do not include the Allways diskettes.

How to Store 1-2-3 on a Hard Disk

1. With your computer on, place the 1-2-3 System disk in drive A, the floppy drive.

2. Make a directory named 123. After the C>, type:

   MD \123

3. Press Enter.

4. To change to the new directory, type:

   CD \123

5. Press Enter.

6. Now copy the 1-2-3 files from the System disk in A into the subdirectory. After the C>, type:

   COPY A:*.* C:

7. Press Enter. This command copies all the files on the floppy disk onto the hard disk.

8. Once the copy is complete, replace the System disk with any of the remaining disks and repeat steps 6 and 7.

9. Leave your computer on and proceed to Lesson 5, "Installing 1-2-3 on Floppy-Disk and Hard-Disk Systems."

5

Installing 1-2-3 on Floppy-Disk and Hard-Disk Systems

FEATURING

The Access System
The arrow keys
The Escape key
F1 (Help)
F9
F10

Assume that you are about to ride a bicycle blindfolded and you do not know what kind of bicycle it is. Knowing whether it is a three-speed, a ten-speed, or a unicycle would probably influence how you attempt to ride it.

1-2-3 is also influenced by the kind of equipment on which it operates, but unlike the blindfolded bicyclist, it cannot depend on trial and error. 1-2-3 must have the information in advance. For example, 1-2-3 needs to know what kind of printer you are using. Do you have a laser printer or a dot-matrix printer?

To tell 1-2-3 about your equipment, you will use the installation procedure to create a file called a *driver set*. Each *driver* in the set identifies some aspect of your equipment. The installation procedure prompts you to identify exactly what kind of equipment you are using. Before you start, therefore, you should know what kind of computer, monitor, monitor card, and printer you have. Check your manuals if you are not sure.

To start the installation procedure, you will select an option from the Lotus Access System menu. A *menu* is a list of options from which you can choose. The Access menu is the first menu that appears when you enter 1-2-3. It is also the menu you use to start 1-2-3.

Although you do not need to install 1-2-3 in order to use it, you will not be able to display graphs or use your printer correctly until you do.

How to Display the Access System Menu

Proceed by following all the instructions that fit your computer's disk system, floppy or hard.

If You Have a Floppy-Disk System

1. Insert the System disk in drive A and be sure the **A**> prompt is displayed. Then proceed to step 2.

If You Have a Hard-Disk System

1. Be sure the **C**> prompt is displayed. Also, be sure you are in the correct subdirectory. (To change subdirectories, type **CD** followed by a blank space, a slash, and the subdirectory name. For example: CD \123. Then press Enter.) Proceed to step 2.

Whether You Have a Floppy-Disk or Hard-Disk System

2. Type:

   LOTUS

3. Press Enter. The Access System menu appears (see Figure 5.1). You will use this particular menu now to install 1-2-3. You can also use the Access menu to start 1-2-3, print graphs,

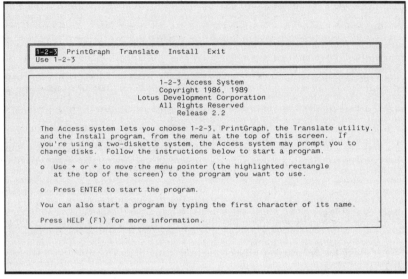

Figure 5.1: *The Access System Menu*

translate files from other programs such as dBASE III or VisiCalc, or exit to the operating system (DOS).

How to Install 1-2-3

4. Using the Right Arrow key, move the highlighted rectangle across the screen until it appears over the word **Install**.

5. Press Enter. It takes a few seconds for Install to begin. You will be prompted to read screens of information, change disks, and follow other instructions. 1-2-3 prompts you with questions, background information, and directions. Read this screen.

6. Press Enter to begin the Install program (see Figure 5.2). You have four options: first-time installation, change selected equipment, advanced options, or exit Install. Read the instructions at the right and bottom of the screen.

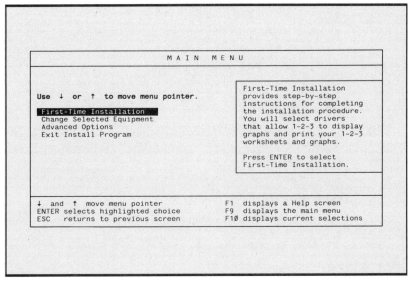

Figure 5.2: Install Menu

- If you are installing 1-2-3 for the first time or you want to create a completely new—and perhaps additional—driver set, select first-time installation on the main Install menu.

- If you want to change some of the information that has been stored already, use the second option on the main Install menu.

- If you want to make one of several driver sets current and change that driver set, or if you want to add new equipment choices to the Install menu, use the third menu option.

7. Proceed through the installation as you are prompted on the screen. Specific keys perform certain functions:

- The arrow (or *pointer*) keys move the cursor.

- The Escape key returns you to the previous screen.

- The F1 (Help) key displays additional explanations of the screen options. (Do not type F and then 1; there is a single key on the left marked F1.)

- The F9 key returns you to the main Install menu.

- The F10 displays the current driver selections.

When you finish, the Access menu returns.

How to Install the Allways Spreadsheet Publisher

The following steps will copy the Allways disks onto your hard disk and install Allways for your printer and monitor. It is necessary to exit the Access menu.

8. Select **Exit** to leave the Access menu.

9. Insert the Allways Setup Disk in drive A.

10. At the DOS prompt, type **A:**

11. Press the Enter key.

12. Type: **AWSETUP**

13. Press the Enter key.

14. Use the arrow (pointer-movement) keys to move the pointer to **First-time Installation**.

15. Press Enter.

16. Follow the instructions on the screen.

17. When through installing Allways, return to the Access menu by typing: **LOTUS** and pressing Enter.

A

C

B

1

3

1

2

2

Part Two

Building a Worksheet

3

LESSON

6

Displaying a Blank Worksheet

FEATURING

*Rows, columns, cells on a
blank worksheet*

You are ready to begin building a worksheet. How you bring up the
worksheet on your computer depends on whether your machine is on
or off.

How to Display a Blank Worksheet

Follow the instructions that fit your computer system, floppy
or hard.

If Your Computer Is On

1. Whether you have a floppy- or hard-disk system, if you are
   continuing from the previous lesson, the Access System menu
   is displayed. Since 1-2-3 is already highlighted on the menu,
   press Enter to select it.

The 1-2-3 logo, the serial number for your copy of 1-2-3, and copyright information appear on the screen. In a moment, the worksheet
will appear.

If Your Computer Is Off

1. If you have a floppy-disk system, place the 1-2-3 System disk in drive A and then place a formatted or prepared disk in drive B. If you have a hard-disk system, drive A must be empty.

2. Whether you have a floppy- or hard-disk system, if your computer is off, turn it on.

3. Enter the date and time if necessary. (See Lesson 1.)

4. Display the Access System menu shown in Figure 6.1. (See Lesson 5.)

5. Since 1-2-3 is already highlighted on the menu, press Enter to select it.

The 1-2-3 logo, the serial number for your copy of 1-2-3, and copyright information appear on the screen. In a moment, the worksheet will appear.

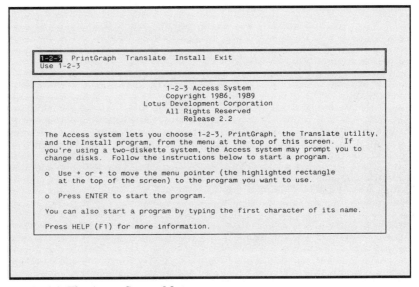

Figure 6.1: The Access System Menu

6. If you have a hard-disk system and a release of 1-2-3 prior to 2.2, you may get the following message: *Insert a disk in Drive B:, press any key to continue.* If so, press the Escape key to continue.

What you see in Figure 6.2 is a blank grid with numbers down the left side that identify *rows,* and letters along the top that identify *columns.* Typically, once the worksheet is put to use, the top row or rows and the left column are filled with titles and headings to identify the contents of all the cells on the worksheet.

Suppose you want to keep a daily record of your out-of-pocket business expenses. You could start by entering the days of the week along row 1, beginning at column B. In column A, you would type the dates for every week of the year next to the numbers. Your worksheet would look like the one in Figure 6.3. Your first dollar entry for the first Monday of the new year would be entered where column B (Monday) and row 2 (Week 1) intersect. This place is called a *cell,* and B2 would be the *cell address* for your first entry. Your worksheet would now look like the one in Figure 6.4.

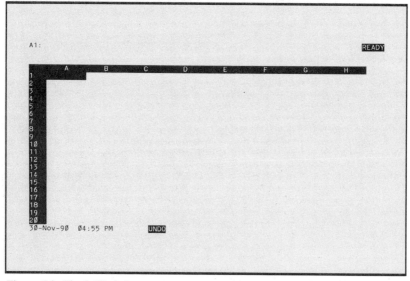

Figure 6.2: Blank Worksheet

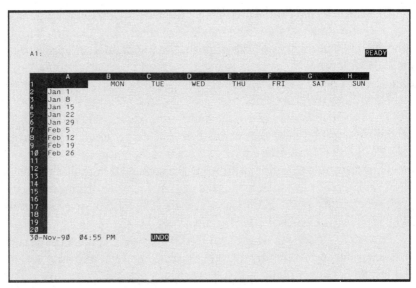

Figure 6.3: *Sample Worksheet*

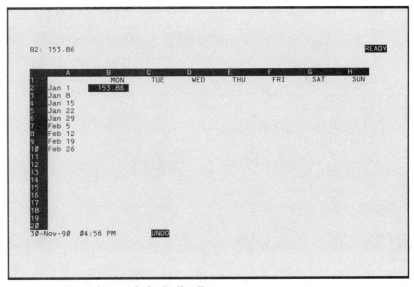

Figure 6.4: *Worksheet with the Dollar Entry*

The *control panel* is the area above the worksheet. On the left side of the control panel, above the blank worksheet, **A1:** appears. This is the current cell address of the *pointer*, the highlighted rectangle that is in cell **A1**. Since the pointer is in **A1**, you can't see the rectangle's top and left borders. In the next lesson, you will be using the pointer to move around the worksheet.

The *mode indicator* is on the right side of the control panel. It announces what 1-2-3 is doing. For example, when it indicates **READY**, 1-2-3 is waiting for you to enter information.

The *status line* is on the bottom of the screen. It contains the date and time, error messages, and indicators, which are displayed under certain circumstances. For example, if the Caps Lock or Num Lock key is pressed, **CAPS** or **NUM** is displayed.

Release 2.2 users will notice that **UNDO** may also appear in the status line. This means that the Undo feature is in effect, allowing you to cancel any changes made to the worksheet since 1-2-3 was last in the **READY** mode. (Undo is explained in more detail in Lesson 11, "Oh No! How to UNDO a Mistake.")

7

Moving Within the Worksheet

FEATURING

The Tab key
The Pointer-movement keys
The Scroll Lock key
The Num(eric) Lock key
The GOTO (F5) function key

The blank worksheet that first appears on your screen is only a small portion of the entire worksheet. Although it appears to have 20 rows and 8 columns, it actually has 8,192 rows and 256 columns, totaling more than 2 million cells. The entire spreadsheet is equivalent to a piece of paper 21 feet wide by 130 feet long. Because it is so large, you can never see the entire worksheet on your screen at once. Viewing it is similar to using a zoom lens to focus on a small part of a huge piece of paper.

To move around the worksheet and view the area that's not visible, you move the pointer, the highlighted rectangle now in cell A1. One way to do this is to press the *arrow keys* on the right side of the keyboard.

These keys, shown in Figure 7.1, move the pointer one cell at a time in a specific direction—up, down, left, or right.

Other keys, shown in Figure 7.2, move the pointer more than one cell at a time. These keys and the arrow keys are called *pointer-movement keys* and are summarized in the list that follows.

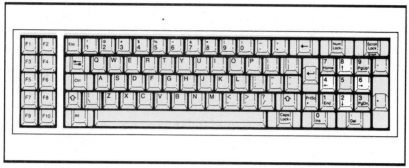

Figure 7.1: *Arrow Keys*

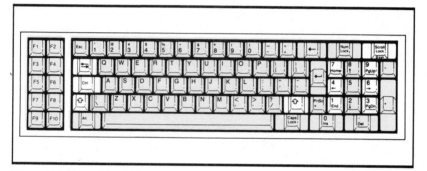

Figure 7.2: *Remaining Pointer-Movement Keys*

↑	Moves the pointer up one cell at a time.
↓	Moves the pointer down one cell at a time.
→	Moves the pointer to the right one cell at a time.
←	Moves the pointer to the left one cell at a time.
PgUp	Moves the pointer up one full "page" or 20 lines at a time.
PgDn	Moves the pointer down one full "page" or 20 lines.

⇆ or Ctrl→	(BIGRIGHT) Moves the pointer to the right one full screen. Holding down the Control key and tapping the Right Arrow key does the same.
⇧ ⇆ or Ctrl←	(BIGLEFT) Moves the pointer left one full screen. Holding down the Control key and tapping the Left Arrow key does the same.
Home	Moves the pointer to cell A1.
End	In conjunction with the arrow keys, moves the pointer in a specific direction to the nearest entry.
End Home	Moves the pointer to the lower-right corner of your work.
GOTO (F5) function key	Allows you to type the address of the cell where you want to move the pointer. After typing, you must press Enter.
Scroll Lock	In conjunction with the arrow keys, moves the worksheet in a specific direction as it pulls the pointer to the edge of the worksheet.

Although it is not a pointer-movement key, you should be aware of the *Num(eric) Lock* key because it changes the pointer-movement keys to number keys. If you are using the pointer-movement keys and numbers appear on the control panel, you have accidentally pressed the Num Lock key. If this happens, press the Backspace key to erase the numbers and then press the Num Lock key again. The pointer-movement keys will move the pointer when **NUM** disappears from the bottom right of the screen.

As you read through the following directions, you may notice that they are extremely explicit. In the beginning, nothing will be left unexplained. As you become more proficient, however, you will be asked to perform tasks without being told how, if you have already performed the task once.

How to Move Within the Worksheet

1. Using the Right Arrow key, move the cell pointer to and then beyond column H. Notice that as you move across the worksheet to the right, columns on the left disappear. Notice also that the cell address on the control panel changes to reflect the cell address of the pointer as it moves across the screen.

2. Using the Left Arrow key, return to cell A1. Hold the key down rather than tap it. The pointer will move more rapidly. 1-2-3 will beep at you when the pointer reaches the left side of the worksheet.

3. With the Down Arrow key, move the pointer to and then beyond row 20. Continue moving the pointer to row 40. This time, notice that rows disappear off the top as you move down the worksheet.

4. Press the key marked Page Up, or PgUp. Notice that the pointer is now on row 20. The PgUp key always moves the pointer up one full screen—or 20 lines—each time you press it.

5. Press the key marked Page Down, or PgDn. The pointer returns to row 40. The PgDn key always moves the pointer down a full screen—or 20 lines.

6. Press the Home key. The pointer is back in cell A1.

7. Press the End key. The word END appears in the lower-right corner of the screen. The End key is a *toggle* key. This means that you can disengage it by pressing it a second time. The End key, on its own, does nothing; it operates only in conjunction with arrow keys as illustrated in the next step.

8. With the End key on (the **END** message is displayed in the bottom right of the screen), press the Down Arrow key. The pointer is now in row 8192—the last row of the worksheet—because the End key, followed by an arrow key, moves the pointer in a specific direction to the first entry on the screen. Since there are no entries yet, the pointer goes directly to the last cell in the column. The word **END** disappears from the screen.

9. Press the Home key again.

10. Press the key marked F5. Do not type the letter F and the number 5; there is a single function key marked F5. This key is called the **GOTO** key because you use it to tell 1-2-3 where you want the pointer to *go to* by typing a cell address. The prompt **Enter address to go to:** appears on the screen. 1-2-3 suggests the current position of the pointer.

11. Type **G10**. If you typed incorrectly, use the Backspace key to erase.

12. Press Enter. The pointer moves to the cell you specify, in this case, **G10**.

13. Press the key marked Scroll Lock in the upper right corner of your keyboard. The word **SCROLL** is highlighted on the screen. The Scroll Lock key is also a toggle key. It operates with the pointer-movement keys to move the screen as it pulls the pointer to the edge of the worksheet. (Moving through rows or columns is also called *scrolling*.)

14. Press the Right Arrow key until several columns scroll off to the left and the pointer is pulled to the left edge of the worksheet.

15. Press the Down Arrow key until several rows scroll off the top of the worksheet and the pointer is pulled to the top edge.

16. Press Home.

17. Press the Scroll Lock key again to release it.

18. Press the Tab key. The pointer moves one full screen to the right.

19. Hold down the Shift key and press the Tab key. The pointer returns Home—that is, moves one full screen to the left.

20. An alternative way to move one screen at a time is to hold down the Control key and tap the Right Arrow key. The pointer moves a full screen to the right again.

21. Hold down the Control key and tap the Left Arrow key. The pointer returns Home—that is, moves one full screen to the left.

8

Labeling the Worksheet

FEATURING

Label-prefix characters
Caps Lock
Escape
READY and LABEL modes

There are endless variations on what might go on a blank worksheet. However, since the worksheet is often used for a budget in one form or another, the following instructions show you how to set up a budget. If you want to set up your own budget later on, the budget you will build in this book, shown in Figure 8.1, will give you the skills and confidence to do so. (Figure 8.1 is the finished worksheet. Do not enter it yet.)

But first things first. A worksheet needs labels or it won't be much help to you. To make sense of the figures you enter on the worksheet, you need to label your rows and columns. Your readers need to know, for example, that the four columns of figures you're presenting to them represent the year's four quarters, and the numbers along the bottom row represent profits, not expenses.

Depending on how you want your worksheet to look, you can align on the left or the right, center, or repeat a label within a column, as shown in Figure 8.2. A repeating label creates a row of characters, such as dashes or asterisks.

To tell 1-2-3 where you want to place your label within the column, you precede the label with a *label-prefix character*. You have four choices:

'	(apostrophe) for a left-aligned label
" (quotation marks)	for right-aligned label
^ (caret)	for a centered label
\ (backslash)	for a repeating label (do not use / (slash))

Be aware that if you do not include a label-prefix character, 1-2-3 will automatically left-align your label unless it begins with any one of the following characters:

$$0\ 1\ 2\ 3\ 4\ 5\ 6\ 7\ 8\ 9\ +\ -\ .\ (\ @\ \$$$

If your label begins with one of these characters, and you forget the label-prefix, 1-2-3 will misinterpret your label and assume that you are entering a number or a mathematical formula.

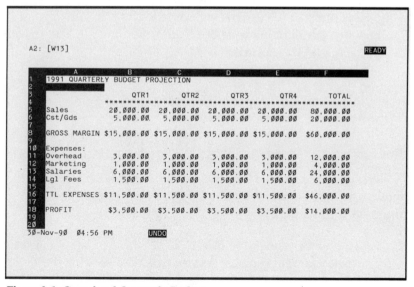

Figure 8.1: *Completed Quarterly Budget*

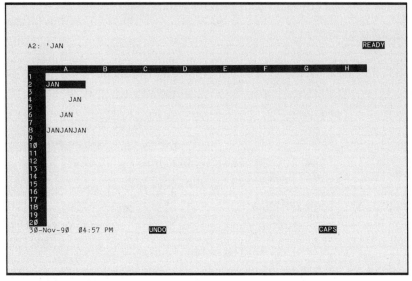

***Figure 8.2:** Examples of Labels in Four Positions*

To avoid this confusion, be sure to precede all labels that start with any of the number or punctuation symbols shown above with a label-prefix character. If your label begins with a letter, you do not need to type a label prefix; 1-2-3 assigns it automatically. You will know that you are correctly entering a label because the mode indicator will change from **READY** to **LABEL**.

How to Enter Labels on the Worksheet

To Construct a Quarterly Budget

When you need to type the label-prefix characters (except for the apostrophe), use the Shift key. Use the Caps Lock key to enter the rest of the labels in capitals.

1. The pointer should be in cell A1. Press the Caps Lock key when you want capitals. As you type the following label, use the numbers at the top of your keyboard. Type:

'1990 QUARTERLY BUDGET PROJECTION

Do not press Enter yet. Notice that you needed a single apostrophe label prefix because the label starts with a number. Notice also that the mode indicator changes to **LABEL**. Until you press Enter, the label remains beneath A1: on the second row of the control panel—the area above the worksheet. As long as your entry is on the control panel, you can easily correct mistakes with the Backspace or Escape key. (Do not confuse the Backspace key with the Left Arrow key.) The Backspace key erases one character at a time to the left. The Escape key erases the entire entry.

2. Correct any errors now, before you press Enter, using the Backspace or Escape key.

3. Press Enter. 1990 QUARTERLY BUDGET PROJECTION now appears at the top left of the worksheet and on the top row of the control panel, next to its cell address. If your label is incorrect and you entered it on the worksheet, the next step will show you how to correct it.

4. This step is added to illustrate one method of correcting errors once they are entered on the worksheet. You move the pointer to the cell containing the error, retype the entry on the control panel, and press Enter. Move the pointer to A1, if it is not already there. Type:

   '1991 QUARTERLY BUDGET PROJECTION

   Press Enter. The revision is entered on the worksheet. The label will span beyond cell A1 unless the cells to the right of it are already filled. Should this be the case, the label would be cut off.

5. Using the Down Arrow and Right Arrow keys, move the pointer to cell B3. The cell address on the control panel reflects the move.

6. Type:

   "QTR1

   Notice that you used double quotes (quotation marks) to align the label on the right. Do not press Enter.

7. Correct errors while the entry is on the control panel. Do not press Enter.

8. Instead of pressing Enter, there is a more efficient method of entering: pressing the Right Arrow key. In one step instead of two the label is entered on the worksheet and the pointer moves to the next cell.

9. Proceed to enter the next labels in cells C3, D3, E3, and F3 in the same way that you entered "QTR1. Be sure to look for mistakes on the control panel before you press the Right Arrow key. Remember to use the Shift key to type the double quotation marks (") before each label. Type:

    "QTR2 and press the Right Arrow key

    "QTR3 and press the Right Arrow key

    "QTR4 and press the Right Arrow key

    "TOTAL and press the Enter key

10. Move the pointer to B4.

11. Type:

    \ *

    Be sure you use the correct slash key. The backslash is the label prefix for repeating a label within a cell.

12. Press the Right Arrow key.

13. Repeat steps 11 and 12 for cells C4, D4, E4, and F4 until you have a row of asterisks beneath all the labels.

14. Move the pointer to A5.

15. Press the Caps Lock key. The CAPS message disappears from the bottom of the screen. Type and check for errors:

    Sales

    Since the label starts with a letter and you want it aligned on the left, it is not necessary to use a label prefix.

16. Press the Down Arrow key.

17. In A6, type and check for errors:

    Cst/Gds

18. Press the Down Arrow key.

19. Enter the following labels in the same way. Check for errors as you type each label on the control panel. Use the Caps Lock key to switch between capitals and lowercase labels.

    - in cell A7—**GROSS MARGIN**
      Press the Down Arrow key. (This label extends past the column; you will correct this later.)

    - in cell A8—**Expenses:**
      Press the Down Arrow key.

    - in cell A9—**Overhead**
      Press the Down Arrow key.

    - in cell A10—**Salaries**
      Press the Down Arrow key.

    - in cell A11—**Marketing**
      Press the Down Arrow key.

    - in cell A12—**Lgl Fees**
      Press the Down Arrow key.

    - in cell A13—**TTL EXPENSES**
      Press the Down Arrow key. (This label also extends past the column. You will correct this too, later.)

    - in cell A14—**PROFIT**
      Press the Down Arrow key.

    When you've completed these steps, the worksheet will look like the one in Figure 8.3.

Now go back and correct any errors by typing and entering the corrections over the errors. If you entered some labels into the wrong cells altogether, leave them for the time being. You will learn how to erase them later.

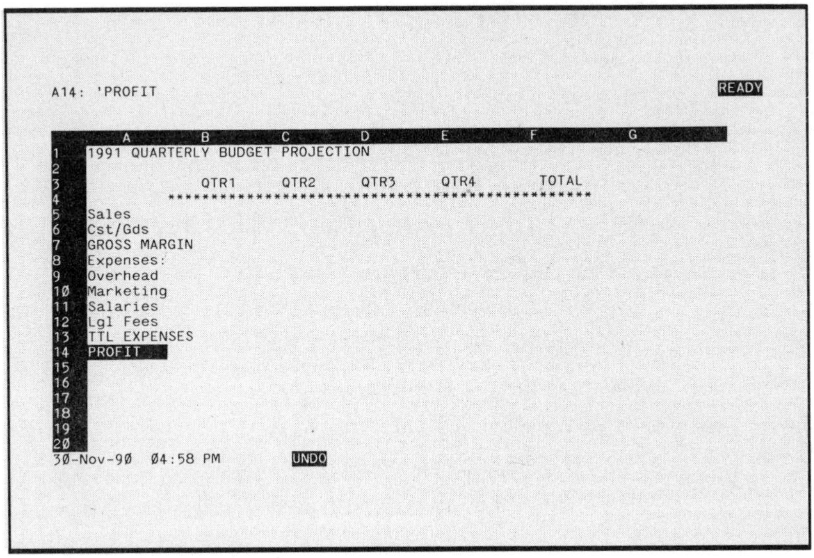

Figure 8.3: *Labeled Worksheet*

LESSON

9

Help! What Do I Do Next?

FEATURING

The HELP (F1) function key

1-2-3 has a lifeguard built into the program to save you from drowning in confusion. In case you don't know or can't remember how to proceed, more than 200 "pages" or Help screens are instantly available.

A common problem at this stage is forgetting which label-prefix character to use. Suppose, for example, that you are confident about your new computer skills and you want to experiment by labeling your own worksheet beneath the first one on the screen. Perhaps you want a monthly rather than a quarterly projection, or perhaps you prefer to break down your overhead expenses into such categories as space and equipment rental. And you want the new labels to be centered or aligned on the right, instead of the standard left-aligned format. You decide to start by typing a label in column A.

Suddenly, you can't remember which label prefix to use. Although you could look it up in the previous section of this book, there's a more efficient way: referring to the Help screens in 1-2-3.

Any time you are in the midst of a problem, you can leave what you are doing on the screen, press the **HELP (F1)** function key, read the relevant Help screen, and return to your work, ready to proceed now that you have the answer to your question.

To explore the Help screens, use the Arrow, Backspace, Enter, Escape, and F1 keys (shown in Figure 9.1).

*H*ow To Get Help Using the Help Screens

1. Press the **HELP (F1)** function key and read the screen. Do not type the letter F and the number 1; there is a single key marked F1. (If you are using Release 2.0 or 2.01, use the Down Arrow key to move the pointer to the phrase **Help Index** and press Enter.)

The Help Index is displayed. Don't worry if you don't understand everything on the screen. The mode indicator in the upper-right corner now says **HELP**. Any time you have a question as to how to proceed, 1-2-3 can instantly provide a Help screen that applies to the task at hand.

2. Since you want to know how to enter labels, move the pointer to **Cell Formats—Number Vs. Label**.

3. Press Enter and read the screen.

4. For more specific information, move the pointer to **Label Formats**.

5. Press Enter and read the screen.

6. Press Backspace to review the previous Help screen. If you wanted, you could continue to read other Help screens and 1-2-3 would remember up to 15, each of which you could review again by pressing Backspace.

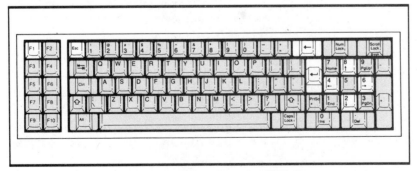

Figure 9.1: *The Arrow, Backspace, Enter, Escape, and F1 Keys*

7. After you finish reading, press **F1** again to return to the first screen that you viewed.

8. Go to the Help Index and select the screen **Using the Help Facility**. Review the use of the Help screen.

9. To return to your work exactly where you left off, press the Escape key.

LESSON

10

Correcting Mistakes in a Cell

FEATURING

The EDIT (F2) function key

In 1-2-3 you can often do one thing several ways, such as correcting a mistake. Until now, you would correct an error by using the Backspace or Escape key before entering data on the worksheet or by overwriting an entry already on the worksheet. **EDIT (F2)** allows you to correct a single error more easily.

For example, if you type **BUDET** on the control panel instead of **BUDGET**, you would have to erase the **T** and **E** and type in **GET** before you entered it on the worksheet. Or, if it were already on the worksheet, you would have to type the entire word over and reenter it. Instead, using the **EDIT** mode, you simply insert the **G** where it belongs.

The F2 key enables you to make corrections any time you notice a mistake. If the error has not been entered on the worksheet, you can press F2 and correct it while it is still on the control panel. Once the entry is on the worksheet, you simply move the pointer to the cell that needs correcting, press F2, and the entry is pulled up to the control panel for editing. In effect, all errors, whether they are on the control panel or already entered on the worksheet, are corrected on the control panel.

At this stage, forgetting to enter a label prefix and making an incorrect entry are the most common errors. The following instructions show you how to correct these mistakes, using the EDIT mode to enter and delete characters.

*H*ow to Correct Errors with the *EDIT (F2) Function Key*

1. To practice on a new screen, tap the PgDn key on the right side of the keyboard. This will bring up rows 21 through 40, where you can enter mistakes in order to learn how to correct them.

If You Forget to Enter a Label-Prefix Character

2. Press the Caps Lock key. **CAPS** is displayed. In the cell where the pointer currently resides, A35, type:

   1991 BUDGET

   Do not type a label-prefix character. Notice that the mode indicator changes to **VALUE**, not **LABEL**.

3. Press Enter. 1-2-3 beeps, your entry remains on the control panel, and the **EDIT** mode is automatically invoked because, although it doesn't recognize all errors, 1-2-3 knows when you forget to enter a label prefix if the label begins with any one of the following characters and contains letters:

   0 1 2 3 4 5 6 7 8 9 + . (@ $

   An entry beginning with one of these characters is normally interpreted as a number or a mathematical formula. This is called a *value*. However, because there are letters in the entry, 1-2-3 recognizes the error and knows that you intended to enter a label.

4. When you are in the **EDIT** mode, the pointer-movement keys respond differently. The Right Arrow and Left Arrow keys now move a small *cursor* along the second line of the control panel. Move the cursor to the first 1 in **1991 BUDGET** and type a single apostrophe.

5. Press the Down Arrow key. **1991 BUDGET** is entered as a label and aligned on the left, and you are in the **READY** mode.

If You Enter a Word or Number Incorrectly on the Worksheet

6. In cell A36, rather than typing **RENTAL COSTS,** type the following incorrect entry:

    TENTA COSTD

7. Press Enter. **TENTA COSTD** appears on the worksheet.

8. Press F2. **'TENTA COSTD** is pulled up to the second line of the control panel. 1-2-3 automatically adds the label prefix.

9. Move the cursor to the first letter: **T.**

10. Press the Del(ete) key located on the right side of the keyboard. The first letter **T** is deleted.

11. Type:

    R

    The **R** is inserted before the **ENTA,** which shifts to the right.

12. Move the cursor to the space between **A** and **C.**

13. Type:

    L

    The **L** is inserted before the blank space.

14. Press the End key. In the **EDIT** mode, it moves the cursor to the space after the last character. (Pressing the Home key moves the cursor to the first character in the line.)

15. Press Backspace to delete the previous character.

16. After the **T** on **COST,** type:

    S

17. Press Enter. The corrected entry, **RENTAL COSTS,** appears on the worksheet. Having pressed Enter, you are back in **READY** mode.

LESSON

11

Oh No! How to UNDO a Mistake (Release 2.2)

FEATURING

The UNDO (Alt-F4) feature

Oh no! You just accidentally erased five columns of important data from your worksheet. And you hadn't gotten around to saving the worksheet before you made the mistake. All your entries are lost. Or are they? With 1-2-3, Release 2.2, you can use the Undo feature to restore the worksheet as it was before you made the error.

When you first access 1-2-3, Undo is in effect and UNDO is displayed at the bottom of the screen. At certain points during your work session, 1-2-3 creates a temporary backup copy of the worksheet in a *buffer,* and it is this backup copy that is restored with Undo. Any action that changes the READY mode will signal 1-2-3 to create a backup copy. For example, when you press the slash (/) key and change to MENU mode or when you enter data into a cell and change to Value or Label mode, 1-2-3 will create a backup copy. Moving around the worksheet, however, will not create a new backup copy because you remain in the READY mode.

Some actions, such as those that affect disk files or the printer, cannot be undone. For example, once a file is erased from the disk, it cannot be restored using Undo. Or once you start printing, you cannot use Undo to stop printing. Also, when using Allways (see Part 8), you cannot use certain commands. (For more information regarding the specific commands that cannot be undone, refer to your 1-2-3 manual.)

How to Use Undo

To do the following steps, UNDO must be displayed at the bottom of the screen.

1. In cell A1, in the READY mode, type **test**.

2. Press Enter. The new title—test—is entered on the worksheet. Because you entered a label, the READY mode changed to LABEL and a copy of the worksheet prior to the change was placed in the buffer.

3. To Undo the previous step, press **UNDO;** hold down the Alt key and press F4. (Do not type F and then a 4; press the key marked F4.) The worksheet is restored and the original title is displayed.

4. Press **UNDO (Alt-F4)** again. The worksheet with the test label is restored.

5. Press **UNDO (Alt-F4)** one more time to restore the original worksheet.

12

Entering Numbers on the Worksheet

FEATURING

The VALUE mode

Now that the worksheet is labeled, you are ready to begin entering numbers. By the time you finish, your worksheet should contain the numbers in Figure 12.1, all of which represent dollar figures.

How to Enter Numbers

If you make a mistake as you type, use either the Backspace or Delete keys to correct the error while it is still on the control panel, or press EDIT (F2) and edit the error (or press UNDO (Alt-F4) if you are using Release 2.2 of 1-2-3).

1. Be sure the pointer is in cell A1. A quick way is to press the Home key.

2. Move the pointer to B5. Without adding a comma, type:

   20000

   VALUE appears as the right-hand mode indicator.

3. Press the Down Arrow key. 20000 appears on the worksheet.

4. Without adding a comma, in B6 type:

   5000

5. Press the Down Arrow key. 5000 appears on the worksheet.

6. Move the pointer to B9, leaving B7 and B8 empty.

7. In the same way that you entered 20000 and 5000, enter the following numbers:

   - in B9:   3000   (Press the Down Arrow key.)
   - in B10:   6000   (Press the Down Arrow key.)
   - in B11:   1000   (Press the Down Arrow key.)
   - in B12:   1500   (Press the Down Arrow key.)

   Never place a label prefix before a number that is to be calculated.

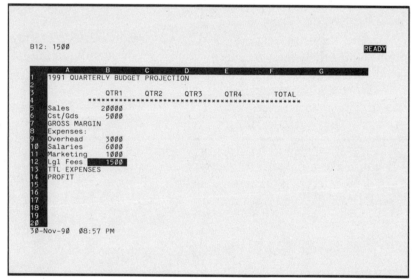

Figure 12.1: Worksheet with Numbers

LESSON

13

Entering Formulas and Functions and Playing "What If"

FEATURING

Formulas and the @SUM function

If you only used 1-2-3 to store information, it wouldn't be much more than a very expensive ledger pad. However, with *formulas,* some as simple as the ones you learned in Algebra 1, you can begin to calculate, analyze, compare, and project.

Placed in individual cells, formulas tell 1-2-3 to perform calculations that can vary in complexity. A formula may be simple, such as one that adds numbers, or it may be complex, such as one that calculates your monthly mortgage payments.

Take a look at the worksheet you've built so far. When you look down through the rows, you will notice three empty cells that are crucial to this particular budget. They raise several questions: What is the profit on sales after the cost of goods is subtracted? What are the total expenses? What is the overall profit? Some simple formulas, entered in those cells, will provide the answers for you. Later, you can play "what if" by changing the numbers on the worksheet, and 1-2-3 will automatically adjust its findings to reflect your changes.

When you enter a formula, 1-2-3 interprets it as a *value,* which includes both formulas and numbers. A value is one of two kinds of entries possible on the worksheet; the other kind is a label, which you are already familiar with.

If you aren't careful, however, 1-2-3 will misinterpret your formula as a label. Since you can use a number's cell address, such as D9, in a formula, rather than the number itself, formulas often begin with letters. This leads 1-2-3 to assume your formula—D9 + D10—is a label. The result is that 1-2-3 simply enters the formula on the worksheet; it doesn't store the formula as a direction to perform a calculation.

To avoid this, you must precede the formula with a specific *operator.* An operator is a symbol representing a mathematical operation, such as a subtraction or division sign. Normally, you will precede your formula with a plus sign, as in + D9 + D10. This way, you don't have to pay attention to whether or not your formula begins with a letter or a number.

There are other operators in addition to the ones already mentioned. The following are some of the most common.

^	Exponentiation
+, −	Positive, Negative
*,/	Multiplication, Division
+, −	Addition, Subtraction
<,>	Less than, Greater than (referred to as logical operators)

Although most of these operators are probably familiar to you, some vary slightly from their counterparts in algebra books. For example, rather than use a traditional division sign, 1-2-3 uses the slash (/).

The operators are listed in order of precedence, that is, in the order in which 1-2-3 calculates them in a formula. 1-2-3 doesn't always calculate a formula from left to right. Instead, it follows the normal algebraic order of operations. Thus, for example, it calculates multiplication and division before it calculates addition and subtraction. This can seem confusing until you learn how to enter a formula correctly.

To illustrate, let's assume that you want to project sales profits over the next two years. Being conservative, you project them at the current rate of sales. Using the worksheet you've built so far, you would apply the formula Sales – Cost of Goods*2 years, or +20000 – 5000*2, or for the sake of efficiency, +B5 – B6*2, where the cell addresses are used to represent the numbers on the worksheet. Calculated by hand, the answer is 30,000 since you know to subtract before you multiply. Calculated by 1-2-3, the answer is 10,000 because 1-2-3 multiplies before it subtracts. Obviously, there's a problem.

The solution is a simple one: you place parentheses around whatever you want 1-2-3 to calculate first. Thus when it calculates (B5 – B6)*2, it will provide the correct answer: 30,000. (The left parenthesis functions the same way as a plus sign here, so the initial plus sign is not needed.)

Something else to consider when entering a formula is the length of the formula. Sometimes a formula can get cumbersome. For example, if you want to calculate overall profits, you would add your expenses and subtract them from the sales profit. One way of writing this formula would be:

Sales – Cst of Gds – (Overhead + Salaries + Marketing + Lgl Fees)

or

+ B5 – B6 – (B9 + B10 + B11 + B12)

Although this formula is quite long, a large spreadsheet might well have even more profit and expense entries. To avoid lengthy, time-consuming formulas, *functions* are used to represent part or all of a formula. For example, the previous formula can be written as +B5 – B6 – @SUM(B9..B12), using the *sum* function. Now the formula reads: the sales income minus the cost of the goods minus the sum of the expenses. The sum function tells 1-2-3 to add all the figures between and including two cells. In addition to the sum function, there are more than 50 other functions, some of which do special tasks, such as rounding off numbers. For a list of all the functions used by 1-2-3, see the appendix in your 1-2-3 manual.

To enter a function, always precede it by @, identify it by name, and enclose the cells included in the formula in parentheses. Whenever a formula starts with a function, you do not need to use a plus sign; the @ symbol serves the same purpose. Neither formulas nor functions can contain any blank spaces. There are two plus keys and two minus keys on the keyboard. You may use any of them in building formulas.

*H*ow to Enter Formulas and Functions

To Calculate GROSS MARGIN Using the Formula:
+B5 − B6

1. Move the pointer to **B7,** to the right of **GROSS MARGIN**.

2. Type:

    + B5 − B6

Notice that the mode indicator changes to **VALUE**. It does not matter whether you use capital or lowercase letters when building formulas.

3. Press Enter. As in Figure 13.1, **15000** appears on the screen. Although the formula does not appear on the screen, 1-2-3 remembers it, and any time you change either of the two cell entries, 1-2-3 will recalculate **GROSS MARGIN**. (The **GIN** in **GROSS MARGIN** disappeared; you will correct this later.)

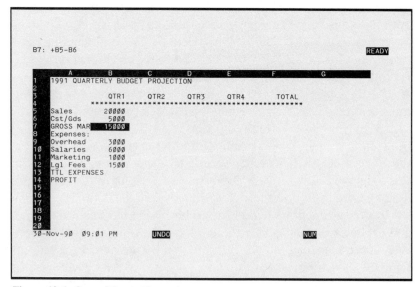

Figure 13.1: Gross Margin Formula

To Calculate TOTAL EXPENSES Using the Function: @SUM(B9..B12)

(Refer to the discussion of *functions* earlier in this lesson.)

4. Move the pointer to **B13**.

5. So far, you have been entering formulas by typing. You will now use the second method of entering a formula, *pointing*. Pointing offers a more visual method of identifying cells to include in the formula. First, type:

   @SUM(

6. Now, point to **B9** by moving the pointer to its cell using the Up Arrow key.

7. Type a period to *anchor* **B9** as the first cell in the formula. Two periods and another B9 appear on the screen. Typing a period prevents the first cell address on the control panel from changing when you move the pointer.

8. Point to **B12** by moving the pointer to its cell. The four cells are highlighted. Notice that the second **B9** is replaced by **B12**.

9. Type a right-hand parenthesis to close the formula. **@SUM(B9..B12)** is displayed.

10. Press the Down Arrow key. As in Figure 13.2, **11500** appears on the screen. Any time you change one of the cell entries, 1-2-3 will recalculate this figure. (The **SES** is erased from **TTL EXPENSES**. This too will be corrected later.)

To Calculate PROFIT Using the Formula: +B7−B13

11. Be sure the pointer is in **B14**.

12. Type only a plus sign. Remember: You can use either of the plus keys and either of the minus keys when building formulas.

13. Point to **B7** by moving the pointer to its cell.

14. Type a minus sign. The pointer will return to the original cell **B14**.

15. Point to **B13** by moving the pointer to its cell.

16. Press Enter. **3500** is displayed on the screen. Since the formula for profit includes all of the cell entries, a change in any one will be reflected in the profit.

To Play "What If"

17. Move the pointer to **B5**.

18. Type:

    30000

19. Press Enter. Notice that the totals for **GROSS MARGIN** and **PROFIT** are automatically recalculated to reflect the change.

20. In **B5,** type:

    20000

21. Press Enter. 20000 returns to the screen, and the totals are recalculated again. See Figure 13.3.

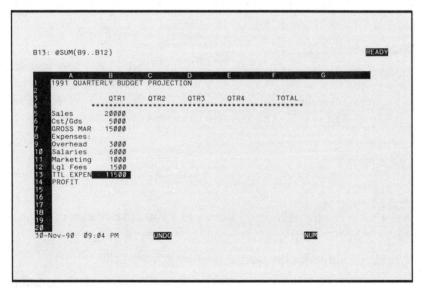

Figure 13.2: Total Expenses Formula

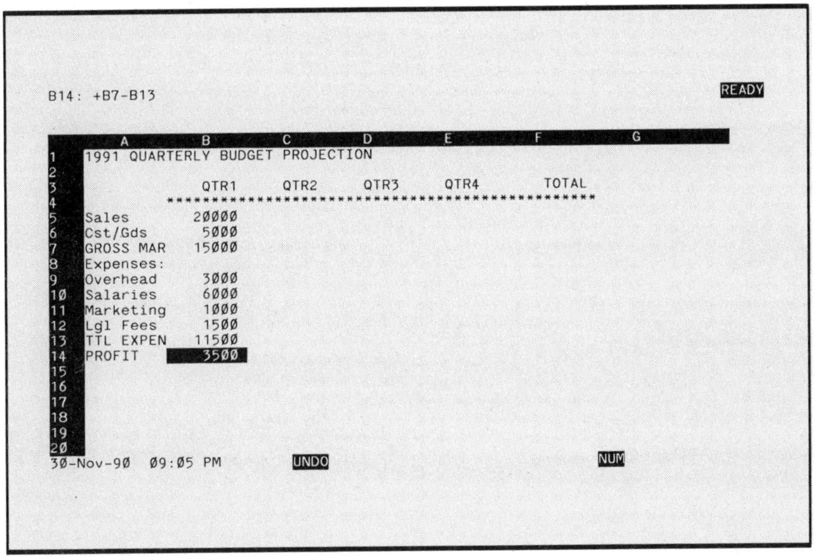

Figure 13.3: Profit Formula

14

Saving a File and Quitting 1-2-3: How to Stop Without Losing Everything

FEATURING

Command menus
Break keys
/File Save
/Quit

You've gotten this far, and you decide you've had enough and want to quit. If you turn off the machine now, everything you've entered up to this point will be erased. Rather than having to start over when you return to 1-2-3, it is a better idea to save your work on a disk.

You'll just skip this step for now? You may be disappointed if you do. A power failure, a sudden surge of power, or an observer curious about your power switch could erase everything you've accomplished to date. (Ironically, we just erased the last ten pages of text by accidentally knocking the power cable with the 1-2-3 manual.)

To be safe, periodic "saves" are a good practice. That way, even if you accidentally turn off the machine as you reach for another cup of coffee or lean to pick up the phone, you will have the last version of your work stored on a disk. Storing is also necessary if you want to file away one worksheet for later reference while you build another.

To store your work, you use a series of *commands*. Commands help you do a variety of operations that are indispensable in the creation of a spreadsheet, such as storing, printing, and retrieving the worksheet, displaying it as a graph, transferring information from one worksheet to another, and erasing data.

Commands are divided into categories by function and are assigned a corresponding name. The major command categories are listed in the *command menu* (see Figure 14.1).

/**Worksheet** commands affect the appearance of the entire worksheet, such as the one that changes a column width.

/**Range** commands affect part of the worksheet.

The /**Copy** command copies one part of the worksheet to another part.

/**Move** commands are used to move data within the worksheet.

/**File** commands allow you to store and retrieve your work, combine worksheets, and list files.

/**Print** commands are used to print worksheets.

/**Graph** commands are used to create graphs.

/**Data** commands are used to create a database.

The /**System** command allows you to exit 1-2-3 temporarily without losing your work, so that you can run other programs or use DOS commands such as **FORMAT, COPY, RENAME,** and **ERASE**.

/**Add-In**, for Release 2.2, enables you to use special software in conjunction with 1-2-3 such as Allways for enhanced printing and the Macro Library for storing macros.

/**Quit** ends the worksheet session, erasing the worksheet from memory in the process.

To access commands, you press the slash (/) key. But be prepared! Pressing the slash key in 1-2-3 is like traveling with Alice down the tunnel to Wonderland. Suddenly, a vast hierarchy of commands is available to you.

Lesson 14

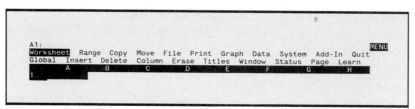

Figure 14.1: The Command Menu

How to Move Through the Command Menu

1. Press the slash (/) key. Be sure you press the forward slash (/), not the backslash (\). The command menu appears on the two lines of the control panel. The mode indicator changes to **MENU**.

2. Before proceeding to save your work, familiarize yourself with operating the command menu. Using the Right Arrow and Left Arrow keys, which now move from command to command, move among the different command options. Notice that the second line on the control panel offers new options or explanations for each command.

3. Move the pointer to **File**. Read the second line on the control panel.

4. Press Enter. The options that were below **File** are now on the top line of the control panel. Each time you choose a command, additional explanations or commands appear on the second line that relate to the highlighted option above. These layers of commands, or submenus, form a tree structure. Choosing one opens up a number of branches; choosing again opens up more branches.

5. Press Escape. You return to the previous command menu. Enter and Escape allow you to move in and out of the command menu, one level at a time.

6. Press Enter again.

7. To exit instantly, rather than one level at a time, hold down the Control key above the left Shift key and tap the Break key in

the top right corner. (*Break* may be written on the front side of the Scroll Lock key.) Do this now.

*H*ow to Save Your Work

8. If you have a hard-disk drive, proceed to step 9. If you have a floppy-disk drive, place a formatted disk in drive B and proceed to step 9. If you do not have a formatted disk, do the following:

   To format a disk without exiting 1-2-3, use the /**System** command. To format a disk now, press /, move the pointer to **System** and press Enter. The **A>** is displayed. Place your DOS disk in drive A. Type **FORMAT B:** and press Enter. When prompted, place a blank disk in drive B and press Enter again. When formatting is complete, type **N** and press Enter. Type **Exit** at the **A>** prompt and your worksheet will be displayed. Replace the DOS disk in Drive A with the 1-2-3 System disk, and leave the newly formatted disk in drive B.

9. Press the slash (/) key again.

10. Move the pointer to **File**.

11. Press Enter. The File Command menu (Figure 14.2) appears.

12. Move the pointer to **Save**.

13. Press Enter. The prompt **Enter name of file to save:** is displayed.

14. *If you have a floppy-disk system* and B:\ is displayed, type:

    91BUDGET

    If B:\ is not displayed, type:

    B:\91BUDGET

    If you have a hard-disk system and 1-2-3 is in a directory called 123, type:

    91BUDGET

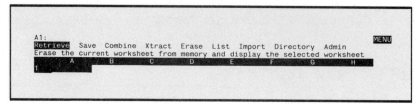

Figure 14.2: *File Command Menu*

The File menu

You use these commands to **Retrieve** a file that you **Save**
on a disk, to **Combine** part or all of a saved worksheet
with the worksheet on the screen, to **Xtract** part of your
worksheet to a new file on the disk, to **Erase** a file on
the disk, to display the names of the files that you've
saved (**List**), to incorporate text or numbers from
another software program into the worksheet (**Import**),
and to save or retrieve from a disk or subdirectory (if you
have a hard-disk system) other than the one you are currently using (**Directory**). For Release 2.2, use the **Admin**
command to share a worksheet on a network, to recalculate formulas that are linked to another file on the
disk, or to create a list of worksheet, graph, print, or
linked files on the worksheet.

If you named your subdirectory with a name other than 1-2-3,
type **C:**, the directory name, ****, then **91BUDGET**. To save on
another disk drive, substitute that drive, for example:

D:\123\91BUDGET

When you choose a name for you worksheet, be sure to
choose a relevant title, such as **91BUDGET**, so that when you
read through the file names in the directory at a later date, you'll

know what you filed under each name. It doesn't matter if you give the file a nickname, a date, a name, or a number, as long as it makes sense to you. But note the following rules:

- 1-2-3 will remember only the first eight characters that you type.

- You can use only letters of the alphabet, numbers, and the underline key.

- You cannot use punctuation or blank spaces.

1-2-3 automatically assigns an extension of **.WK1** to the file name. Thus your budget will be named **91BUDGET.WK1**.

15. Press Enter. When the mode indicator says **READY**, the worksheet or file is saved.

16. Saving the file again offers new options. Repeat steps 9 through 13. This time around, 1-2-3 knows the file name: **91BUDGET**.

17. Press Enter.

After a file is saved once, you have several options. You can **Cancel** saving the worksheet file, **Replace** the first version with a new version, or, for Release 2.2, make a **Backup** by copying the worksheet on the disk to a new file called **91BUDGET.BAK** and saving the worksheet on the screen to the file **91BUDGET.WK1**.

From now on, it is a good idea to save your work after each lesson in this book unless otherwise instructed. This will prevent you from having to retype more than a few steps if you accidentally erase the screen. If you want to stop working, now is the best time to do so—*after* you have saved your work.

Changing the File Directory

When working with floppy-disk systems, some releases of 1-2-3 will attempt to save and retrieve worksheets from the A drive. Normally you will want to use drive B for storing worksheets. On hard-disk systems, 1-2-3 will save and retrieve from the drive and directory where the 1-2-3 program files are. You may want to store the worksheets in a different directory.

Use /**File Directory** to change where 1-2-3 normally saves and retrieves worksheets. This change will last only until you quit 1-2-3. (To change the directory permanently, refer to Lesson 33, "Checking and Changing 1-2-3 Default Settings.")

18. Press the slash (/) key.

19. Move the pointer to **File**.

20. Press Enter.

21. Move the pointer to **Directory**.

22. Press Enter.

23. For floppy-disk systems, if B:\ is not displayed type:

    B:

    For hard-disk systems, if C:\123 is not displayed type:

    C:\123

    (Substitute 123 with the correct directory if necessary.)

24. Press Enter.

Saving a Worksheet Under a Different Name— a Quick and Painless Way to Back Up Your Work

25. When you save a worksheet again, 1-2-3 suggests the drive, directory, and file name that it was originally saved under. To save a worksheet under a different name, just type in a new name.

    Use /**File Save** to display the current file name. Type in a new name: **BUDGET2**. Notice that **91BUDGET** was over-written by the new name. Press Enter to save the worksheet.

Saving a Worksheet in a Different Directory or Disk Drive—Another Way to Back Up Your Work

26. To save a worksheet in a different area of your hard disk or on a different floppy drive, go through the following steps. Older releases of 1-2-3 will differ slightly in the following steps.

     Use /**File Save** to display the current file name, now **BUDGET2**. Press Escape once to display all worksheet files on the current drive in the current directory.

     If you have a floppy-disk computer you will see:

     B:\∗.wk1

     (or .WK? for older releases).

     If you have a hard-disk computer and the current drive is C and the current directory is named 123, you will see:

     C:\123\∗.wk1

     (or .WK? for older releases).

     A list of worksheet files for Release 2.2 of 1-2-3 is displayed. For older releases, the list will include all worksheets ending in .WKS, .WK1, or .WK3.

27. Press Escape again to clear the current file name from the control panel.

28. Press Escape one more time to clear the drive and directory. **Enter name of file to save:** is still displayed.

29. *For a floppy-disk system,* place another "backup" diskette in drive A. If you don't have one, move the disk in drive B to drive A temporarily. (You will need to take out the System disk—it is only necessary when starting 1-2-3 or when using the Help screens.) Then type **A:\BUDGET2** and press Enter. This will create a backup copy on the other diskette. Now remove the diskette from A (reinsert it in B, if necessary), and reinsert the System disk in drive A.

30. *For a hard-disk system,* you can save the worksheet on a floppy as in the prior step for floppy-disk systems, or you can

save it in a different directory on the same disk. To save it in the main, or root, directory, type **C:\BUDGET2**.

31. Now save the worksheet one more time under its original name and in the default directory. Using **/File Save**, save it as **B:\91BUDGET** for floppy-disk systems or **C:\123\91BUDGET** for hard-disk systems.

32. You will need to **Replace** the first version of the worksheet with the new one. Alternatively, you could select **Backup** to save the last version of the file under a file name with an extension of .BAK.

Quitting the Worksheet

33. To leave the worksheet use the **Quit** command. Press slash (/).

34. Move the pointer to **Quit**.

35. Press Enter.

36. Move the pointer to **Yes**.

37. Press Enter again. (Release 2.2 only: If you have changed the worksheet and not saved it, you will be asked whether you want to quit without saving. Answer Yes, if necessary.) The Access menu is displayed. From here, you can exit the Access System and exit to DOS, return to 1-2-3, or use any of the utility programs available from the Access menu.

LESSON

15

Retrieving Work That You've Saved

FEATURING

/File Retrieve

You stored your worksheet, turned off your computer, went out for a luncheon appointment, and returned to your desk, ready to review your work. Another file command, **/File Retrieve**, quickly returns your worksheet to the screen.

How to Retrieve a File

1. Bring up the blank worksheet on the screen. If you turned off the computer in the last section, you must turn it on again, then enter the date and time, if necessary. From the Access System menu, press Enter to display the 1-2-3 worksheet. For further instructions, see Lesson 6, "Displaying a Blank Worksheet."

2. Press the slash (/) key.

3. Move the pointer to **File**.

4. Press Enter.

5. Since the pointer is already on **Retrieve,** press Enter.

   Beneath the **Name of file to retrieve:** prompt is a list of any worksheet files that were saved previously. To see additional files, use the Right Arrow or Left Arrow key to scroll through the list. Alternatively, the Tab and Shft-Tab keys will move through the list a screen at a time.

6. With the pointer on **91BUDGET,** press Enter. The worksheet is displayed on screen. (Alternatively, you could type the drive and file name and press Enter rather than point to it.)

If, at a later date, you are working with one worksheet and want to retrieve another worksheet that you've saved, remember to save the worksheet you have made changes to before you attempt to retrieve another worksheet. If you don't, the changes in the current worksheet will be lost. For instructions on how to save a file, refer to Lesson 14.

16

Changing a Column Width and Hiding and Displaying Columns

FEATURING

/Worksheet Column
Set-Width
Reset-Width
Hide
Display
Column-Range (Release 2.2)

There is a problem with the worksheet. When you entered numbers in column B, some of the labels in column A were cut off. In order to read the complete labels, you have to widen column A. Since changing a column affects the appearance of the entire worksheet by shifting all of the columns to the right, you use a /**Worksheet** command, rather than a /**Range** command, which is reserved for changes affecting only part of the worksheet.

How to Change a Column Width

1. Move the pointer to any cell in the column that you want to widen. In this case, move it to **A5**.

2. Press the slash (/)key.

3. Since the pointer is already on **Worksheet,** press Enter. The **Worksheet** command menu, shown in Figure 16.1, appears on the screen.

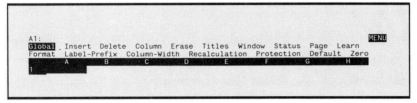

Figure 16.1: Worksheet Command Menu

The Worksheet Command Menu

- change **Global** settings—such as column-width—that affect the appearance of the entire worksheet

- **Insert** columns and rows

- **Delete** columns and rows

- change the width or hide or display a **Column**

- **Erase** the entire worksheet

- ensure that your labels don't scroll off the screen when you move the pointer **(Titles)**

- split the screen into two screens or **Windows**

- check **Status**

- set a *page break* anywhere in your worksheet **(Page)**

- store macros in a special macro library (Release 2.2) **(Learn)**

4. Move the pointer to **Column.**

5. Press Enter.

6. The following menu is displayed:

Set-Width Reset-Width Hide Display Column-Range

Since the pointer is on **Set-Width**, press Enter. The prompt **Enter column width (1..240): 9** appears. Nine is the preset, or *default,* width of a column.

7. Using the Right Arrow key, widen column A to 13. The labels that were cut off in column A reappear. You could also type 13.

8. Press Enter. The worksheet now matches the one in Figure 16.2.

   Notice that **[W13]** is displayed above the worksheet in the control panel. This shows that column A has been set with **Worksheet Column** for a width of 13. At this point, if you wanted to change the column back to its original width, called the global default setting—*global* because it affects the entire worksheet, *default* because it is the original setting that comes with the 1-2-3 program—you would select **Reset** instead of **Set** after doing **Worksheet Column** again. After pressing Enter, 1-2-3 would automatically return the column back to its original setting.

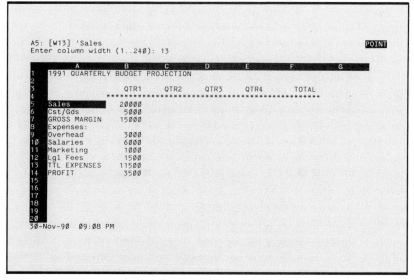

Figure 16.2: *Widening the Column*

How to Hide and Display a Column

You can hide one or more columns so they are not displayed on the screen or included in the worksheet when it is printed. Hiding a column can keep sensitive data secure while the data is used to build and calculate worksheets that will be distributed to others. Hiding columns also makes it easy to print only selected portions of a large worksheet.

9. Use **Worksheet Column** again to hide a column. Press /.

10. Press Enter at **Worksheet**.

11. Move the pointer to **Column**.

12. Press Enter.

13. Move the pointer to **Hide**.

14. Press Enter.

15. The **Specify column to hide: A5** prompt is displayed. Press Enter. Column A will disappear.

16. To redisplay the column, use **Worksheet Column Display**. Column B will be prompted. Move to column A. Column A will be displayed with an asterisk. This identifies it as a hidden column. Press Enter and column A is hidden again.

How to Widen Several Columns at Once (Release 2.2)

If you are not using Release 2.2 of 1-2-3, skip to the next lesson.

17. Move the pointer to any cell in column B.

18. Press the / key.

19. Press Enter.

20. Move the pointer to **Column**.

21. Press Enter.

22. Move the pointer to **Column-range**.

23. Press Enter.

24. Press Enter again. You are prompted to enter the **range** of the columns to be adjusted. (Ranges are explained in the next lesson.)

25. Move the pointer to column E. The column range should be Bx..Ex where x is any cell.

26. Press Enter. You are prompted to enter a column width.

27. Type **15**.

28. Press Enter.

29. Repeat the process to set columns B through E back to 9.

17

Copying Data from One Area of the Worksheet to Another

FEATURING

/Copy

While building a worksheet, you often run into the problem of having to retype formulas or data that you have already entered on another part of the same worksheet. The /**Copy** command eliminates tedious retyping by copying information for you. It enables you to copy a single cell or a group of cells across the worksheet or down through a column.

Let's assume, for the sake of illustration, that the company for which you are building the 1991 Budget Projection is extremely consistent; in fact, it is so consistent that you expect the income and expenses to stay the same for the remaining three quarters. To save yourself time, you would copy all the figures across the worksheet, from QTR1 into the remaining three columns or quarters.

As soon as you finish entering the figures for all four quarters, though, other questions will come to mind. What are the total sales for the year? What are the total salary costs? The total marketing costs? Column F is the place to answer these questions. After entering a formula in F5, and copying the formula down through the column, you will have the annual totals for every item in column A.

To use the /**Copy** command, you will specify what **range** you want to copy and where you want to copy it to. A range may be a single cell, part of a column, part of a row, or a combination of columns and rows. Be sure, when you copy a range, that there are plenty of blank cells to copy to; the /**Copy** command will copy over existing data if you don't.

How to Copy Data from One Area of the Worksheet to Another

Hint: If you lose your way in the following steps, remember that the Escape key takes you out of any menu. Also, you can always start over by retrieving the file 91BUDGET if you need to. Release 2.2 users can use UNDO (Alt-F4) to restore the prior version of the worksheet.

If You Want to Copy a Single Cell Across to Several Cells

1. Move the pointer to the cell you want to copy; in this case, it is **B5**.

2. Press the slash (/) key.

3. Move the pointer to **Copy**.

4. Press Enter. The prompt **Enter range to copy FROM: B5..B5** appears on the screen (Figure 17.1), and the mode indicator changes to **POINT**, indicating that you will point to or type the *range.*

A range is either a single cell or a group of cells arranged in a rectangular block, such as part of a column or row, or a combination of both. You can perform many 1-2-3 features using ranges, including printing, erasing, formatting, graphing, moving, and copying.

Since the pointer was already on B5 when you pressed the slash (/) key, 1-2-3 assumes that it is the only cell you are copying. There are no others between B5 and B5.

5. Since you are copying **B5**, press Enter. The prompt **Enter range to copy TO: B5** appears. 1-2-3 assumes you are copying to the same cell until it is told otherwise.

6. Move the pointer to **C5**.

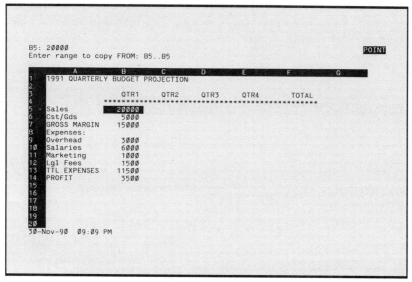

Figure 17.1: *Copying a Cell*

7. Type a period to anchor the cell. Two periods appear.

8. Move the pointer to **E5**. All the cells into which you are copying are highlighted. **C5..E5** is also displayed in the control
   panel (see Figure 17.2).

9. Press Enter. The number **20000** is copied to cells **C5, D5,** and
   E5, as shown in Figure 17.3, and the pointer returns to the
   original cell.

If You Want to Copy More Than One Cell Across the Worksheet

Now copy the rest of the numbers in column B to columns C, D,
and E all at once.

10. Move the pointer to **B6,** 5000.

11. Press the slash (/) key.

12. Move the pointer to **Copy.**

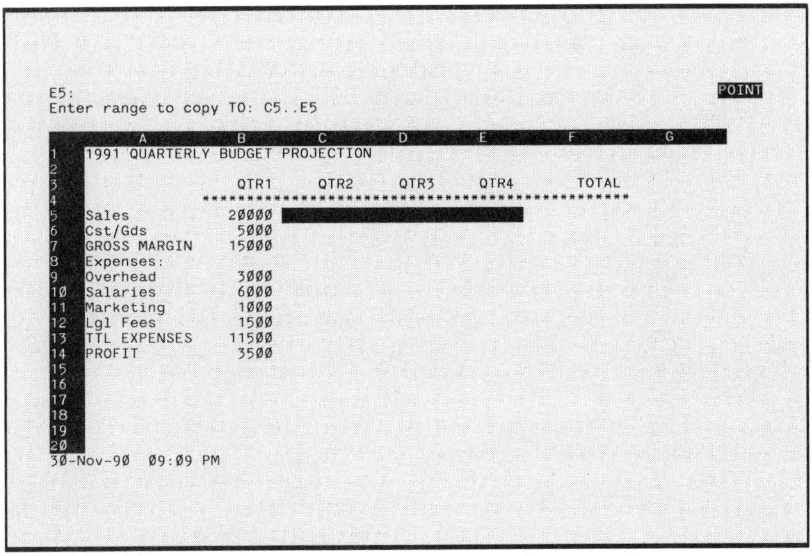

```
E5:
Enter range to copy TO: C5..E5                                    POINT

            A         B         C         D         E         F         G
1    1991 QUARTERLY BUDGET PROJECTION
2
3                    QTR1      QTR2      QTR3      QTR4      TOTAL
4              **********************************************
5    Sales           20000
6    Cst/Gds          5000
7    GROSS MARGIN    15000
8    Expenses:
9    Overhead         3000
10   Salaries         6000
11   Marketing        1000
12   Lgl Fees         1500
13   TTL EXPENSES    11500
14   PROFIT           3500
15
16
17
18
19
20
30-Nov-90   09:09 PM
```

Figure 17.2: *Copying to Multiple Cells*

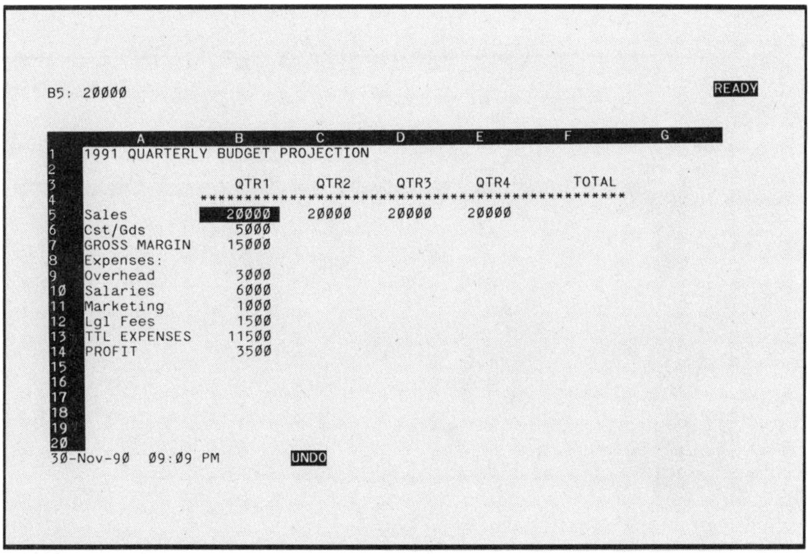

```
B5: 20000                                                        READY

            A         B         C         D         E         F         G
1    1991 QUARTERLY BUDGET PROJECTION
2
3                    QTR1      QTR2      QTR3      QTR4      TOTAL
4              **********************************************
5    Sales           20000     20000     20000     20000
6    Cst/Gds          5000
7    GROSS MARGIN    15000
8    Expenses:
9    Overhead         3000
10   Salaries         6000
11   Marketing        1000
12   Lgl Fees         1500
13   TTL EXPENSES    11500
14   PROFIT           3500
15
16
17
18
19
20
30-Nov-90   09:09 PM              UNDO
```

Figure 17.3: *Worksheet with Copied Numbers*

13. Press Enter. 1-2-3 displays **Enter range to copy FROM: B6..B6**.

14. Since you are copying more than one cell, move the pointer to **B14** before pressing Enter. Cells **B6** through **B14** are highlighted (see Figure 17.4).

15. Press Enter. The **copy TO:** prompt appears. Notice that this prompt does not display the cell addresses separated by periods. You must decide at this point whether you want to move the pointer first, *before* anchoring it to a particular cell.

16. Move the pointer to **C6**.

17. Type a period to anchor it.

18. Move the pointer to **E6**. When you copy a column, you only need to specify the top of the range you are copying to. When you copy a row down, you only need to specify the left side of the range you are copying to (see Figure 17.5).

19. Press Enter. The numbers and formulas are copied across the worksheet, as in Figure 17.6, and the pointer returns to

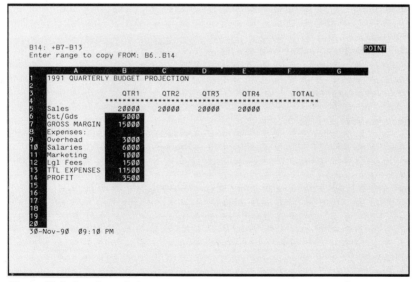

Figure 17.4: Copying a Column

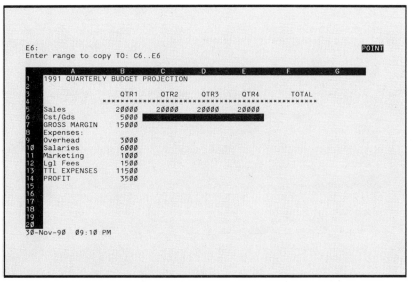

Figure 17.5: *Copying to Multiple Columns*

the original cell. Now save the budget in case you make mistakes in the following steps. If this happens, you can then abandon the later version and retrieve what you have done so far.

20. Use /**File Save**. Press the slash (/) key.

21. Move the pointer to **File**.

22. Press Enter.

23. Move the pointer to **Save**.

24. Press Enter.

25. Press Enter again to accept the same name.

26. Since you have already saved the budget once, **Replace** it with the new version. Move the pointer to **Replace**. For Release 2.2, you may use **Backup** to keep a copy of the older version in a file called **91BUDGET.BAK**.

27. Press Enter.

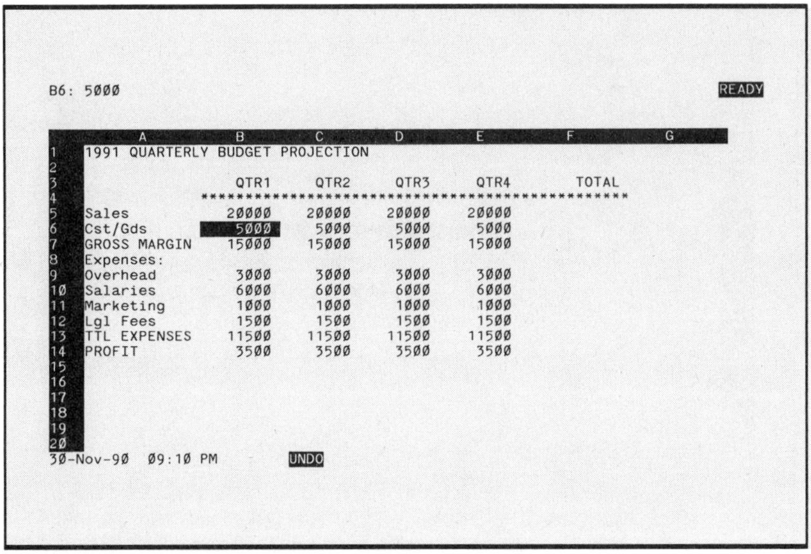

Figure 17.6: Second Worksheet with Copied Numbers

If You Want to Copy Down Through a Column

There are two ways to create formulas in column F that will total the quarterly amounts into yearly amounts. One way is to type in one formula for each row of numbers; the other is to type in one formula and copy it into the other rows. The second way is more efficient.

28. Cell F5 is empty. Before you copy it, you need to enter a formula. Since you want to total each row, type the **@SUM** function in **F5**:

    @SUM(B5..E5)

29. Press Enter. **80000** appears in **F5**.

30. Press the slash (/) key.

31. Move the pointer to **Copy**.

32. Press Enter. 1-2-3 prompts you to identify the range you are copying from. It suggests **F5..F5**.

33. Since you are copying the single cell down through the column, press Enter. 1-2-3 asks for the range to copy to.

34. Move the pointer to **F6**.

35. Type a period.

36. Move the pointer to **F14**. The range you are copying to is highlighted.

37. Press Enter. Your worksheet should look like the one in Figure 17.7. The totals for each row are entered in column F. A zero is entered in row 8 since there were no numbers to add in this row. Proceed to the next lesson in order to erase the zero.

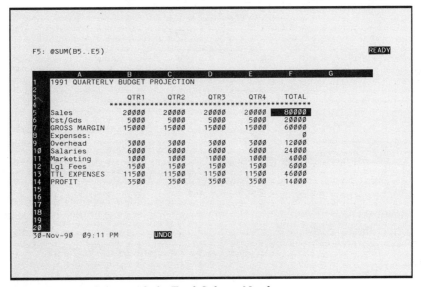

Figure 17.7: Worksheet with the Total-Column Numbers

18

Erasing Part of the Worksheet

FEATURING

/Range Erase

A few seconds ago, a colleague walked into your office with revised figures. It turns out that you've been making predictions with out-dated information. With **/Range Erase**, you can quickly erase all the old figures before you enter the new data.

Depending on your needs, you can erase one or many cells with **/Range Erase**. You may have noticed that you can't completely erase a cell with the **EDIT (F2)**; you can only change the entry. You must use **/Range Erase** if you want to leave one or several cells completely blank.

How to Erase Part of the Worksheet

If You Want to Erase a Single Cell

1. Move the pointer to **F8**.

2. Press the slash (/) key.

3. Move the pointer to **Range**. The Range command menu, shown in Figure 18.1, appears on the screen.

4. Press Enter.

5. Move the pointer to **Erase**.

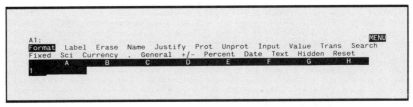

Figure 18.1: Range Command Menu

The Range Command Menu

You use these commands to

- change the **Format** of some of the numbers (by adding dollar signs for example)

- right-, left-justify, or center labels within a column (**Label**)

- **Erase** part of the worksheet

- assign a **Name** to a range of cells

- apply word-wrap to long labels (**Justify**)

- **Protect** a cell so you can't enter anything in it

- **Unprotect** a cell so you can enter data into it

- restrict pointer-movement and data entry to unprotected cells (**Input**)

- convert formulas to their values with the **Value** command

- **Transpose** columns and rows on a worksheet

- **Search** for text in labels or formulas (and replace, if desired) (Release 2.2.)

6. Press Enter. The prompt **Enter range to erase: F8..F8** appears. 1-2-3 always suggests the single cell where the pointer currently resides.

7. Press Enter to erase **F8**.

If You Want to Erase a Range of Cells

8. Press the slash (/) key.

9. Move the pointer to **Range**.

10. Press Enter.

11. Move the pointer to **Erase**.

12. Press Enter. The range-to-erase prompt appears again.

13. Press Escape. The second half of the range is erased from the prompt. You have just *unanchored* the range.

14. Move the pointer to the cell where you practiced making corrections earlier, **A35**.

15. Type a period to anchor **A35**.

16. Use the Down Arrow key to include **A36**. The cells are highlighted, and the control panel reflects the range.

17. Press Enter. The range is erased.

18. Press the Home key.

19. Be sure to save your worksheet now. You will be erasing the entire worksheet in the next lesson. Saving it will enable you to return to the worksheet as it appears at this time. **Replace** the previously saved version with your new version.

If You Want to Create a Template

A template includes a worksheet's labels and formulas but excludes numbers. By creating a template, you will already have, for example, a head start when preparing next year's budget.

20. Erase the numbers in your budget. Move the pointer to **B5**.

21. Press the slash (/) key.

22. Move the pointer to **Range**.

23. Press Enter.

24. Move the pointer to **Erase**.

25. Press Enter. 1-2-3 displays **Enter Range to erase: B5..B5**.

26. Move the pointer to **E6**. The **Sales** and **Cst/Gds** numbers are highlighted.

27. Press Enter to erase the range.

28. Do the same with expenses, **B9..E12**. Do not erase the formulas.

29. Save this under a new file name: **91TEMP**. Do not save it as **91BUDGET**; you will need the worksheet in succeeding lessons. Refer to Lesson 20, "Formatting the Entire Worksheet," for tips on changing how formulas are displayed in the template.

19

Erasing the Entire Worksheet

FEATURING

/Worksheet Erase

When you've finished with a worksheet and saved it, you can erase it from your screen by using the /**Worksheet Erase** command.

How to Erase the Entire Worksheet

1. Press the slash (/) key.

2. Since the pointer is already on **Worksheet**, press Enter.

3. Move the pointer to **Erase**.

4. Press Enter. The prompt **No Yes Do not erase the entire worksheet; return to READY mode** is displayed as a safeguard to prevent you from erasing the worksheet in case you forgot to save it first.

5. Move the pointer to Yes.

6. Press Enter. The entire worksheet is erased from the screen— not only the entries, but also the column-width setting that you changed.

If you are using Release 2.2 and you did not save before erasing, 1-2-3 will display an additional prompt asking you if you are sure you want to erase the worksheet.

In addition to /**Worksheet Erase**, the /**File Retrieve** and /**Quit** commands will erase a worksheet from the screen. /**File Retrieve** will erase whatever is displayed before retrieving a new worksheet, and /**Quit** will let you exit 1-2-3, if you choose, without saving the current worksheet.

Do not save your worksheet now. Whenever you save, the previously saved file is overwritten with the new save. This means that you would be saving the blank worksheet over the budget worksheet. Since you want to retrieve the worksheet that you saved earlier, not a blank worksheet, don't save it now.

20

Formatting the Entire
Worksheet: Changing the Way
Numbers Are Represented

FEATURING

/Worksheet Global
   Format
   Zero
   Default Other International
Settings Sheets (Release 2.2)
NAME (F3) key

At some point you may want to share a worksheet with your co-workers. Before you do, though, you will want it to be as clear and straightforward as possible. A few changes will enhance its appearance.

Whenever you change the appearance of the cell entries, you are *formatting* the worksheet. There are a variety of ways to format the worksheet. You can change the appearance of all the cells with **/Worksheet Global Format** commands, or you can change only part of the worksheet using **/Range Format** commands.

An important point to remember about formatting is that **Range** commands take precedence over **Worksheet** commands. Once you alter part of the worksheet with a **Range** command, it will not be affected by **Worksheet** commands. In other words, you can't display some of the numbers on the worksheet as currency and then expect to change all of the numbers, including those already formatted as currency, to percentages. Therefore, although you can change your mind and the worksheet several times, it is easier if you plan your changes so that you use **/Worksheet Global Format** commands before you use **/Range Format** commands.

Returning to your worksheet, you will first want to change the way your figures are represented on the entire worksheet. You can choose any of the following ten formats:

Fixed displays numbers with a specified number of decimal places (e.g., 2.0).

Scientific displays all numbers in exponential form with a specified number of decimal places (e.g., 2.00E + 01).

Currency displays all numbers with a $, commas, and a specified number of decimal places (e.g., $2,000.00).

, (Comma) displays all numbers with commas and a specified number of decimal places (e.g., 2,000.00).

General displays numbers in the most abbreviated way possible (e.g., if you entered 2000.00, 2000 will be displayed). This is the standard format, also known as the default format.

+/− displays numbers as a pictograph; that is, positive numbers are represented by plus signs (5 = + + + + +) and negative numbers are represented by minus signs (−3 = − − −). Zeros are displayed as periods. As always, numbers that are too large for the column are not displayed; instead, asterisks fill the column.

Percent displays numbers as multiples of 100 with a percent sign, and with a specified number of decimal places (e.g., 2 = 200.0%).

Date causes special Julian numbers to be displayed in one of five date formats or one of four time formats. Julian numbers represent the number of days since the beginning of the century and range from 1 (for January 1, 1900) to 73049 (for December 31, 2099). A fraction is attached to the number to represent the time of day. For example, the

Julian number for noon, January 1, 1900 is 1.5. To generate the number that represents the current day, use the @DATE or @NOW function. To generate a number that represents a particular time, use @TIME or @NOW. (Refer to Lesson 59, "Using Key Names" and Lesson 66, "Applying Commonly-Used Functions" for further explanation.) The date and time formats are as follows:

/Range Format Date	Produces
D1	15-JAN-91
D2	15-JAN
D3	JAN-91
D4 (long int'l)	01/15/91
D5 (short int'l)	01/15
DT1	10:15:20 PM
DT2	10:15 PM
DT3 (long int'l)	22:15:20
DT4 (short int'l)	22:15

Text displays formulas as they were entered on the screen and displays numbers in **General** format.

Hidden allows you to hide the contents of one or more cells from the screen or from print.

In addition to /**Worksheet Global Format**, there are several other ways to format numbers. If, for example, some of your formulas calculate to zero, you can display them as blank cells using /**Worksheet Global Zero** or you can display a message of your choice if you are using Release 2.2. Using /**Worksheet Global Default Other International**, you can change the currency symbol and display it before or after the number, change the period in the numbers to a comma, change the international date and time formats, and change how negative numbers are displayed.

In Release 2.2, certain commands cause 1-2-3 to display a **setting sheet** (see Figure 20.1) that temporarily replaces your worksheet. It is

1-2-3's way of telling you the current settings, such as whether or not you have chosen to display commas in the numbers in each cell. The **/Worksheet Global** setting sheet is the same screen as that shown for **/Worksheet Status**. (See Lesson 33, "Checking and Changing 1-2-3 Default Settings.")

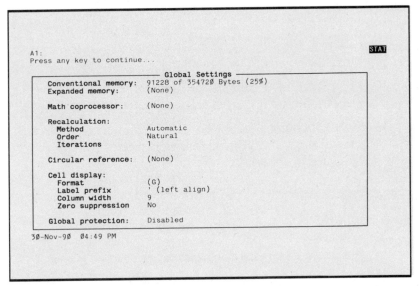

Figure 20.1: Setting Sheet

*H*ow to Format the Entire Worksheet

To Add Commas and Decimal Places to the Numbers

1. First, retrieve the worksheet. Press the slash (/) key.

2. Move the pointer to **File**.

3. Press Enter.

4. Press Enter again to select **Retrieve**. A list of file names is displayed. If you are using Release 2.2, press the NAME (F3) key to list as many file names as possible on the screen.

5. Move the pointer to **91BUDGET**.

6. Press Enter.

7. Press the slash (/) key.

8. Press Enter to select **Worksheet**.

9. Press Enter again to select **Global**. If you are using Release 2.2, review the setting sheet. Is the format under Cell Display (G) for general? This is the default setting that you will change.

10. Press Enter to select **Format**.

11. Move the pointer to the **,** (comma).

12. Press Enter. 1-2-3 prompts you to enter the number of decimal places you want displayed on your worksheet.

13. Since your numbers represent dollar figures, leave the 2 on the control panel. Press Enter. Your worksheet will match the one in Figure 20.2.

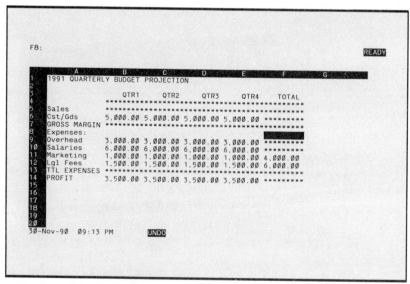

Figure 20.2: *Formatted Worksheet*

The comma format adds four characters to each number. Those numbers that are now too large to display are replaced by asterisks. To correct this, you will use the **/Worksheet Global Column-Width** command, introduced in the next lesson.

LESSON

21

Widening All the Columns on the Worksheet

FEATURING

*/Worksheet Global
Column-Width*

Since many display formats add several characters to each number—commas, decimal points and places, and dollar signs—numbers often grow too large for their column and thus it becomes necessary to widen all the columns. But wait a minute! You already learned how to adjust a column width in an earlier section. Why do you need to learn how to do it again?

The reason is that when you widened column A to fit all of the labels, the rest of the worksheet only shifted to the right; the other columns didn't get any wider. Now you will widen all the columns.

How to Widen All the Columns

1. Press the slash (/) key.

2. Since the pointer is on **Worksheet,** press Enter.

3. Since the pointer is on **Global,** press Enter.

4. Move the pointer to **Column-Width.**

5. Press Enter. The prompt **Enter column width (1..72): 9** appears. As explained earlier, nine is always the number of characters in a 1-2-3 column unless you specify otherwise; it is the default setting.

6. Use the Right Arrow key to expand the columns to 11. You could also type the desired width.

7. Press Enter. Your worksheet will now match the one in Figure 21.1. Notice that column A didn't widen. You widened it earlier with the /**Worksheet Column-Width** command, which takes precedence over the /**Worksheet Global Column-Width** command. To adjust column A, you need to use /**Worksheet Column Reset**.

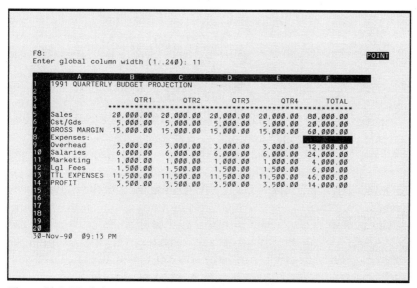

Figure 21.1: Worksheet with Widened Columns

LESSON

22

Formatting Part of the Worksheet: Changing the Way Numbers Are Represented

FEATURING

/Range Format
/Worksheet Global Default
   Other International
   Currency

Perhaps you want to emphasize particular areas of the worksheet to give them more impact. Using **/Range Format** you have the same options that you had in **/Worksheet Global Format**, but you can use them to change the way a single cell or range of cells is displayed. For example, you can play up the most relevant details on the worksheet by adding dollar signs to the gross margin, total expenses, and profit figures.

How to Format Part of the Worksheet

To Change the GROSS MARGIN, TTL EXPENSES, and PROFIT Rows to Currency

1. Press the slash (/) key.

2. Move the pointer to **Range**.

3. Press Enter.

4. Since the pointer is on **Format**, press Enter. The **Range Format** menu, shown in Figure 22.1, appears on the screen. Notice that there is one command in /**Range Format** that is not in /**Worksheet Global Format: Reset**. It is used to return the range setting that you specify back to the global format—which in this case is the comma format.

5. Move the pointer to **Currency**.

6. Press Enter. This prompt appears:

   Enter number of decimal places (0..15): 2

7. Since you still want two decimal places, press Enter. A prompt asking you to enter the range to format appears.

8. Press Escape. The range is unanchored.

9. Move the pointer to the first cell in the range; in this case, it is **B7**.

10. Type a period to anchor the cell again.

11. Move the pointer to **F7**.

12. Press Enter. Dollar signs are added to the figures in row 7. **(C2)** appears on the control panel above the worksheet. It tells you that the cell is formatted as currency and two decimal places and appears only in front of cells that have been formatted using /**Range Format**. (To see **(C2)**, you must move the pointer to a cell in row 7 if it is not already on one.)

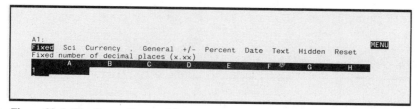

Figure 22.1: The Range Format Menu

13. To add dollar signs to the **TTL EXPENSES** and **PROFIT** rows, repeat the process beginning with step 1 and type in or point to the appropriate cell ranges. When you are done, the worksheet will look like the one in Figure 22.2.

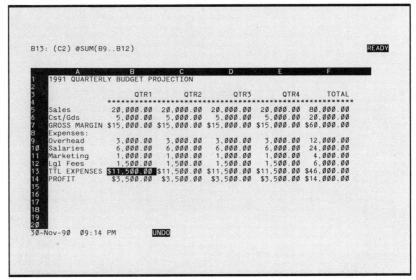

Figure 22.2: Worksheet with Numbers in Comma and Currency Formats

23

Shifting Labels Within Their Columns

FEATURING

/Range Label

After you have entered your labels on the worksheet, you may decide that you want to shift them, especially if you have widened the columns. Although you could go back to individual cells and reenter each label to center it, shifting labels with the **/Range Label** command is much faster.

How to Shift Labels Within Columns

1. Press the slash (/) key.

2. Move the pointer to **Range**.

3. Press Enter.

4. Move the pointer to **Label**.

5. Press Enter. You now have a choice of making all the labels centered or aligned on the left or the right.

6. Move the pointer to **Center**.

7. Press Enter. A prompt asks you to enter the range.

8. Press Escape to unanchor the range on the control panel.

9. Move the pointer to **B3**.

10. Type a period to anchor the cell.

11. Move the pointer to **F3**.

12. Press Enter. The labels are centered. At a later date, if you decide you want all of your labels automatically aligned on the right or centered, use the /**Worksheet Global Label-Prefix** command to change the default setting so that 1-2-3 doesn't automatically align them on the left. /**Worksheet Global Update** would then save the new setting. You must use this command before you enter any labels because it will not realign labels already on the worksheet.

LESSON

24

Inserting Columns and Rows

FEATURING

/Worksheet Insert

After you finish building the worksheet, or while you are still in the midst of building it, you may want to insert columns or rows. Perhaps you need to add figures you neglected to include, or you might want to move a column or row that you've already entered, or set apart a column or row by surrounding it with blank space. You don't simply want to add to the right or bottom of the worksheet; you want to insert columns and rows between columns and rows that already contain information.

For example, looking at the budget, you realize you haven't answered an important question: What percent of the total expenses does each item represent? And you still don't like the appearance of the worksheet; the numbers are too crowded. What can you do? You need to add another column of figures and insert some blank rows so there is more space between the rows of numbers.

Where should you put the new column? One option is to add the figures between the fourth quarter and total columns. But first you have to insert a blank column between the two columns. To do so, you use the **/Worksheet Insert** command. The same command enables you to add blank rows above and below **GROSS MARGIN** and **TTL EXPENSES**.

*H*ow to Insert Columns and Rows

To Insert a Blank Column

1. Move the pointer to **F3**.

2. Press the slash (/) key.

3. Since the pointer is on **Worksheet,** press Enter.

4. Move the pointer to **Insert**.

5. Press Enter. The prompt **Column Row Insert one or more blank columns to left of cell pointer** is displayed.

6. Since you want to insert a column to the left of the **TOTAL** column, column F, you press Enter. The prompt **Enter column insert range:F3..F3** appears. You need only specify one cell in the column. 1-2-3 always inserts an entire column. You expand the range to the right only if you want to insert more than one column.

7. Since you want to insert only one column, press Enter.

8. Move the pointer to the right to see that everything from column F shifts to the right to make room for the blank column. (Had there been more columns with entries, they too would have shifted to the right.) All the formulas are adjusted to reflect the change. The worksheet now looks like the one in Figure 24.1.

To Insert a Blank Row

9. Press the slash (/) key.

10. Since the pointer is on **Worksheet,** press Enter.

11. Move the pointer to **Insert**.

12. Press Enter. 1-2-3 offers you the option of inserting a column or a row.

13. Move the pointer to **Row**.

14. Press Enter. 1-2-3 asks you to identify the range of the row and suggests the cell where the pointer currently resides.

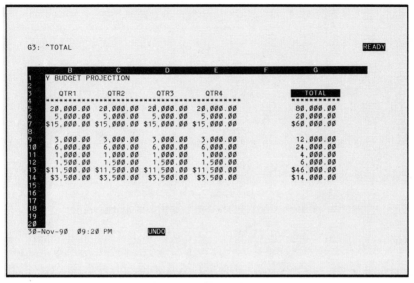

Figure 24.1: *Worksheet with a Blank Column*

15. Press Escape to unanchor the range.

16. Move the pointer to a cell in the row where you want to insert a row. Move it to **A7**. It's not necessary to specify any more than one cell in the row. 1-2-3 automatically inserts an entire row. You expand the range only when you want to insert more than one row.

17. Press Enter. A blank row appears between **Cst/Gds** and **GROSS MARGIN**, and the worksheet shifts down. Formulas adjust automatically to reflect the change.

18. Repeating steps 9 through 17, insert blank rows between **Expenses** and **GROSS MARGIN**, between **TTL EXPENSES** and **Lgl Fees**, and **PROFIT** and **TTL EXPENSES**. Remember as you enter each row that 1-2-3 adds a blank row *above* the row that you specify.

19. Press the Home key. The budget should now look like the one in Figure 24.2.

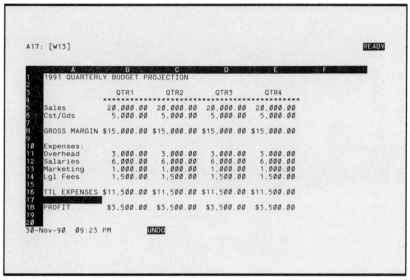

Figure 24.2: *Worksheet with Blank Rows*

25

Entering Absolute Formulas

FEATURING

The ABSOLUTE (F4)
function key

Column F is empty. You still need to calculate each expense item as a percentage of the total expenses. To arrive at the percentages, you need to enter a formula and copy it down through the expenses, similar to the way you entered and copied formulas across the worksheet. However, there is one major difference that has to do with the cell addresses being *relative* or *absolute*.

When you first entered formulas, you typed or pointed to the different cell addresses to create the gross margin, total expenses, and profit formulas. You then copied them, along with the rest of the figures, across the worksheet.

When you copied, 1-2-3 automatically adjusted, or made relative, the cell addresses in the formula. More specifically, 1-2-3 adjusted the total expenses formula in column B—@SUM(B9..B12)—to @SUM(C9..C12) for column C, @SUM(D9..D12) for column D, and @SUM(E9..E12) for column E. 1-2-3 does this automatically to all formulas whether it's copying across the worksheet or down through columns.

Because of this, a problem arises when you build the formula to calculate the percent of total expenses. In the formula, Expense Item divided by Total Expenses, the cell address for total expenses must remain constant, while the expense items change. Therefore, you need to instruct

1-2-3 *not* to automatically adjust the total expenses figure when it copies the formula. To do this, you precede both parts of the cell address with a dollar sign, and the formula is written: +G11/$G$16. This makes the cell address of the total expenses absolute, rather than relative.

Not only is it possible to make a cell address absolute, it is also possible to make part of it absolute. Since a cell address consists of two parts, a column letter and a row number, you can make either component absolute. This is called a *mixed cell address.*

Why would you want to do this? Suppose you want to know how much of the sales for each quarter is spent on marketing. After you find what percentage of the total expenses is represented by marketing, you would multiply sales by the percentage figure— +B5*G11.

If you want the percentage for the sales figures for every quarter, though, you need to enter a formula in which the columns change, but the rows do not so that you can copy the formula across the worksheet. In this case, you designate the row number as absolute, but the column letter remains relative. Thus when you enter the formula +B$5*$G$11, the formulas are copied across as +C5*G11, +D5*G11, and +E5*G11. Only the column changes because the first cell address in the original formula is a mixed cell address.

Mixed cell addresses are considered to be a more advanced use of 1-2-3. In this lesson, you will be using only absolute cell addresses. However, as you become more skilled, understanding mixed cell addresses will help you put them into practice.

How to Enter Absolute Cell Addresses

1. First, enter the following labels:

   in F3   **% of TOTAL**

   in F4   *

2. In F11, type a plus sign to begin the formula.

3. Move the pointer to the right, to the first expense total in **G11**.

4. Press the slash (/) key. The forward slash key, not backslash. This time it acts as a division sign because you are building formulas and you are in the **VALUE** mode. Also, the pointer returns to the original cell.

5. Move the pointer to the entire year's total expenses, **G16**.

6. Press the Absolute (F4) function key. The following appears on the control panel:

    + G11/$G$16

    G16 is now absolute. The Absolute (F4) function key can also be used to enter a mixed or relative cell address. Pressing it once, as you did, makes both the column and row absolute. Pressing it once or twice more makes the cell address mixed, and pressing it a fourth time returns the cell to its original relative setting.

Press once	Absolute	$G$16
Press twice	Mixed:Relative column, absolute row	G$16
Press three times	Mixed:Absolute column, relative row	$G16
Press four times	Relative	G16

    Return to absolute by pressing **F4** once more.

7. Press Enter. **O.26** appears in **F11**, and you return to the **READY** mode.

8. To copy the formula for the other three expenses, press the slash (/) key.

9. Move the pointer to /**Copy**.

10. Press Enter. Do not change the range to copy from.

11. Press Enter to specify the range to copy to.

12. Specify **F12..F16**.

13. Press Enter. The percentages appear, and the worksheet now matches the one in Figure 25.1.

14. Use **/Range Erase** to erase the zero in row 15.

15. Use **/Range Format** to change the numbers in **F11..F16** to **Percent** format with two decimals (see Figure 25.2).

16. Move the pointer up and down through the five cells. Notice on the control panel that the first cell address in the formula changes but the second does not. It remains absolute. The formulas should look like this:

   in F11:   +G11/$G$16

   in F12:   +G12/$G$16

   in F13:   +G13/$G$16

   in F14:   +G14/$G$16

   in F16:   +G16/$G$16

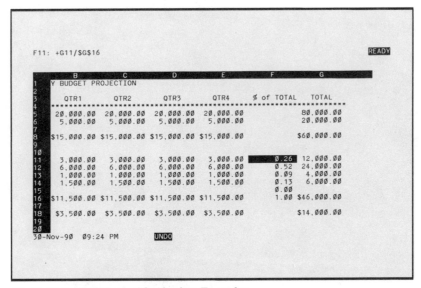

Figure 25.1: Worksheet with Absolute Formulas

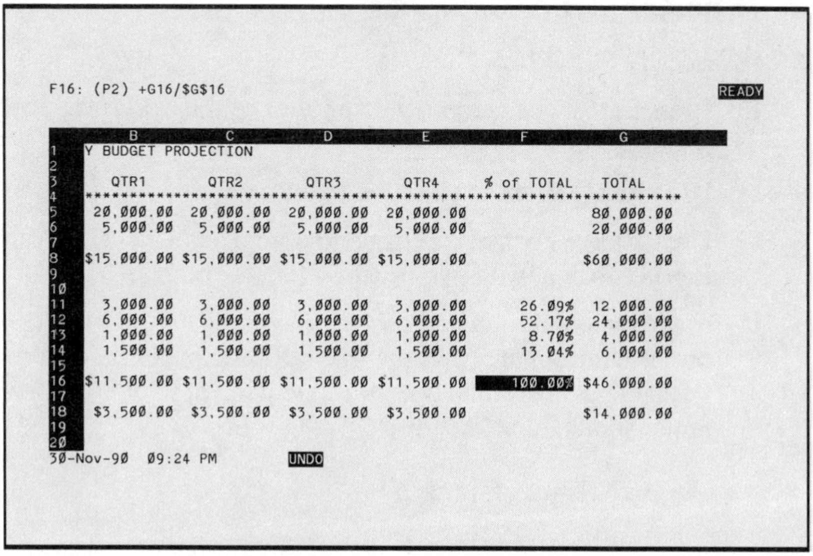

Figure 25.2: Worksheet Formatted with Percentages

Alternatively, you can type the dollar signs in a formula rather than use the Absolute (F4) key.

LESSON

26

Moving Columns and Rows

FEATURING

/Move

Note: Save your worksheet again before you begin this lesson and after you finish each of the following lessons. A small error in these lessons can delete valuable information. If you have Release 2.2, use **UNDO (Alt-F4)** if you make a mistake. Otherwise, use **/File Retrieve** to erase your current work and restore the last saved version.

In the last lesson you inserted the **% of TOTAL** column between the **QTR4** and **TOTAL** columns. But you don't like how it looks. It might make more sense, you think, to put it after the **TOTAL** column. It might also be a good idea to move the row of marketing data above the row of salary data, since both marketing and overhead expenses have risen dramatically this year, while salaries and legal fees haven't changed. With the **/Move** command you can easily make both changes.

/Move works much like the **/Copy** command. You specify a range of cells to move from and another range of cells to move to. You can move a single cell, part of a column, part of a row, or a combination of columns and rows. When you move a range, make sure that there are plenty of blank cells to move it to; the **/Move** command will copy over existing data if you don't.

How to Move Columns and Rows

To Move a Column

Since you are moving the % **of TOTAL** column to the right end of the worksheet, there is space. You do not have to insert a blank column first.

1. Press the slash (/) key.

2. Move the pointer to **Move**.

3. Press Enter. 1-2-3 asks you where you want to move from.

4. Press Escape. The range is now unanchored.

5. Move the pointer to **F3**.

6. Type a period. The cell is now anchored again.

7. Move the pointer down to row **F16**. The range of cells to move is highlighted.

8. Press Enter. 1-2-3 asks you where you want to move to.

9. Move the pointer to **H3**. You do not have to specify more than the first cell in the column you are moving to.

10. Press Enter. The column moves to the right of the **TOTAL** column, and a blank column is left in its place. The worksheet now looks like the one in Figure 26.1.

To Move a Row

11. Since you are moving the row up, above **Salaries,** you first need to insert a blank row. Using the /**Worksheet Insert** command, do so now in cell **A12**. If you've forgotten how, refer to Lesson 24, "Inserting Columns and Rows."

12. Press the slash (/) key.

13. Move the pointer to **Move**.

14. Press Enter. 1-2-3 asks you where you want to move from and displays a range.

15. Press Escape.

16. Move the pointer to **A14.** The range is unanchored and shows a single Marketing cell.

17. Type a period. The cell is anchored.

18. Move the pointer to **H14.** The range of numbers to move is highlighted.

19. Press Enter. 1-2-3 asks you where you are moving to.

20. Move the pointer to **A12,** the blank cell. You do not have to specify more than the first cell in the range.

21. Press Enter. The row moves up, and row 14 is left blank. The worksheet now looks like the one in Figure 26.2.

22. Save your worksheet.

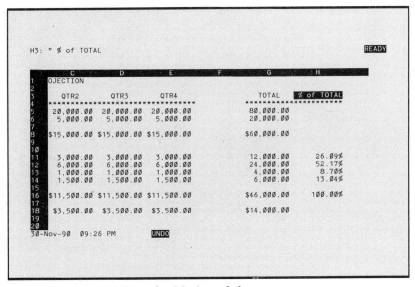

Figure 26.1: *The Worksheet after Moving a Column*

Be careful when moving formulas! If moved correctly, your formulas should calculate correctly. However, if you moved a row containing a cell that had been entered as the first or last cell in a formula, you would disrupt the formula and produce inaccurate results or get an error message. For example, the Legal Fee amounts in row 14 could not have been moved without causing an **ERR** message in the Total Expenses and Profit formulas. The same is true with the row of Overhead figures. This is because the Total Expense formulas refer directly to rows 11 and 14, which are the Overhead and Legal Fee rows. Thus if you were to move either of them you would get one of these formulas: **@SUM(ERR..B14)**, **@SUM(B11..ERR)**, or **@SUM(ERR..ERR)**. In the future, if you move cells that contain formulas, be aware that you might have to correct the formulas to reflect the moves. That is why it is a good idea to save the worksheet before using the **/Move** command.

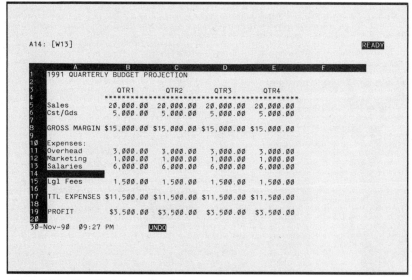

Figure 26.2: The Worksheet after Moving a Row

LESSON

27

Deleting Columns and Rows

FEATURING

/Worksheet Delete

Having moved a column and a row, you are left with a blank column and row on the budget. Obviously, they both need to be deleted. The /**Worksheet Delete** command handles this task.

Deleting part of the worksheet is not the same as erasing it. Erasing entries simply leaves the cells blank. Deleting does more. It erases the entries in a column or row *and* deletes the space occupied by the column or row.

How to Delete Columns and Rows

Note: In case of an accidental deletion, retrieve the worksheet that you saved in the last section. Or, if you are using Release 2.2, use **UNDO (Alt-F4)**.

To Delete a Column

1. Press the slash (/) key.

2. Since the pointer is on **Worksheet**, press Enter.

3. Move the pointer to **Delete**.

4. Press Enter. You have the choice of deleting columns or rows.

5. Since the pointer is on **Column**, press Enter. 1-2-3 asks you the range of columns to delete.

6. Press Escape.

7. Move the pointer to a cell in column F. You need to specify only one cell in the column.

8. Press Enter. The blank column disappears from the screen, and the columns on the right shift to the left.

To Delete a Row

9. To delete row 14, repeat the steps above, but select **Row** instead of **Column**, and designate a cell in row 14. When you've finished, the worksheet will look like the one in Figure 27.1.

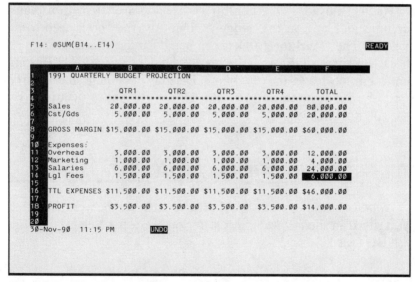

Figure 27.1: The Worksheet without the Blank Column and Row

$\overline{\quad}$ *A*

$\overline{\quad}$ *C*

$\overline{\quad}$ *B*

$\overline{\quad}$ *1*

$\overline{\quad}$ *3*

$\overline{\quad}$ *1*

$\overline{\quad}$ *2*

$\overline{\quad}$ *2*

Part Three

Using a Worksheet

3

28

Keyboard Shortcuts: A Faster Way to Enter Commands

FEATURING

Saving time as you type

Now that you're experienced, it's time to start saving time. Just as you can both type or point to a cell when building a formula, you can type or point to a command. Typing, however, saves keystrokes and time.

How do you type a command? Simply type the first letter of the command. This selects the command and enters it automatically. For example, if you want to save a file, you only need to press the slash (/) key and type **FS**, for File Save, before you enter the file name.

Throughout the remaining lessons, you will be asked to *select* commands, rather than press the slash key, move the pointer to the command, and press Enter. For example, you will see the instruction **Select /File Retrieve**. Whenever you see the instruction to select, you have a choice: You can press the slash key (/), move the pointer to the command name and press Enter, or you can save time by pressing the slash key (/) and then typing the first letter of each command.

Be careful, though! It's much easier to enter a wrong command by typing than it is by pointing.

29

Adding Comments to the Worksheet: Simple Word Processing

FEATURING

/Range Justify

Want to add a short comment or note to your worksheet? Simple! Use **/Range Justify** to "wrap" your text within one or more columns. You may enter up to 256 characters at one time in a cell. **/Range Justify** will then reformat the text within margins that you specify.

How to Enter a Comment in the Worksheet

1. Select **/File Retrieve** to retrieve **91BUDGET** if it is not already displayed.

2. Type the following sentence in cell **A20:**

   This budget projection was created on November 30, 1990 by Fred Jones, Vice-President Finance, ABC Incorporated.

3. Press Enter.

4. Select **/Range Justify** to contain the text in columns A through E only.

5. Specify the range as **A20..E20**. Press Enter.

6. Move the pointer down several rows to view the rest of the text.

7. Select **/File Save Replace** to save the file.

LESSON

30

Splitting the Screen: Viewing Two Areas of the Worksheet Simultaneously

FEATURING

/Worksheet Window
WINDOW (F6)

A worksheet can get very large, with most of its columns not visible on the screen. This can be inconvenient, especially if you want to compare figures in a visible area to figures that are not on the screen. Scrolling through the worksheet isn't the solution since you have to scroll back and forth every time you want to look at a number off the screen.

Instead, you can divide the screen in two—horizontally (as shown in Figure 30.1) or vertically—with the **/Worksheet Window** command. This way you can scroll through two areas of the worksheet and analyze distant figures side by side. To move the pointer back and forth between the two screens or windows, you press the **WINDOW (F6)** function key.

Lesson 30

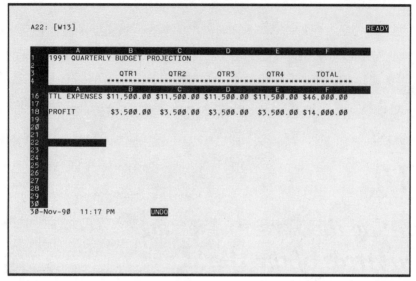

Figure 30.1: Horizontally Split Screen

*H*ow to View Two Areas of the Worksheet Simultaneously

To Split the Screen Horizontally

1. Press Home to display the beginning of the worksheet if it is not already on your screen.

2. Move the pointer to a cell in the row where you want to split the screen; in this case, move it to **A5**.

3. Select **/Worksheet Window**. Remember: You can move the pointer to the command and press Enter or type the first letter of the command. The Window menu, shown in Figure 30.2, appears on the screen.

4. Select **Horizontal**. The screen is divided into two windows. Notice that the column letters are inserted across the middle of the screen.

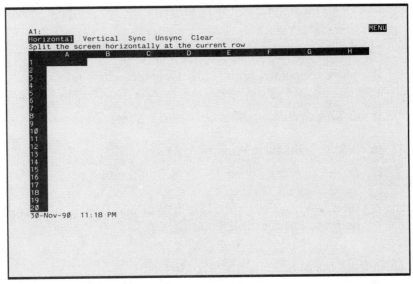

Figure 30.2: *The Window Menu*

5. Move the pointer down. Now the pointer moves only in the top window.

6. Press the **F6** function key. Notice that the pointer switches windows.

7. Move the pointer down again.

8. Press **F6**. The pointer switches back to the top window.

To Return to One Window

9. Select **/Worksheet Window Clear**. The single window returns to the screen.

To Split the Screen Vertically

10. Press Home.

11. Move the pointer to a cell in the column where you want to split the screen; in this case, move it to column B.

12. Select **/Worksheet Window Vertical**. The screen splits vertically.

13. Move the pointer to the right. Only the left window scrolls. Press the Home key.

14. Press the **F6** key to move the pointer into the right window.

15. Move the pointer to the right. Only the right window scrolls.

To Scroll Through Both Windows at the Same Time

16. Select /**Worksheet Window Sync**.

17. Move the pointer down to row 40. Notice that both windows scroll together and the labels scroll off the top of the worksheet. (When the screen is split horizontally, you can scroll both windows to the left and right.)

To Release the Synchronized Scrolling

18. Select /**Worksheet Window Unsync**.

19. Move the pointer up or down. Notice that you are scrolling through only one window.

20. Select /**Worksheet Window Clear** to return to one window.

31

Fixing Titles So They Don't Scroll Off the Worksheet

FEATURING

/ Worksheet Titles

When you view column G, the labels in column A scroll off the screen. Unless you have the labels for each column and row memorized or written down somewhere, this can be disconcerting. It becomes difficult, if not impossible, to interpret or alter unidentified figures.

The **/Worksheet Titles** command remedies this before or after you split the screen by ensuring that designated columns or rows—called *titles*—remain on the screen or are *fixed*; hence the term *fixing titles*. A worksheet with fixed titles is shown in Figure 31.1. Normally, you would fix labels or headings; however, you can designate more than one column or row as long as it borders the top or left edges of the worksheet.

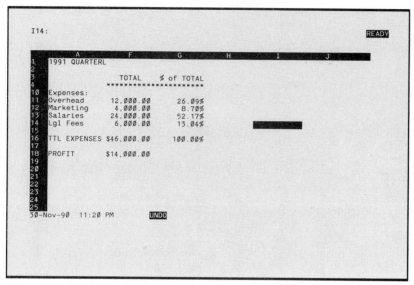

Figure 31.1: Worksheet with Fixed Titles

How to Fix Titles

To Fix Rows Across the Top (Horizontal Titles)

1. Press Home. Move the pointer to a cell in the row *below* the titles you want to remain fixed. To fix all the labels on the top of the worksheet, move the pointer to row 5.

2. Select /**Worksheet Titles Horizontal**.

3. Move the pointer to row 35. Notice that rows 1 through 4 do not scroll off the top of the screen.

To Release Fixed Rows and Columns

4. While you are still in row 35, select /**Worksheet Titles Clear**. Notice that the titles have disappeared off the top of the screen. Press Home.

To Fix a Column on the Left (Vertical Titles)

5. Move the pointer to a cell in the column to the right of what you want to remain fixed. To fix the left column, move the pointer to column B.

6. Select /**Worksheet Titles Vertical**.

7. Move the pointer to column L. Notice that column A remains on the screen.

8. Release the left column using /**Worksheet Titles Clear** again.

9. Press Home.

To Fix both Rows and Columns Simultaneously

10. Move the pointer below and to the right of everything that you want to remain fixed. To fix all of the labels on the budget, move the pointer to **B5**.

11. Select /**Worksheet Titles Both**.

12. Move the pointer to column L. Notice that everything in column A remains.

13. Press Home. The pointer returns to **B5**.

14. Move the pointer down to row 35. Now everything in the top four rows remains fixed.

15. Press Home. Notice that the pointer does not return Home to A1. It is in B5 again because pointer-movement keys will not move the pointer into fixed titles. Other than clearing titles, the only way to move into a title—to edit it, for example—is to use the **GOTO (F5)** function key.

16. Press the **F5** function key. 1-2-3 asks you to enter the cell address of the cell you want to go to.

17. Press the Left Arrow key once. Notice that a copy of the fixed titles is brought out for editing. Press Enter to complete the process.

18. Move the pointer down to **Cst/Gds**. Change the title to **Cost/ Goods,** using the **EDIT (F2)** function key. When you finish, press Enter.

19. Move down to **Lgl Fees**. Again using the **F2,** change this to **Legal Fees**. When you finish, press Enter.

20. To eliminate duplicate titles, move to column E.

To Release Fixed Columns and Rows

21. Use **/Worksheet Titles Clear.**

LESSON

32

Protecting the Worksheet: Making Some Entries Permanent

FEATURING

/Worksheet Global Protection
/Range Unprotect

If you plan to update only some of the cells on the worksheet, while others, particularly formulas, remain unchanged, it is a good idea to *protect* those cells that will remain constant. By protecting them, you cannot change or erase cell entries, accidentally or otherwise, without first *unprotecting* the cells.

Protecting is a safety measure to ensure that you, or other people who have access to your files, don't alter certain entries. For example, you may want to be sure that if your co-workers enter new sales figures on the worksheet, they won't accidentally erase the formulas.

When you unprotect cells they become highlighted. This distinguishes the unprotected cells from the protected ones. In fact, even if you do not plan on protecting the rest of the worksheet, highlighting can make it easier to find the cells that you want to work with.

Lesson 32

Protecting cells is a two-step process. First, you protect the entire worksheet with the **/Worksheet Global Protection** command. Then you unprotect the cells where you will continue to work with the **/Range Unprotect** command. You can do this in the reverse, as well: First unprotect the cells you want to work in and then protect the rest of the worksheet; the result will be the same.

How to Protect the Worksheet

1. Select **/Worksheet Global Protection**. The menu in Figure 32.1 is displayed on the screen. Until you change it, **/Worksheet Global Protection** is disabled; that is, not in effect.

2. Select **Enable**. The entire worksheet is now protected; you cannot make any changes. Later, if you wanted to turn off the protection, you would select **Disable**.

3. Move the pointer to **B5**, and type your first name.

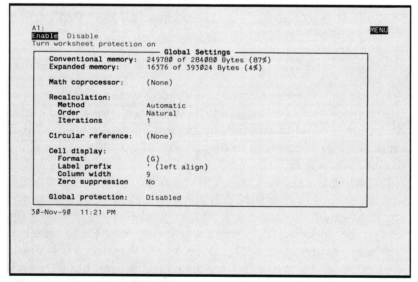

Figure 32.1: Global Protection Menu

4. Press Enter. 1-2-3 beeps and **ERROR** and **Protected cell** appear on the screen. 1-2-3 is reminding you that you cannot enter anything in that cell.

5. Press Escape to clear the control panel. When you get an error message, pressing Escape returns you to the **READY** mode.

To Unprotect Individual Cells

6. Select /**Range Unprotect**. 1-2-3 asks you to identify the range that you want to unprotect.

7. Press Escape to unanchor the range.

8. Move the pointer to **B5,** if it's not already there.

9. Type a period.

10. Move the pointer to include rows 5 and 6 from column B through column E.

11. Press Enter. Notice that the unprotected cells are highlighted after you press Enter. (Adjust the contrast knob on your monitor to see the highlighted cells.)

12. Repeat steps 6 through 11 to specify a second range. Include rows 11 through 14 from column B across to column E.

13. Press Enter. The cells in these two ranges do not have labels or formulas.

To Disable Global Protection

14. Use /**Worksheet Global Protection** to **Disable** protection. The unprotected ranges will remain highlighted. /**Range Protect** would change this, though it is not necessary.

Regardless of whether Global Protection is enabled or disabled, the unprotected cells will remain highlighted. (See Figure 32.2.)

Lesson 32

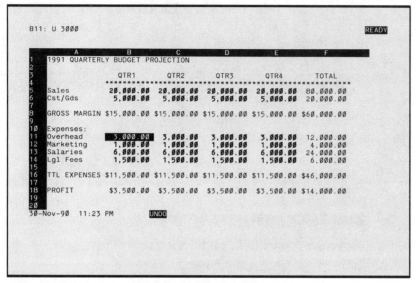

Figure 32.2: *Worksheet with Unprotected Cells Highlighted*

LESSON

33

Checking and Changing 1-2-3 Default Settings

FEATURING

/Worksheet Status
/Worksheet Global Default
   Status
   Update
   International Currency
COMPOSE (F1)

The budget you have built is not so large that you have to worry about running out of memory (RAM) inside the computer. However, long before you fill all of 1-2-3's 8,192 columns and 256 rows, you'll confront a **MEM** (memory full) message. How can you find out, before you do run out, how much memory is available? And, if you don't remember, how can you find out whether the global column-width is set at 9 or 11? And what about the global format? Is it set at a comma with two decimal places or is it set at Currency?

The /**Worksheet Status** command displays the answers to all of these questions on the screen. In addition to indicating available memory, it displays global settings—that is, the settings for the features that affect the entire worksheet, such as recalculation, format, label-prefix, column-width, and protection.

The /**Worksheet Global Default Status** command displays the startup—or default—settings whenever you begin working with 1-2-3. It comes in handy when you want to know how 1-2-3 is set up for printing, saving and retrieving files, and for displaying formats for dates, times, and numbers. The /**Worksheet Global Default** commands enable you to change these settings.

*H*ow to Check the Worksheet Status

1. Select /**Worksheet Status**. 1-2-3 displays the menu in Figure 33.1. Since you have already changed several settings, such as **Global Column Width** and **Global Protection**, the settings you have will not necessarily match the default settings—the settings that originally came with the 1-2-3 program. Descriptions of the various settings follow.

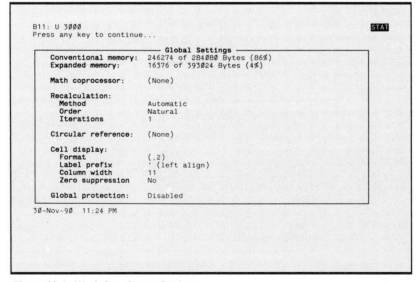

Figure 33.1: Worksheet Status Settings

Conventional memory is the amount of memory (RAM), up to 640K, that is available in your computer after the disk operating system (DOS), 1-2-3 itself, and the current worksheet have been loaded.

Expanded memory is the amount of memory above 640K and up to 4 Mb that is available. You can increase the amount of memory available in both conventional and expanded memory by erasing data you don't need, by deleting blank rows, and by using **/Range Format Reset** to get rid of unnecessary formatting, especially of blank cells. Also, place your work toward the top of the worksheet; blank cells above your work will take up additional memory. To regain memory after you make these changes, you must save your worksheet and then retrieve it again.

Math coprocessor tells you whether your computer has an 8087 coprocessor. Some calculations, especially complex ones such as those using the @IRR and @NPV functions, are substantially speeded up with an 8087 coprocessor.

The following three settings are set using **/Worksheet Global Recalculation**.

Recalculation: Method specifies whether a worksheet will calculate **Automatically** each time you enter new data or change existing data, or **Manually** when you press the **CALC (F9)** function key. Manual recalculation is useful when a worksheet is large and the continual recalculation of the automatic method slows down your work.

Recalculation: Order will almost always be left to **Natural** order. When calculating a formula that depends on the results of another formula, this setting makes 1-2-3 wait until the results of the first formula have been calculated. Exceptions may occur when you have translated a worksheet from another software program that depends on **Column** or **Row** order, or if a 1-2-3 worksheet has been set specifically to calculate in one of these alternative orders.

Recalculation: Iterations is useful when a worksheet needs to be calculated a number of times in order to derive correct results (for example, if you use formulas that calculate internal rates of return). You can set up the number of times you want a worksheet to be calculated.

Circular reference displays any cell address where a formula refers to itself. For example, a formula in cell B4 that reads $+B2+B3+B4$ is a circular reference. In many cases circular references will produce inaccurate results. **CALC** will display on the screen whenever there is one or more circular reference. If there are multiple circular references, correcting the one that is displayed in the Status menu will display any others.

Cell display: Format refers to the **/Worksheet Global Format** setting for all numbers and formulas. **Label Prefix** refers to the **/Worksheet Global Label Prefix** setting that determines if labels are centered, right-aligned, or left-aligned when first entered into the worksheet. **Column width** displays the **/Worksheet Global Column Width** setting, and **Zero suppression** refers to whether formulas will display a 0 or be displayed (and printed) as blank when the value of the formula is 0. This is set using **/Worksheet Global Zero**.

Global protection displays whether **/Worksheet Global Protection** has been enabled or disabled. Refer to Lesson 32, "Protecting the Worksheet."

2. To return to the worksheet, press any key.

*H*ow to Check and Change 1-2-3 *Global Default Settings*

3. Select /**Worksheet Global Default Status**. 1-2-3 displays the screen in Figure 33.2.

    Printer displays the printer interface (serial or parallel), the setting for automatic line feed, the default margins, page length, any setup codes, and the name of the printer. These default settings will be used for all worksheets unless they are changed here or changed individually in a worksheet using the /**Print Options** command.

    Add-In (Release 2.2) lists any additional programs that are set up to run when you start 1-2-3. See Lessons 65, "Using the Macro Library Manager,"and 67, "Allways Spreadsheet Publishing," for more about Add-Ins.

    Directory displays the drive and subdirectory used for retrieving and storing files.

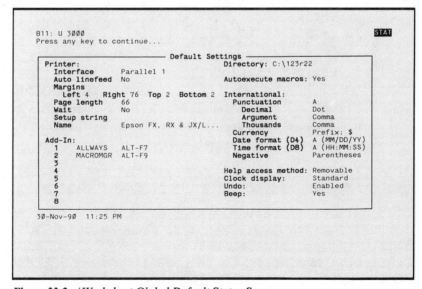

Figure 33.2: /Worksheet Global Default Status Screen

International reflects the types of formatting for numbers, currency, dates, and times.

Help access method reflects whether 1-2-3 has been set up to allow removal of the System disk from drive A, while still allowing use of the Help screens. This is useful for floppy-disk systems.

Clock display reflects the type of time format displayed in the bottom left of the screen. Alternatively, the current file name can be displayed. This clock can be turned off.

Undo (Release 2.2) is **Enabled** (in effect) or **Disabled** (not in effect).

Beep tells 1-2-3 to beep (YES) or not to beep (NO) when you make an error.

4. Press any key when you finish with this screen. The worksheet is displayed.

5. Experiment with changing some of the Global Default settings such as **Directory** or **Printer** as follows:

   If you change the default directory (where your worksheets reside), you want to save the changes permanently, and you are using a floppy-disk system, you must remove any write-protect tab on the System disk in drive A first. Then use **/Worksheet Global Default Update**.

   If you specified several printers when you installed 1-2-3, you could use **/Worksheet Global Default Printer Name** to switch to another printer. When you finish, select **Quit** twice to return to the worksheet.

How to Change the Currency Sign for Formatted Numbers

The budget totals are currently formatted with dollar signs. What if your currency were the Japanese yen or the British pound? How would you change the currency symbol? Using **/Worksheet Global Default Other International Currency** in conjunction with **COMPOSE (Alt-F1),** you can type symbols that do not appear on the keyboard. You can change the currency symbol to ¥ for Yen.

6. Select /**Worksheet Global Default Other International Currency**.

7. Use the Backspace key to erase the dollar ($) sign.

8. Use **COMPOSE**. Hold down the Alt key and tap the F1 key.

9. Type **Y =** . The two letters will be displayed one over the other.

10. Press Enter. You will be prompted to select **Prefix** or **Suffix**. This allows you to put the currency symbol in front of numbers (Prefix) or after numbers (Suffix).

11. Select **Prefix**. Press Quit twice. The symbols on your worksheet reflect the change.

12. Repeat steps 6 through 11 to set the currency symbol back to the dollar ($) symbol.

How to Disable the UNDO Feature

Because UNDO reserves half of your system's available memory in order to maintain a backup copy of your worksheet, you may need to **Disable** it and free up the memory in order to work on large worksheets.

13. First check that no Add-In programs are being run now. If they are, do not do the following steps; you may not be able to enable UNDO again without additional steps.

    Select /**Worksheet Global Default Status**. If any programs are listed under Add-In, Select **Quit** and go to the next lesson. Otherwise, select **Quit** and do the following steps.

14. Select /**Worksheet Global Default Other Undo Disable**. The **UNDO** message at the bottom of the screen has disappeared.

15. Select /**Worksheet Global Default Other Undo Enable**. The **UNDO** message is displayed again.

LESSON

34

Handling Large Worksheets by Turning Off Automatic Recalculation

As worksheets expand, 1-2-3's ability to calculate slows down. Usually this happens when a worksheet is many times the size of the one you have built.

Large worksheets force 1-2-3 to do more work. Each time you enter a piece of information—whether it's a label, number, or formula—1-2-3 automatically recalculates the entire worksheet. Although the only changes you see are the new entries and calculations, every formula has been recalculated. As a result, very large worksheets may take as much as a minute or more to recalculate after every entry.

If you are using Release 2.01 with Speedup or Release 2.2, 1-2-3 calculates faster because it recalculates only formulas affected by changes you make. Nevertheless, you may still want to save time by turning off the automatic recalculation setting. When you do this, 1-2-3 does not recalculate until you press **CALC (F9)**. So that you don't forget to calculate, before printing or saving, for example, 1-2-3 reminds you by displaying **CALC** at the bottom of the worksheet.

How to Turn Off Automatic Recalculation

1. Select **/Worksheet Global Recalculation**. 1-2-3 offers six setting options—automatic, manual, natural, column, row, and iteration—all of which were explained in Lesson 33.

2. Select **Manual**.

3. Move the pointer to **B5**.

4. Type: **30000**

5. Press Enter. Notice that 1-2-3 did not recalculate any formulas and **CALC** appears at the bottom of the screen.

6. Press **CALC (F9)**. All the formulas are recalculated and **CALC** disappears.

To Turn On Automatic Recalculation

7. Select **/Worksheet Global Recalculation**.

8. Now select **Automatic**.

9. In B5, type: **20000**

10. Press Enter. 1-2-3 automatically recalculates.

When automatic recalculation is off, you can calculate one cell at a time. To do this, you would move to the cell with the formula, press **EDIT (F2)**, and then press Enter.

35

Printing the Worksheet

FEATURING

/Print
Printer
/Worksheet Global Default
Stop printing (Ctrl-Break)

Note: Even if you don't have a printer, follow the instructions in this section. The information will be useful when you do have access to a printer.

The **/Print** command enables you to print all or part of the worksheet. In addition, 1-2-3 offers a variety of formatting options that transform the worksheet into a fancy report.

With printing options, you can add a *header* or *footer* or both to the worksheet page. Either one might include the report's title, author, date, and page number. You can also *fix* columns and rows at the top and left of each page of the report, just as you fixed titles on the screen, in case the worksheet is so large that parts of it are printed on separate pages. You can adjust the printout to fit different paper sizes, making the report pages longer or shorter, wider or narrower. You can also vary the size of the characters, their type style, and the printing shade from light to dark, depending on your printer.

1-2-3 prints each page with margins on four sides and fits as many columns as it can within the standard or default left and right margins. Columns that don't fit are printed on a new page.

In this lesson, you will experiment with three types of printouts. You will first print the worksheet simply, without any additions to the page. Then, you will print it using a variety of format options that change the appearance of the report. After that, you will print the formulas in the worksheet.

In the steps that remain, you will use the /**Worksheet Global** command to change the printer default settings. Since many 1-2-3 users will consistently use certain print options, it makes sense to save time by making them permanent. For example, if the majority of your work consists of large budget projections, you will probably want to print as much as you can on wide paper, with a wide printer, and with small type. By changing the default settings to suit your needs, you don't have to set these options each time you want to print a worksheet.

*H*ow to Print the Worksheet

To Print a Simple Report

1. Prepare your printer. Make sure that the top of the first page is lined up with the print head. Turn on your printer.

2. Save your worksheet. This is always a good idea before you print.

3. Select /**Print**. You have two choices: **Printer** and **File**. /**Print Printer** sends your work to a printer. /**Print File** saves the worksheet on disk as it appears on the screen and without formulas. This enables you to include the worksheet in a document created by a word processing program.

4. Select **Printer**. The Print menu (Figure 35.1) appears.

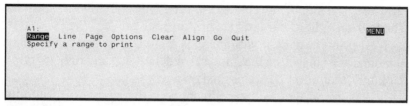

Figure 35.1: Print Menu

The Print Menu

- **Range** specifies the cells that you want to print.

- **Line** advances the printer a single line.

- **Page** advances the paper to the top of the next sheet.

- **Options** offers a menu of printing options, such as headers and footers.

- **Clear** clears any print settings that you may have set previously.

- **Align** tells the printer where the top of the page is, once you've aligned the perforated area with the head.

- **Go** tells the printer to print.

- **Quit** exits the Print menu.

For Release 2.2, you will also see the **Print Settings Sheet**. This displays the current settings for the Print commands. When you exit the Print menu or press **WINDOW (F6)**, the worksheet is redisplayed.

5. Select **Range**. 1-2-3 asks you to enter the print range and displays the cell where the pointer resides.

6. Press the Home key to move the pointer to the top left corner.

7. Type a period.

8. Move the pointer down to row 22 and across to column G.

9. Press Enter. The Print menu returns to the control panel.

To Start and Stop Printing

10. Select **Align** to tell 1-2-3 that the top of the paper is aligned correctly in the printer.

11. Select **Go**. If you have a printer, the worksheet begins to print. If you don't, 1-2-3 will beep and **ERROR** will flash on the screen. If this happens, press Escape to return to the worksheet.

12. To stop printing prematurely, hold down the Control key and tap the Break key on the right side of the keyboard. The printer stops. The Print menu is erased.

13. Select **/Print Printer Page**. If you have a printer, the paper advances to the top; otherwise, nothing happens.

14. Select **Go** again. If you have a printer, the worksheet is printed.

15. Select **Page** to advance the printout.

Because the worksheet is wider than the screen, it will not fit on the paper using the current print settings. When this happens, the columns that don't fit will be printed at the end. There are two ways to solve this problem.

To Repeat Columns on Each Page

With the extra column printed on the last page, it is difficult to determine which numbers refer to which expenses. To solve this, you can use the **Borders** command to print column A again on the last page. You must not include column A in the print range, however.

16. From the Print menu, select the **Options**. The Options menu, shown in Figure 35.2, is displayed.

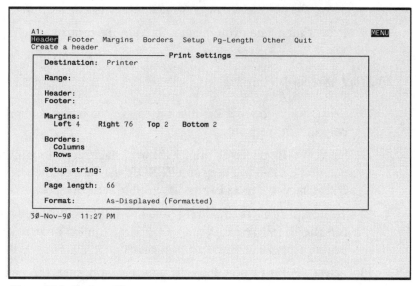

Figure 35.2: *Options Menu*

The Options Menu

- **Header** adds the date, time, or page to the top of each page.

- **Footer** is similar to a header but prints at the bottom of each page.

- **Margins** adjusts the space at the top, bottom, left, and right of the page.

- **Borders** prints specified columns and/or rows on each page. For example, if the worksheet is so large that you need to print it in sections, you might want to print the column headings from row 1 at the top of each page.

- **Setup** tells your printer the size, style, and shade of print to use.

- **Page-Length** is used to adjust the printer in case your paper is shorter or longer than 11 inches.

- **Other** offers more options, such as printing the worksheet formulas instead of the numbers.

17. Select **Borders Columns**.

18. Type **A1** to specify a Border column. This will cause column A to print on each page.

19. Press Enter and then Escape to exit the options menu.

20. Change the print range so that it does not include column A. Select **Range**. Type: **B1..G22** and press Enter.

21. Select **Go** to print the worksheet.

22. Select **Page**. Column A should print next to the extra column on the last page. Notice that the title is cut off; it is possible to fix multiple columns, if necessary. It is also possible to print a row or rows at the top of each page using **Borders Rows**.

To Change the Top, Left, and Right Margins

In addition to printing specified columns or rows on each page of a worksheet to make it easier to read, you can also change the left and right margins to increase the number of columns that will print. You will also change the top margin to center the worksheet on the page more.

23. From the **Printer** menu, select **Options**.

24. Select **Margins**. 1-2-3 offers four margin locations.

25. Select **Top**. 1-2-3 displays the default setting: 2 for two lines.

26. Type: **10**

27. Press Enter.

28. Select **Margins** again.

29. Select **Left**. 1-2-3 displays the default left margin setting: 4 (characters).

30. Type: **0**

31. Press Enter.

32. Select **Margins**

33. Select **Right**. 1-2-3 displays the default right margin setting: 75.

34. Type: **136**

35. Press Enter. This expands the margins to include 136 charac-ters. When you have a wide-carriage printer and use smaller print, you may use the maximum width of 240.

To Change the Size of the Print

In addition to changing the margins, you can also change the print size in order to fit more on a page.

36. Select **Setup**. 1-2-3 prompts you to enter a setup string. The **Setup String** is a three-digit code preceded by a \ (backslash) that tells your printer the type or size of print to use. This includes bold, underlined, italicized, and double-spaced print and different pitches and fonts. (To create setup codes, refer to the *printer control codes* in your printer manual. Then translate your control characters into 1-2-3's setup codes, using the 1-2-3 Setup Strings Table in the appendix of the 1-2-3 manual.)

37. To compress the print to roughly half the size, type one of the following codes:

Printer Type	Setup String(s)
Epson compatible/IBM	\015
HP Laserjet	\027(s16.66H

(If your printer does not match either of the two listed, do not type in a setup string.)

38. Press Enter.

39. To return to the main **Print** menu, select **Quit**.

40. Select **Go**. If you have a printer, 1-2-3 prints the new version of the report.

41. Select **Page** to advance the page.

To Add a Header

42. Select **Options Header**. 1-2-3 asks you to enter the header.

43. Type: **Widgets Division Budget ¦¦@**
    The vertical lines are added to tell 1-2-3 how to distribute the header across the page. They are created with the Shift and backslash (\) keys. The header is divided into three parts: the left third, the center third, and the right third. Anything that is typed before the first vertical line is printed in the left corner of the page. Whatever is entered between the vertical lines is centered, and what comes after the vertical lines is printed in the right corner. The @ symbol will print today's date. The two vertical lines tell 1-2-3 to place Widgets Division Budget in the left third and the date in the right third.

44. Press Enter. The **Options** menu returns to the screen.

To Add a Footer

45. Select **Footer**. 1-2-3 prompts you to enter a footer.

46. Type:

    ¦#

    This tells 1-2-3 to print page numbers in the center of the bottom of each page.

47. Press Enter. The **Options** menu returns to the screen.

48. Select **Quit,** then **Go** to print.

49. Press **Page** to print the page number in the footer. (The page number will be set to 1 when you exit the Print menu and return.)

To Print the Formulas of a Worksheet

50. Select **Options Other**.

Print Options Other Menu

- **As-Displayed** prints the worksheet as it is displayed on the screen. This is the default setting.

- Use **Cell-Formulas** to audit your formulas by printing each cell's contents on a separate line.

- **Formatted** tells 1-2-3 to print the worksheet with the standard or selected options, such as headers, footers, and margins. This is also the default setting.

- **Unformatted** tells 1-2-3 to print without headers, footers, margins, and page length. Use this when printing the worksheet to a file using **/Print File** for use in a word processor. This allows you to use your word processor to create the proper margins and page breaks.

51. Select **Cell-Formulas**.

52. Press Escape to return to the **Print** menu.

53. Select **Go**. If you have a printer, 1-2-3 prints the worksheet with each cell on a separate line.

54. When it's finished, select **Options Other** to return the setting to **As-Displayed** for normal printing later on. The **Options** menu returns to the screen.

55. Press Escape to return to the **Print** menu.

56. Select **Page** to advance the page if necessary.

To Clear the Print Options

To return the worksheet to its default print settings to print other worksheets, you can clear the print options.

The Print Clear Menu

- **All** cancels all options and the print range that you last used.
- **Range** cancels only the range.
- **Format** cancels the Margins, Page-Length, and Setup options.
- **Borders** cancels the column's and row's border options.

57. Select **Clear**.

58. To clear **Options** but retain the **Print** range, select **Format**. The **Print** menu returns.

To Make Options Permanent by Changing the Print Default Settings

Next, you will change 1-2-3's print settings permanently to match those above.

59. Use Ctrl-Break to return to **READY** mode. In addition to stopping printing, Ctrl-Break will break out of the menus and return 1-2-3 to the **READY** mode.

60. Select **/Worksheet Global Default**. 1-2-3 offers seven choices.

61. Select **Printer Right**.

62. Type: **136**. This widens the right margin.

63. Press Enter.

64. Select **Quit** to return to the **Default** menu.

65. If you have a floppy-disk system, remove the write-protect tab from the 1-2-3 System disk, if necessary. Place the System disk back in drive A.

66. Select **Update**. The new settings are permanently saved as part of the 1-2-3 program until you change them again.

67. Select **Quit**.

Note: If you are using a printer that can print only 80 columns, change the /**Worksheet Global Default Printer Right** margin setting back to the initial 75 setting. Use **Update** to save the change.

36

Naming Parts of the Worksheet

FEATURING

/Range Name
NAME (F3)

With the **/Range Name** command it's possible to use everyday English, rather than cell addresses, when you need to specify a range of cells.

Suppose, for example, you have a very large worksheet and you want to print only one section of it. Instead of having to remember the cell addresses of that one section, say C462..P512, you can assign a name, say "Summary," to the entire range of cells. Later, when you want to print it, all you have to do is specify the name "Summary," not the range.

You can also use names in formulas. For example, if you hadn't already entered a **PROFIT** formula, you could assign a name "MAR" to B8, the cell containing the **GROSS MARGIN** figure, and another name "EXP" to B16, the cell containing the Expenses figure. Then, instead of entering the PROFIT formula as +B16-B8, you could enter the formula in English: +**MAR-EXP**.

Once a range is named, you can /**Copy**, /**Move**, /**Range Erase**, and /**Range Format** the cells in the named range. You can also use names with the **GOTO (F5)** to go to the top left corner of the range. Thus whenever 1-2-3 asks you to specify a range, you can enter its name instead of its cell addresses.

What you name a range is entirely up to you given the following limitations:

- Range names cannot be more than 15 characters.

- They may not include spaces, commas, semicolons, or the characters + * − / & > < @ #.

- They should not be similar to cell addresses (e.g., A1 or EQ500), to avoid confusion.

- They should not contain @function names (e.g., @**sum**), macro commands (e.g., {**QUIT**}), or key names (**CALC**).

- They should not begin with a number (e.g., 1991.)

How to Assign a Name to a Range

To Print the Expenses Summary

1. Select /**Range Name**. The **Range Name** menu is displayed.

The Range Name Menu

- **Create** assigns a name to a range.

- **Delete** erases a range name.

- **Labels** allows you to use a label that already exists on the worksheet as a name for a range.

- **Reset** erases all the range names from the worksheet.

- **Table** creates a list of all the range names that you have created.

2. Select **Create**. 1-2-3 asks for the name of the range.

3. Type:

    EXPENSES

4. Press Enter. 1-2-3 asks for the range you want to name.

5. Press Escape to unexpand the range.

6. Move the pointer to the label **Expenses** in cell A10.

7. Type a period.

8. Move the pointer to **TTL EXPENSES** in **A16**.

9. Move across to the **% of TOTAL** figures in column G, row 16.

10. Press Enter.

To Print the Named Range

Even if you don't have a printer, complete the following steps.

11. Select **/Print Printer Range**. 1-2-3 asks for the range to be printed and displays the last range you printed. The entire worksheet is displayed.

12. Press the **NAME (F3)** function key. All the range names that have been created—in this case, one—are displayed.

13. Since the pointer is already on **Expenses:**, press Enter. You could also type the name on the control panel. The **Print** menu returns to the screen, and the new range is specified, including the range name, e.g., EXPENSES.

14. To check that the range is specified, press Enter again at the **Range** command. Although the name is not displayed, the range is. Notice that the Expense range you named is now highlighted as the Print range.

15. Press Enter to return to the **Print** menu.

16. To print the summary, select **Page** to advance the paper in the printer.

17. Select **Go**. If you have a printer, 1-2-3 prints the Expenses summary. If not, you will get an Error message; press Escape.

18. When printing is completed, select **Page**.

19. To return to the **READY** mode, select **Quit**.

37

Transferring Data from One Worksheet to Another

FEATURING

/File Combine
/File Xtract

It's often useful to transfer data from one worksheet file to another where the data will be combined with new information. For example, let's assume that you've created the budget projection for one of two stores, and you would like to compare the two stores' profits in another worksheet file, one that summarizes the profit figures for all four quarters.

The **/File Combine** command accomplishes this by transferring data from one worksheet into the worksheet on the screen without erasing it from the original worksheet.

First, you must name the range that you want to transfer before you can transfer it. Then, in order to compare profits for two stores, you will create a budget in a second file for the second store. Finally, you will create a third file into which you will transfer each store's profits using the **/File Combine** command.

In addition to /**File Combine,** Release 2.2 offers file linking to auto-mate the consolidation of worksheets. File linking is explained in Lesson 38.

How to Transfer Data from One Worksheet to Another

To Name the Range

1. Select /**Range Name Create.** 1-2-3 displays the range that you've already named: **EXPENSES.**

2. Type:

    PROFIT

3. Press Enter. 1-2-3 asks you to specify the range you are naming.

4. Press Escape to unexpand the range.

5. Specify the PROFIT row or bottom-line figures (row 18), columns B through F. Do not include the label in Column A.

6. Press Enter.

7. Save the current worksheet. Use /**File Save** and save the worksheet under the name **STORE1** by typing in the name and pressing Enter.

To Create the Budget for the Second Store

8. Enter the following numbers in place of the current ones. (They will automatically be converted to the comma, decimal format.)

Sales	100000	110000	120000	130000
Cst/Gds	40000	45000	50000	55000
GROSS MARGIN				
Overhead	15000	15000	15000	15000
Marketing	10000	10000	10000	10000

| Salaries | 30000 | 30000 | 30000 | 30000 |
| Lgl Fees | 8000 | 8000 | 8000 | 8000 |

TTL EXPENSES

PROFIT

The gross margin, total expenses, and profits adjust automatically. Two numbers in column F are not displayed because they are too wide for the column; instead, asterisks are displayed.

9. Select /**Worksheet Global Column-Width** to widen the columns to 12. Notice that column F shifts off the screen.

10. Select /**File Save** again and save the current worksheet under the name **STORE2**. Notice that you did not have to define the Profit range again. You will use the one you defined earlier.

11. Select /**Worksheet Erase**.

12. When prompted, select **Yes**.

13. Press Enter.

14. Enter the labels in Figure 37.1 on the new summary worksheet. Use quotation marks (") before the QTR headings to right-align the column headings.

15. To prepare the worksheet before you transfer numbers, enter the following formulas in B8, to the right of **TOTAL**, and in F5, beneath **TOTAL**.

    In B8:   @SUM(B5. .B6)

    In F5:   @SUM(B5. .E5)

After you press Enter, a zero appears because no numbers have been entered in B5 or B6.

16. Select /**Copy** to copy the formula in B8 across to the remaining columns, including the **TOTAL** column, and the formula in F5

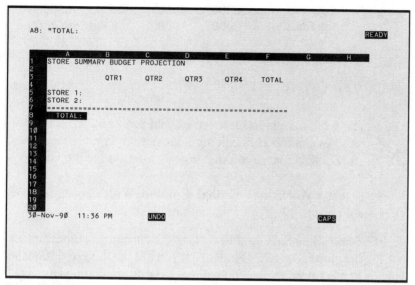

Figure 37.1: Summary Worksheet Labels

down to F6. The worksheet now looks like the one in Figure 37.2. An alternative is to type in formulas manually beneath each quarter and the Total column. Use the two formulas in step 15 as models for the others, but change the cell addresses appropriately. Save the new worksheet as **SUMMARY**.

17. Move the pointer to the cell where STORE1 and QTR1 intersect: **B5**. This is the first cell of the range where you will use **/File Combine** to copy in the profits.

18. Select **/File Combine**. 1-2-3 displays three choices: **Copy**, **Add**, and **Subtract**.

    Copy erases existing entries and replaces them with incoming data. **Add** adds incoming values to the existing values and produces totals. If the existing entries are labels, incoming values are discarded. **Subtract** is similar to **Add**, except that incoming values are subtracted from existing values. Use **Add** since **Copy** will incorrectly bring in the formulas from each store worksheet.

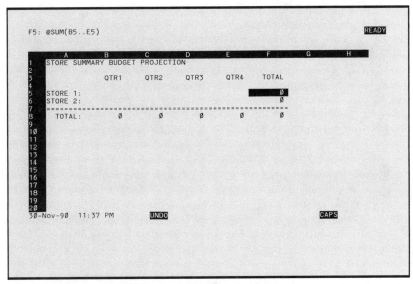

Figure 37.2: Summary Worksheet with Formulas

19. Select **Add**. 1-2-3 displays two more choices: **Entire-File** and **Named/Specified-Range**.

20. From **STORE1,** you will transfer the profit range that you named; therefore, select **Named/Specified-Range**.

21. Type:

    PROFIT

    After you press Enter, 1-2-3 prompts you to enter a file name.

22. Select **STORE1**. After you press Enter, the worksheet will look like the one in Figure 37.3. If there were numbers already present in row 5, /**File Combine Add** would add them to the numbers you are copying. In the future, be sure that you erase whatever is in the row you are copying to unless you want the figures added together.

23. Use /**Worksheet Global Column-Width** to expand the columns to **12**. After you finish, the worksheet will look like the one in Figure 37.4.

24. Move the cursor to the cell where **STORE2** and **QTR1** intersect: **B6**.

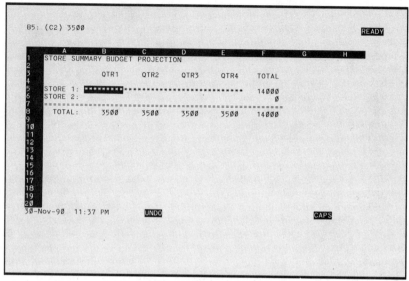

Figure 37.3: Summary Worksheet with STORE1 Profit Figures

25. Select **/File Combine Add Named/Specified-Range**.

26. Type the name of the second range:

    PROFIT

    Since the profit figures were in the same rows in each work-sheet, the same name is used to transfer both ranges.

27. Press Enter.

28. Select the name of the second file: **STORE2**. The summary file, shown in Figure 37.5, is complete. **/File Combine** brings in the **Currency** format.

29. Select **/Range Format Currency** to change all numbers to the same format.

30. Select **/File Save Replace** and save the file under the name **SUMMARY**.

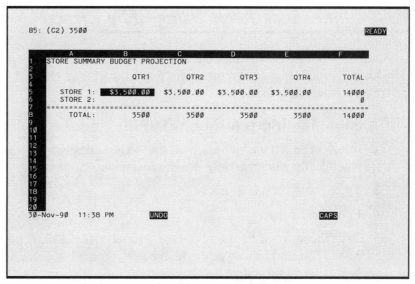

Figure 37.4: *Summary Worksheet with Expanded Columns*

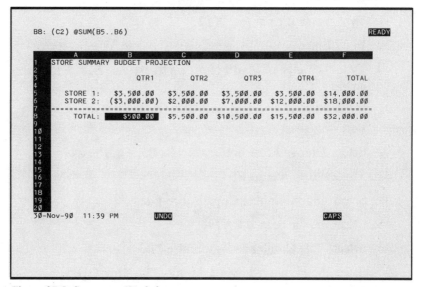

Figure 37.5: *Summary Worksheet*

To Combine Worksheets Using /File Xtract

Another way of transferring data between worksheets is to use /
File Xtract before using **/File Combine**. **/File Xtract** puts a copy of a
range of cells in a new file.

31. Select **/File Retrieve** to retrieve **STORE1**.

32. Select **/File Xtract Values**. Selecting **Values** means that you
    will save the numbers only, not the formulas.

33. Type a new file name: **EXT1**.

34. Press Enter.

35. Type the range of **Profit** numbers to extract: **B18..F18**. Press
    enter. (You could also type **Profit** in place of the cell addresses.
    You assigned this range name earlier.)

36. Select **/File Retrieve** to retrieve **STORE2**.

37. Select **/File Xtract Values** again.

38. Type a new file name: **EXT2**.

39. Press Enter.

40. Type the range of **Profit** numbers to extract: **B18..F18**. Press
    enter.

41. Select **/File Retrieve** to retrieve **SUMMARY**, the consolida-
    tion worksheet.

42. Select **/Range Erase** and erase cells **B5..E6**. Press enter.

43. Move the pointer to **B5**.

44. Select **/File Combine Copy Entire-File**.

45. Select the file named **EXT1**.

46. Select **/File Combine Copy Entire-File**.

47. Select the file named **EXT2**. Using **/File Xtract,** you have cre-
    ated the same **SUMMARY** file as you did previously. It is not
    necessary to save the file since you already have a copy.

LESSON

38

Linking Worksheets (Release 2.2)

FEATURING

*/File Admin Link-Refresh
/Worksheet Global Default
Other Clock*

1-2-3 Release 2.2 offers an efficient means of transferring data between worksheets. Rather than using **/File Combine** as explained in the previous lesson, you can *link* worksheets by entering formulas in a *target* worksheet where data is to be consolidated. These formulas will refer to *source* worksheets that contain detailed information. Then, whenever you retrieve the target worksheet, it will be updated automatically to reflect any changed values in the source worksheets.

But what if you are working with 1-2-3 on a network and someone else changes the source worksheets after you retrieve the target? No problem. Use **/File Admin Link-Refresh** to update the formulas in the target worksheet.

In order to link worksheets, you use formulas. The syntax of a linking formula is

+ <<file reference>>cell reference

where the file reference can include the drive and/or directory and the name of the worksheet file in which the cell reference is located. For example:

+ <<C:\123\BUDGET>>A10

The + sign tells 1-2-3 that you are entering a formula. The brackets < < > > enclose the file reference. The file reference need not include an extension if the extension is .WK1. However, if the file reference is a 1-2-3 Release 1A worksheet (.WKS), or a Symphony worksheet (.WRK or .WR1), for example, you must add the extension. For example, the file reference for a 1A worksheet might look like + <<C:\123\BUDGET.WKS>>A10.

The cell reference can be a cell address, + <<**BUDGET**>>**A10**, for example, but it is better to assign and use a range name such as + <<**BUDGET**>>**Q1 PROFIT**. If the cell reference is a cell address and you move the contents of cell A10 to a new location by inserting, deleting, copying, or moving, the linking formula will not adjust; it will still refer to cell A10. However, a range name will adjust and keep your formulas accurate. When the range name refers to multiple cells, only the value of the top left cell is used. Therefore you must assign a name to each cell in a linking formula.

Although linking requires a bit more work up front, it pays off in the end as you do not need to use /**File Combine** each time you want to update the worksheet.

In order to distinguish between the various worksheets you will be working in, you will use another feature of Release 2.2. You will display the current worksheet file name on the screen.

How to Link Worksheets

To Display the Current File Name on Screen

  1. Select /**Worksheet Global Default Other Clock**.

The Worksheet Global Default Other Clock Menu

This menu controls the date displayed in the lower left-hand corner.

- **Standard** and **International** allow you to switch between two different formats for the date and time.

- **None** displays no date.

- **Clock** turns on the date and time.

- **Filename** replaces the date and time with the the name of the current worksheet.

2. Select **Filename**. Notice that **File name** is now displayed on the default setting sheet.

3. Select **Quit**.

To Set Up the Source Worksheet

4. Select **File Retrieve** to retrieve **STORE1**. You will assign range names to the four quarter profit numbers.

5. Move to cell **B18**.

6. Select **/Range Name Create**.

7. Type: **Q1 PROFIT**.

8. Press Enter.

9. Since B18 is the range you want, press Enter again.

10. Repeat steps 5 through 9 and name the following cells:

Cell	Name
C18	Q2 PROFIT
D18	Q3 PROFIT
E18	Q4 PROFIT

11. Select /**File Save Replace** to save the worksheet.

12. Select /**File Retrieve** and retrieve **STORE2**.

13. Repeat steps 5 through 9 for the same cells in **STORE2**. Use the same range names.

14. Select /**File Save Replace** to save the worksheet.

15. Select /**File Retrieve** to retrieve **SUMMARY**.

16. Select /**Range Erase** to erase the Store 1 and Store 2 numbers in cells **B5..E6**. This will get rid of the existing numbers and make it easier to type in the linking formulas.

17. Enter the following formulas:

In cell:	Enter:
B5	+ < <STORE1 > >Q1 PROFIT
B6	+ < <STORE2 > >Q1 PROFIT
C5	+ < <STORE1 > >Q2 PROFIT
C6	+ < <STORE2 > >Q2 PROFIT
D5	+ < <STORE1 > >Q3 PROFIT
D6	+ < <STORE2 > >Q3 PROFIT
E5	+ < <STORE1 > >Q4 PROFIT
E6	+ < <STORE2 > >Q4 PROFIT

The numbers will appear as you enter the formulas.

18. On a network, if the **STORE1** and **STORE2** worksheets were updated while you were working in **SUMMARY**, you could use /**Worksheet Admin Link-Refresh** to update the **SUMMARY** worksheet.

19. Use /**File List Linked** to display a list of linked worksheets.

20. Save the **Summary** worksheet.

If you get an error message when trying to enter a formula, or if **ERR** appears in place of a number, consider the following.

- Is the source worksheet in the current drive and directory?

- Has the source worksheet been erased or renamed?

- Has the range name in the source worksheet been deleted?

- Are the source worksheets (STORE1 and STORE2) password protected?

- If you are on a network, is the source worksheet being saved or retrieved by someone else?

- Have you mistakenly included a linking formula within another formula? For example, + < <**STORE1**> >**Q1 PROFIT**∗**10%** is not valid. Place the linking formula in one cell and, in another cell, place a formula that includes the cell containing the linking formula.

- Does the linking formula refer to a worksheet that refers to another worksheet? If so, retrieve the middle worksheet to update the formulas before you retrieve the first worksheet.

- If you referenced worksheets created in other releases of 1-2-3 (Release 1A, 2.0, 2.01) and Symphony (versions 1.1, 1.2, 2.0), did you use the correct extension?

LESSON

39

Transferring Data Between 1-2-3 and Other Programs

FEATURING

/File Import
/Print File
/Data Parse
The Translate utility

Do you ever need to create reports that include 1-2-3 worksheet data? What about adding 1-2-3 data to another database program? Or do you have another accounting program from which you might want to transfer data to 1-2-3 in order to analyze it? Depending on whether you want to transfer data *from* or *to* 1-2-3 and depending on the type of data being transferred, you will use different commands.

There are two methods of transfering data *out of* 1-2-3 to another program: (1) through a *text file* using the **/Print** command, and (2) using the **Translate** utility. Text files contain only text and numbers, not formulas. Many programs can use a text file directly, while others will need to translate the text file into their own special file format.

(For additional instructions on how to transfer a 1-2-3 worksheet to another program, consult the user manual for that program.) The **Translate** utility, listed on the System Access menu, translates 1-2-3 worksheets into several of these special formats: dBase II and dBase III, DisplayWrite 3 and 4, Manuscript Release 1 and 2, 1-2-3 Release 1A, DIF, and Symphony Releases 1, 1.01, 1.1 and 1.2. In this lesson, you will use data from the **91BUDGET** worksheet to create a text file using /Print File. In addition, you will change the **91BUDGET** into a 1-2-3 1A worksheet file using the Translate utiltity.

There are also two methods of transfering data *in to* a 1-2-3 worksheet: (1) through a text file using /**File Import**, and (2) using the **Translate** utility. Most programs can create a text file that 1-2-3 can import. In some cases it may be easier to use the Translate utility with the following programs: dBase II or dBase III, DisplayWrite 3 or 4, Manuscript Release 1 or 2, DIF formatted files, or Multiplan Releases 1 and 2. In this lesson, you will import the text file that you will have created using /Print File.

How to Prepare 1-2-3 Text Files For Use With Other Programs

To Create a Text File

1. Select /**File Retrieve** to retrieve **91BUDGET**.

2. Select /**Print File**. This command does not use your printer. Any files with a **.PRN** extension are listed.

3. Create a new file name. Type: **TEXTFILE**. If the file exists, you must replace it.

4. Press Enter. 1-2-3 automatically adds the .**PRN** extension. The **Print** menu will be displayed.

5. Select **Range** to specify the range to print.

6. Type: **A1..F18**.

7. Press Enter.

8. Select **Options Other Unformatted**. This eliminates headers, footers, and page breaks from the text file.

9. From the Options menu, select **Margins Left**.

10. Type: **0** (zero) to set the left margin to zero.

11. Press Enter.

12. Select **Margins Right**.

13. Type: **76** to set the right margin. If 76 is already displayed, proceed to the next step.

    This margin conforms to the page width for an 8-$\frac{1}{2}$-by-11-inch page. If the worksheet is wider than the margin, the columns to the right will be printed below the rest of the worksheet.

14. Press Enter.

15. Press Escape.

16. Select **Align Go**. A text file with the specified range is created.

17. Select **Quit**.

Note: If you wanted to include multiple ranges in the text file, you would specify the additional ranges and press **Go** before you press **Quit** to exit the **Print** menu.

Once the text file is created, you may use it with another program.

To Transfer a Worksheet Using the Translate Utility

Another way of transferring data to other programs is with the Translate utility. You will translate the **91BUDGET** worksheet into a 1-2-3 Release 1A formatted worksheet.

18. In the **READY** mode, select **/Quit**. When prompted, select **Yes** to exit to the System Access menu.

19. From the Access menu, select **Translate**.

20. Move the pointer to the *source* program, that is, the program with the data that you want to translate. For example, if you are using Release 2.2, select **1-2-3 2, 2.01 or 2.2**. See Figure 39.1.

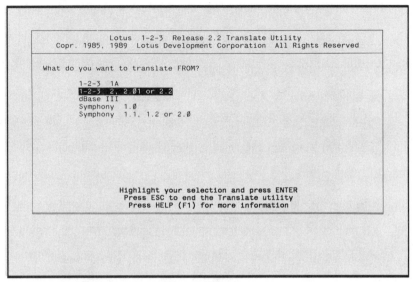

Figure 39.1: Translate Utility Source Program

21. Press Enter.

22. Since the pointer is already on the *target* program, the program to which you will be transferring the data—1-2-3 1A—press Enter. See Figure 39.2.

A series of message screens appears. They contain information on possible translation problems for different programs.

23. Press Escape to exit the message screens. A list of files is displayed.

24. Select **91BUDGET.WK1**. A file named **91BUDGET.WKS** is displayed. The 1-2-3 1A file extension .WKS has been assigned.

25. Press Enter again.

26. Select **Yes** to begin translating data.

27. When the translation is complete, press **Escape** twice.

28. Select **Yes** to exit. The Access menu will be displayed.

29. Select **1-2-3** to display the worksheet.

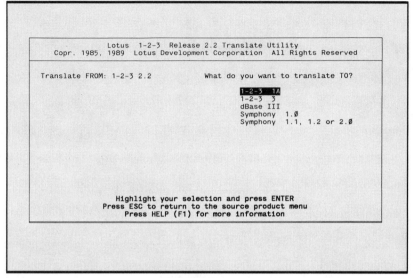

```
              Lotus  1-2-3  Release 2.2 Translate Utility
         Copr. 1985, 1989  Lotus Development Corporation  All Rights Reserved


   Translate FROM: 1-2-3 2.2          What do you want to translate TO?

                                            1-2-3   1A
                                            1-2-3   3
                                            dBase III
                                            Symphony  1.0
                                            Symphony  1.1, 1.2 or 2.0






                       Highlight your selection and press ENTER
                       Press ESC to return to the source product menu
                             Press HELP (F1) for more information
```

Figure 39.2: *Translate Utility Target Program*

How to Transfer Data from Other Programs to 1-2-3

To Transfer Data in to 1-2-3 from a Text File

You will now transfer the text file you created earlier—
91BUDGET.PRN—for use with another program back in to 1-2-3.
This will simulate transferring data from another program.

30. With a blank worksheet displayed, select **/File**.
    You could also add data to an existing worksheet rather
    than a blank one, but you would need to be sure that the
    incoming data does not overwrite existing data.

31. Select **Import**. You will be prompted to select **Numbers** or
    Text. See Figure 39.3.

Select **Numbers** when the incoming text file contains only numbers,
or when labels are enclosed in quotation marks and separated by a

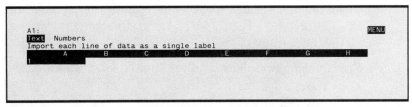

Figure 39.3: The Import Menu

space, comma, colon, or semicolon. An incoming number cannot have a comma or it will be split into multiple numbers.

Select **Text** when incoming labels are not enclosed in quotation marks, separated by the proper punctuation, or when numbers are formatted with commas. With **text,** each incoming line of data is interpreted as one long label (up to a maximum of 240 characters) and entered into a single cell. This creates a worksheet that is composed of a single column of long labels.

32. Select **Text**. For the text file TEXTFILE.PRN this choice is best, because the labels are not enclosed in quotations marks and would be discarded if you were to select **Numbers**.

33. Select **TEXTFILE.PRN**.

34. Notice how the new worksheet differs from the original worksheet 91BUDGET. Move the pointer down column A looking at the control panel above the worksheet. Notice that all the text and numbers in each row are contained in one cell only. In addition, there are no formulas. You will need to enter them later. First, however, the long labels must be split into separate columns.

35. Move to column B and move the pointer up and down the column. Look at the control panel; notice that all cells in column B are empty.

To Separate a Long Label into Columns

/Data Parse splits a label into columns based on a *format line*. The format line determines how many columns to parse—or split—the label into, how much of the label each column will contain, and what type of data each column will contain: value, label, date, or time.

36. Move to cell **A5,** the first row in the worksheet that has numbers. The rows above this can remain as they are; they will not be used in formulas.

37. Select **/Data Parse Format-Line Create**. 1-2-3 inserts a row and creates a format line based on the data it found in the Sales row. See Figure 39.4.

The first character is the label-prefix ¦, which instructs 1-2-3 not to print the row. The **L** denotes the start of a column of labels, the **V** the start of a column of values. Where applicable, **D** reflects dates and **T** reflects times. The format line is correct; however, if it were not, you could edit it using **/Data Parse Format-Line Edit**.

38. Select **Input-Column**. You will specify the range of cells that contains the imported text, including the format line, A5.

39. Specify cells **A5..A19**. You do not need to include any other columns; all the data is stored in column A.

40. Press Enter.

41. Select **Output-Range**.

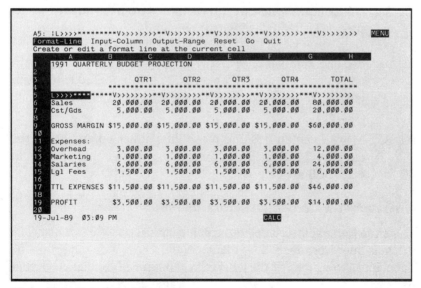

Figure 39.4: Data Parse Format Line

42. Specify a new area to copy the parsed data to. Press Page Down to go to **A25** in the next screen.

43. Press Enter.

44. Select **Go**.

45. Press Page Down to view the parsed data. Notice that no formatting exists: no dollar signs, commas, or decimals. Blank rows were also discarded.

46. Move to column B of the parsed data and move the pointer down the column; there are now numbers.

Using the imported and parsed data, you could now build formulas to calculate the columns of numbers, add column headings, change the formatting to include dollar signs and commas, and widen column A to display the complete text. In addition, the imported text on the first screen could be deleted, including the format line. These steps would create a worksheet similar to your original **91BUDGET**.

47. Use /**File Save** to save this file under a new name, if desired.

48. Select /**File Retrieve** to retrieve **91BUDGET**.

A

C

B

1

3

1

2

2

Part Four

Graphing the Worksheet

3

LESSON

40

Converting the Worksheet to a Graph

FEATURING

/Graph Type
/Graph ABCDEF
/Graph View

A key feature of 1-2-3 is its ability to display worksheet data as a graph, both on the screen and in print. You can choose from a variety of graph types: line, bar, scatter, stacked bar, and pie chart. And, just as you added information to the worksheet to make it easier to interpret, you can enhance a graph's appearance by adding such things as titles, symbols, legends, and a horizontal or vertical background grid.

You can view a graph if you have a graphics card or a color/graphics card in your computer. You can view a graph and worksheet simultaneously if you have two monitors, and you can display a graph in color if you have a color monitor. You cannot view a graph with a monochrome card and monitor. You can print a graph regardless of what kind of monitor and card you have—even if you can't see it on screen, though the process will be tedious!

Converting the worksheet to a graph is a simple matter of only a few steps. First, create the type of graph you want. Then, when you can see where labels need to be added, add the labels.

*H*ow to View the Graph

1. Use **/File Retrieve** to retrieve **91BUDGET**, if necessary.

2. Change the following cell entries on the worksheet

Change:	C5	to	**30000**
	D5	to	**40000**
	E5	to	**50000**
	C12	to	**7000**
	D12	to	**8000**
	E12	to	**9000**

3. Select **/Graph**. See Figure 40.1.

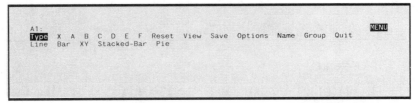

Figure 40.1: The Graph Menu

In Release 2.2, the Graph settings sheet will be displayed. This displays all settings for the current graph. You can toggle between the settings sheet and the worksheet with the WINDOW (F6) key.

4. Select **Type**.

5. Select **Bar**. The Graph menu is displayed again.

6. Select **A**.

7. Enter the first data range to be graphed, the **GROSS MARGIN** figures: **B8..E8**. Press Enter.

8. Select **B**.

9. Enter the second data range, the **TTL EXPENSES** figures: **B16..E16**. Press Enter.

The Graph Menu

There are five **Types** of graphs: line, bar, xy, stacked-bar, and pie chart.

- **X-axis** creates labels along the horizontal axis of a graph.

- The **A** through **F** ranges are used to graph up to six ranges of data.

- **Reset** clears the range settings.

- **Save** creates a picture of the graph for printing.

- **View** diplays the graph on the screen.

- **Options** is used to add legends, titles, and labels to a graph.

- **Name** is used to remember graph settings.

- **Group** (new to Release 2.2) allows you to specify several settings at once.

10. Select **C**.

11. Enter the third data range, the **PROFIT** figures: **B18. .E18**. Press Enter.

12. Select **View**. The graph in Figure 40.2 is displayed. In order to view the graph, you must have a graphics card installed in your computer. If you don't, you can create and print the graph, but you can't view it.

13. Press any key to return to the Graph menu. The Graph menu remains on the screen until you press Escape or select Quit.

14. To view the same data displayed in a different type of graph, select **Type Stacked-Bar**.

15. Select **View** again. The graph in Figure 40.3 is displayed. Notice that the scale has changed to include the three totals in one bar.

16. To return to the Graph menu, press any key.

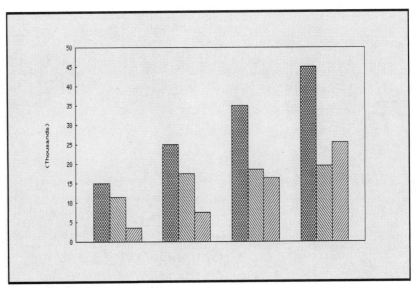

Figure 40.2: Bar Graph

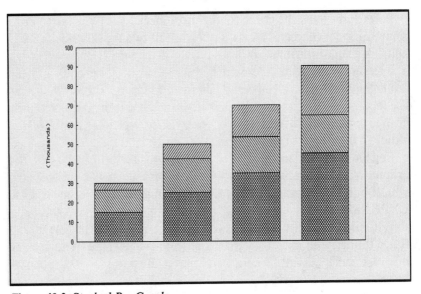

Figure 40.3: Stacked-Bar Graph

41

Labeling the Graph

FEATURING

/Graph Options Legend
/Graph Options Titles
/Graph X

Before you show the graph to anyone, especially if you plan to print it, it's a good idea to add labels. Labels are of two types: *titles* and *legends*. A graph is difficult to interpret without them.

Titles are added to put the entire graph in context. For example, on the graph you just viewed, you could add the title *Budget Projection* across the top. Along the bottom and left sides of the screen, but not on the graph, you could add titles such as *January-December* and *Dollars*, although these aren't really necessary to understand the graph.

Legends are added to explain what is inside the borders of the graph. With the stacked-bar graph, for example, you need to know which bar shadings refer to **MARGIN** and which refer to **TTL EXPENSES**.

With the **Graph X** command, you can add more specific titles along the X (horizontal) axis. Currently, the four quarters are identified by tick marks. The Graph X command places the names of the quarters beneath each tick mark.

Note: The X-axis is the independent variable; that is, the number of items along this axis will not change unless you manually change it. The Y-axis is calculated automatically by 1-2-3 and will vary as the data vary.

*H*ow to Add Labels to the Graph

To Add Legends

The Graph menu should still be on your screen. If not, select /**Graph**.

1. Select **Options**. The Graph Options menu appears (see Figure 41.1).

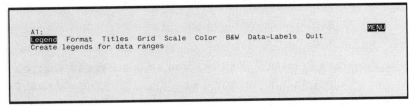

A1:
Legend Format Titles Grid Scale Color B&W Data-Labels Quit
Create legends for data ranges

MENU

Figure 41.1: The Graph Options Menu

The Graph Options Menu

Legend documents which shading or symbol represents which data on the graph. Use **titles** to add text along the top, bottom and left-hand side of the graph. You can add a background **grid,** change the **scale** of the numbers on the axes, display the graph in **color** or **black and white,** and add **data-labels** or labels within the graph.

2. Select **Legend**. A prompt asks you to set the legend for the first range, the A range. The only limitation is the number of characters: 19. However, because of space limitations, it's a good idea to use fewer than 19 characters. **Legend** appears at the bottom of the screen to show what is represented by the various bar shadings.

3. Select **A**.

4. You can enter legends directly from the worksheet by typing a backslash (\) and the cell address. Type : **\A8**. This instructs 1-2-3 to use the contents of A8 as the legend GROSS MARGIN. If you change the text in A8, the legend will change as well. If you want to use a legend that is different than what is on the worksheet, you can type in the text here.

5. Press Enter. The pointer returns to **Legend**.

6. Select **Legend** again and repeat the process, typing the following names for the B and C ranges:

    \A16
    \A18

   Note: Release 2.2 allows you to use **Legend Range** to specify multiple legends at one time if they are adjacent on the worksheet.

To Add Titles

7. Select **Titles**. You have a choice of giving the graph a one- or two-line graph title. Again, the only limitation is the number of characters: 39 per line. As with legends, you can enter titles directly from the worksheet by typing a backslash (\) and the cell address.

8. Select **First**.

9. Type:

    BUDGET PROJECTION

10. After you press Enter, select **Titles** again.

11. Select **Second**.

12. Type: **1991.**

13. Press Enter.
    Note: It is also possible to title the X- and Y-axes.

14. Select **Quit** to return to the Graph menu.

To Add Labels Along the X-axis

Now specify the column headings as X-axis labels.

15. Select **X**.

16. Since you graphed the four quarters, you will now enter the titles you want on the X-axis. Specify the range for the QTR titles on the worksheet: **B3..E3**.

17. Press Enter.

18. Select **View** to view the graph again, this time with titles and X-axis labels. See Figure 41.2.

19. Press any key to return to the commands and the worksheet.

20. Select **Type Bar**.

21. Select **View** again. A bar graph similar to Figure 41.2 is displayed.

22. Press any key.

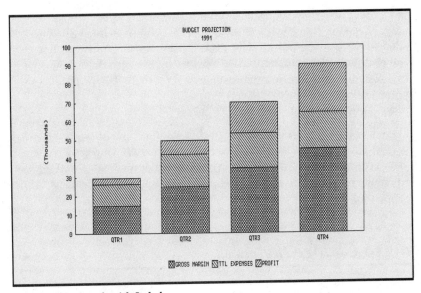

Figure 41.2: *Graph with Labels*

42

Changing the Scales on the Axes

FEATURING

/Graph Options Scale

Unless directed otherwise, 1-2-3 automatically scales the X- and Y-axes to accommodate the graphed range values. The high and low ends of each are based on the highest and lowest values in the data ranges that you entered from the worksheet. As with the other settings in 1-2-3, though, automatic scaling can be turned off. This enables you to set manually the scales on the axes.

When might you want to do this? Any time that you want two graphs to be scaled in the same way. For example, assume that you are preparing a report and you've included your 1991 Budget Projection graphs as a means of predicting trends in expenditures. To avoid confusing your readers, you adjusted the Y-axis manually so that all of the graphs are similar.

*H*ow to Change the Axes

1. Select **Options Scale** from the Graph menu. The menu enables you to set the scale of the numbers along the X- or Y-axes. You

can also skip some of the X-axis labels. For example, if you are graphing the 12 months along the X-axis you may only want to display the name of every other month.

2. Select **Y**. See Figure 42.1.

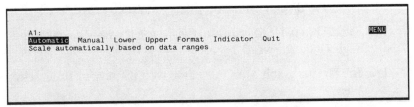

Figure 42.1: The Options Scale Y-axis/X-axis Menu

The Options Scale Y-axis/X-axis Menu

- Lotus scales the axes **Automatically**.

- **Manual** allows you to set Lower and Upper scales.

- **Lower** refers to the number on the bottom of the scale.

- **Upper** refers to the number at the top of the scale.

- **Format** displays graph numbers similarly to the Range Format and Worksheet Global Format commands.

- **Indicator** allows you to turn on and off the ticks, or indicator marks, along the X- and Y-axes.

---

3. Select **Manual**. The same menu returns, but 1-2-3's automatic scaling is not in effect, so you must now set the upper and lower limits and the format for the numbers on the scale.

4. Select **Upper**.

5. Enter a number twice the highest GROSS MARGIN on your worksheet. Type:

   90000

6. Press Enter.

7. You will not change the lower scale. Select **Format**. The standard format menu appears.

8. Select **Currency**. This will display the numbers on the Y-axis with dollar signs and commas.

9. Type **0** to display whole numbers, and then press Enter.

10. Select **Quit** twice to return to the Graph menu—the menu that begins with the word *Type*.

11. To view the graph again, this time with the revised scale, select **View**.

Notice in Figure 42.2 how the enlarged scale has changed the graph's appearance. Also, the numbers have dollar signs.

12. Press any key to return to the worksheet. The Graph menu remains on the control panel.

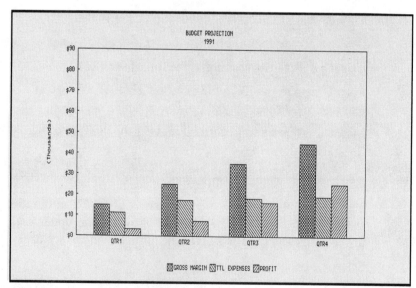

Figure 42.2: *Graph with Revised Scale*

LESSON

43

Adding a Background Grid

FEATURING

/Graph Options Grid

In addition to changing the scale, you can add a background grid to your graph. You have the choice of adding either vertical or horizontal lines, or both. As you will see, the grid is another way of making interpretation easier. For example, with horizontal lines, it's much simpler to see which bar on a bar graph represents the largest figure—or the smallest.

How to Add a Background Grid

1. In the Graph menu, select **Options Grid Both**. You will add both horizontal and vertical background lines to your graph.

2. Select **Quit** or press Escape to return to the Graph menu.

3. Select **View**. The graph is now displayed with a background grid, as shown in Figure 43.1.

4. Press any key to return to the worksheet.

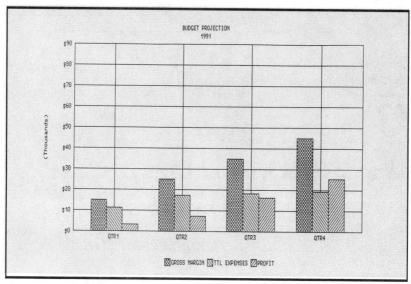

Figure 43.1: Graph with Grid

LESSON

44

Using Color or Black and White

FEATURING

/Graph Options Color
/Graph Options B&W

If you are using a black-and-white (monochrome) monitor, use the **B&W** setting for viewing graphs in order to get the crosshatching seen on the previous graphs. If you are using a color monitor, you can use either the **B&W** or the **Color** setting. Some monochrome monitors can use the Color setting and will display different shades instead of cross-hatching. In the exercise below, you will check to see if your monitor has this capability. Don't skip this section if you don't have a color monitor. You might be surprised to see what happens.

For printing, use the **B&W** setting unless you are using a color plotter or color printer. In that case use the **Color** setting.

How to Display in Color

1. Select **Options Color**.
2. **Quit** the Options menu.

3. Select **View**. If you have a monochrome monitor, the cross-hatching will be changed to solid bars.

4. Press any key to return to the Graph menu.

To Return to Black and White

5. Select **Options B&W**.

6. **Quit** the Options menu.

7. **View** the original graph again. The crosshatching has replaced the solid shades of green.

8. Press a key to return to the worksheet.

LESSON

45

Naming, Saving, and Using Graphs

FEATURING

/Graph Name
/Graph Save

Saving graphs is one of the most misunderstood areas of 1-2-3 because the methods vary depending on what you want to do with your graph. You may want to view only one graph for a worksheet, view multiple graphs per worksheet, or save and print one or more graphs on a printer or plotter.

If you want to view a single graph, and not print it, you need only the **File Save** command to save it—the same command you use to save the worksheet itself. The graph settings are saved along with the worksheet, and you can view the graph when you retrieve the worksheet.

If you plan to save more than one graph per worksheet, you must use **Graph Name** to name them so that 1-2-3 will save the settings for each one.

If you want to print a graph, you must follow several steps: Name the graph if you have more than one, save a *picture* of it with the **Graph Save** command, and save the settings with the **File Save** command.

How to Name, Save, and Use Graphs

To Name the Graph

1. The Graph menu should still be on your screen. Select **Name** and press Enter. 1-2-3 displays the Graph Name menu.

The Graph Name Menu

- **Use** is the command that calls up a particular graph you have already named.

- **Create** names a graph. Use Create to rename a graph when you change any settings—titles, legends, type.

- **Delete** and **Reset** delete either a single graph name or all graph names. Beware! Along with the name, all of the settings, including the graph, are also erased.

---

2. Select **Create**. 1-2-3 asks you to enter the name of the graph.

3. Type:

   BAR CHART

   When naming a graph, the only limitation is the number of characters: 14. Also be sure not to use a name that you have already used unless you want that graph replaced by the current graph.

4. Press Enter. The Graph menu returns to the screen.

To Save the Graph for Printing

5. Select **Save**. 1-2-3 asks you to enter the name of the file.

6. Type:

   BARCHART

Notice that there are no spaces in the Graph Save file name. Unlike the procedure for the Graph Name, the Graph Save file name is entered the same way as all file names: eight characters that can be letters, numbers, or underlined, but no blank spaces and no punctuation. The graph file name is saved with a graph extension (.PIC), whereas a worksheet is saved with a .WK1 extension using File Save. You will not be able to retrieve and work with this graph file; it is a static picture created for the purpose of printing the graph. If you change the graph at all on the screen, you must use Graph Save to save the graph again, with the same or a different name, in order to reflect the changes when you print it.

7. Press Enter.

To Name and Save Additional Graphs

To create another graph, such as a stacked-bar chart, you must change the type, name the graph with a new name so as not to overwrite the original bar chart settings, and then save the graph as a new graph file.

8. First, select **Type**.

9. Select **Stacked-Bar**.

10. Select **View**.

11. Press any key to return.

12. Select **Name Create**.

13. Type in the following graph name:

    STACKED BAR

14. Press Enter. The settings for this graph have now been assigned a name.

15. Select **Save**.

16. Type in the following graph file name:

    STACKBAR

Again, no spaces and a maximum of eight letters are allowed in a file name.

17. Press Enter. The graph is saved to the disk.

Using Named Graphs

18. Now that you've named two graphs, it is easy to switch between the two for viewing. In the Graph menu select **Name**.

19. Select **Use**. The two graph names are listed.

20. Move the pointer to **BAR CHART** and press Enter. The bar chart is displayed.

21. Press any key to return to the **Graph** menu.

22. Select **Name Use** again.

23. Point to **STACKED BAR** and press Enter. The stacked bar chart is now displayed.

To Save the Graphs Along with the Worksheet

24. Select **Quit** to leave the Graph menu.

25. Use /**File Save** to save the entire worksheet, including all the graph settings and names you have created.

26. Use the current file name, **91BUDGET**.

27. **Replace** (or **Backup** for Release 2.2) the old version with the new one.

46

Playing "What If": Reflecting Worksheet Changes on the Graph

FEATURING

GRAPH (F10) key

Just as 1-2-3 automatically recalculates figures after new data are entered on the worksheet, it automatically updates graphs to reflect the new worksheet entries. Thus, "what if" scenarios on the worksheet can also be displayed graphically. To do so, you return to the worksheet, alter numbers, and press the GRAPH (F10) function key, which instantly displays the current graph. Pressing the GRAPH (F10) key saves you from having to enter the Graph command menu to view the graph.

How to Reflect Worksheet Changes on the Graph

1. Change the following cell entries on the worksheet.

   Change: B5   to   **30000**

   B6   to   **7000**

C5	to	**25000**
C6	to	**6000**
B11	to	**1300**
B12	to	**3000**

2. Press the **GRAPH (F10)** function key. The changes are reflected in the graph, as shown in Figure 46.1.

3. Press any key to exit the graph.

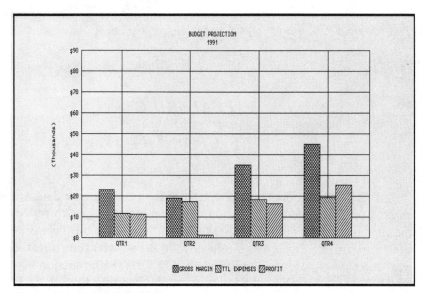

Figure 46.1: Updated Graph

LESSON

47

Displaying a Line Graph with Symbols and Data-Labels

FEATURING

/Graph Options Format

To experiment further with graphs, you can create a line graph using several options. You can add a variety of symbols to represent each range, instead of the bar shadings you saw in your bar graphs. This is possible only with line and XY graphs. In addition, you can display all of the numbers that you graphed to make the graph more specific. You can do this with all graph types except pie graphs.

How to Create a Line Graph with Symbols and Data-labels

To Create a Line Graph

1. Select /**Graph Type Line**.

2. In the Graph menu, select **Options Grid Clear** to clear the grid.

3. **Quit** the Options menu.

4. **View** the graph (Figure 47.1). The lines are based on the previous graph, or the graph after you made the worksheet changes. Notice that each line or data range has a unique set of symbols placed at each quarter's data point. The bottom line, the profit line, intersects each quarter with diamonds. The total expenses line intersects with crosses. And the gross margin line intersects with squares.

5. Press any key to return to the /Graph menu.

6. Use **Options Scale Y-Axis Automatic** to reset the Y scale to automatic scaling.

7. **Quit** the Scale Menu.

8. **Quit** the Options menu.

9. **View** the graph again.

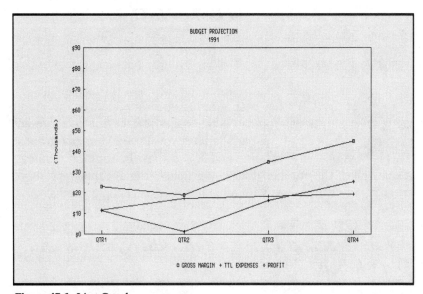

Figure 47.1: Line Graph

To Change the Symbols Inside the Graph

10. Press any key to return to the Graph menu.

11. Select **Options Format** (Figure 47.2). This command is used with line and XY graphs. The graph defaults to both. The

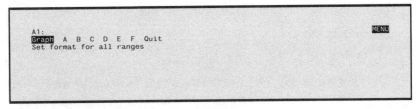

Figure 47.2: Options Format on Graph Menu

Graph command here is used to set the format of the entire graph. Each letter is used to set the format for individual ranges.

12. Select **Graph**.

13. Select **Symbols**.

14. **Quit** the Format menu.

15. **Quit** the Options menu to return to the Graph menu.

16. **View** the graph. As shown in Figure 47.3, only the symbols are displayed on the graph.

17. Press any key to return to the worksheet.

18. Select **Options Format Graph Both** to restore the lines to the graph.

19. Select **Quit** twice to exit the Format and Options menus.

To Add Data-Labels

20. In the Graph menu, select **Options Data-Labels**. 1-2-3 displays the letters A through F. Each letter refers back to the data range you entered when you first created the bar graph. In Release 2.2, **Group** allows you to specify multiple data-labels at one time if they are adjacent in the worksheet.

21. Select **A**.

22. Specify the original A-range, the GROSS MARGIN figures: **B8..E8**. This will display the actual gross margin numbers right on the graph.

23. Press Enter.

24. To specify the data labels, select **Above**.

25. Select **Quit**.

26. **Quit** again to the main Graph menu.

27. **View** the graph. The gross margin figures from the worksheet are now displayed on the graph directly to the right of the gross margin data points, as shown in Figure 47.4.

28. Press any key to return to the Graph menu.

29. Select **Options Data-Labels** to create labels for the B (Total Expenses) and C (Profit) ranges.

30. Select **B** to set the labels for the B-range.

31. Type in or point to **B16..E16**.

32. Press Enter.

33. Specify **Center** to display the labels above the data points.

34. Select **C** to set the labels for the C-range.

35. Type in or point to **B18..E18**.

36. Press Enter.

37. Specify **Below**.

38. Select **Quit** twice until you return to the Graph menu.

39. **View** the graph.

40. In the Graph menu, use **Save** to save the graph. If you don't remember how, refer back to Lesson 45, "Naming, Saving, and Using Graphs," for instructions.

41. Save the graph under the name **DATALBLS**. (Remember that file names have a maximum of eight characters.)

42. Name the graph using **Name Create**. Again, refer back to Lesson 45 if necessary.

43. Name the graph as **DATA LABELS**. (Remember that graph names can be up to 14 characters long, including spaces.)

44. Leave the Graph menu by using the Escape key or selecting **Quit**.

45. Save the worksheet using **/File Save**.

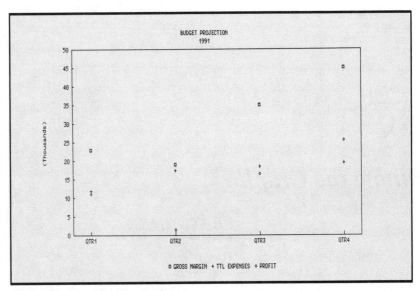

Figure 47.3: Graph with Symbols

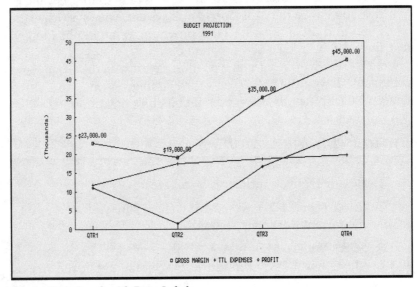

Figure 47.4: Graph with Data-Labels

48

Printing the Graph

FEATURING

PrintGraph

Printing a graph requires several more steps than simply viewing it. Whether you have a hard- or floppy-disk system, you must leave the worksheet and use a separate 1-2-3 program: PrintGraph. Floppy-disk users will be using a new program disk.

Before you can print a graph, you must save it with the **Graph Save** command, as you did in Lesson 45, "Naming, Saving, and Using Graphs." Complete this lesson even if you don't have a printer.

How to Print the Graph

1. Be sure that your printer is on and ready.

2. Select **/Quit**. 1-2-3 asks you if you are sure you want to quit the current worksheet session.

3. Select **Yes**. The Lotus Access menu appears. See Lesson 5, "Installing 1-2-3," for further discussion about the Access System.

4. Select **PrintGraph**. If you have a floppy-disk system, 1-2-3 will ask you to insert the PrintGraph disk in drive A and press Enter. Do so now. The PrintGraph menu should appear (Figure 48.1).

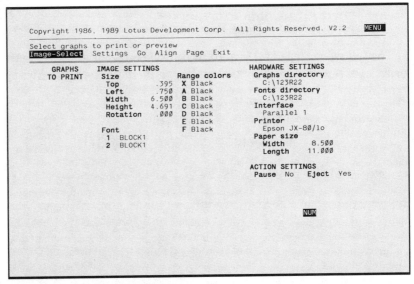

Figure 48.1: The PrintGraph Menu

Note: You may get a message stating that the "printer driver" is incompatible with the PrintGraph program. If so, exit this menu and return to the Access menu. Use Install to specify a graphics printer. Refer to Lesson 5 on installing 1-2-3 on your computer.

The PrintGraph Menu

- **Image-Select** allows you to select one or more of the graph files that you create and save in the 1-2-3 worksheet.

- **Settings** enables you to change the graph's size, color, rotation, and type fonts, and to identify the printer(s) in use and the directories in which the graph files are located.

- **Go** instructs printing to begin.

- **Align** synchronizes the PrintGraph program with your printer before printing.

- **Page** advances the paper in the printer.

- **Exit** takes you out of the PrintGraph program.

To Set Up the PrintGraph Program for Your Computer and Printer

The following steps (5–15) need to be done only if the PrintGraph program is not yet set up. If you are unsure, do these steps; otherwise, skip to step 16.

5. Before selecting graphs, use the **Settings** command to instruct 1-2-3 where to look for them. Select **Settings** (Figure 48.2).

6. Select **Hardware** (Figure 48.3).

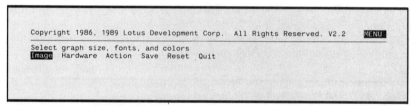

Copyright 1986, 1989 Lotus Development Corp. All Rights Reserved. V2.2   MENU

Select graph size, fonts, and colors
Image Hardware Action Save Reset Quit

Figure 48.2: PrintGraph Settings menu

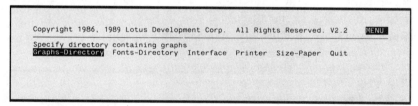

Copyright 1986, 1989 Lotus Development Corp. All Rights Reserved. V2.2   MENU

Specify directory containing graphs
Graphs-Directory Fonts-Directory Interface Printer Size-Paper Quit

Figure 48.3: PrintGraph Hardware menu

7. Select **Graphs-Directory**. 1-2-3 prompts you to type in the directory that contains the graphs. If you have a floppy-disk system, type:

   B:

   If you have a hard-disk system, you must specify the directory where the graph files have been saved. If you installed 1-2-3 as instructed in Lesson 5, type:

   C:\123

   If the files are saved in another directory, replace \123 with the correct directory name.

8. Press Enter.

9. Select **Fonts-Directory**. Again, 1-2-3 prompts you to type in the directory that contains the fonts files. If you have a floppy-disk system, type:

    A:

    If you have a hard-disk system, type:

    C:\123

    If your directory's name is not \123, replace \123 with the correct name.

10. Press Enter.

Next you need to select the printer that you will use to print graphs during this session. You can always change to another printer later on. The choices available depend on the printers that you specified during the installation procedure using Install in the initial Lotus Access menu. (Refer to Lesson 5, "Installing 1-2-3.")

11. Select **Printer**. If the program gives you a beep with a message, you may need to reinstall 1-2-3 for a graph printer. If so, do that now, referring to Lesson 5 and then returning to this lesson. You will need to exit the PrintGraph program. Insert the Installation disk when prompted, if you are using 1-2-3 on floppies.

12. A menu of one or more printers is displayed. Move the pointer next to the printer you want and press the spacebar to select a printer.

13. Press Enter to leave the Printer menu and return to the Hardware menu. If you wanted to print using a serial interface, you could select Interface. To change the size of the paper you are printing on, you could select **Size-Paper**. Do not perform these steps now, however.

14. Select **Quit**.

15. Select **Save** to store the directory and printer settings. After saving, 1-2-3 returns you to the initial PrintGraph menu.

To Select Graphs

16. Select **Image-Select**. A list of graph files is displayed. In it are your three files: BARCHART, DATALBLS, and STACK-BAR (see Figure 48.4).

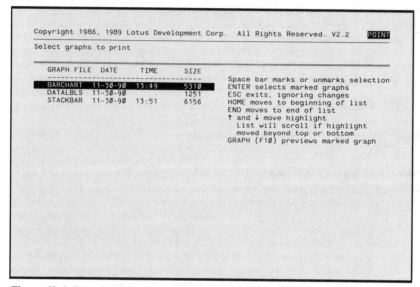

```
Copyright 1986, 1989 Lotus Development Corp.  All Rights Reserved. V2.2    POINT

Select graphs to print


  GRAPH FILE  DATE      TIME     SIZE
  ------------------------------------------
  BARCHART   11-30-90  13:49    5310    Space bar marks or unmarks selection
  DATALBLS   11-30-90           1251    ENTER selects marked graphs
  STACKBAR   11-30-90  13:51    6156    ESC exits, ignoring changes
                                        HOME moves to beginning of list
                                        END moves to end of list
                                        ↑ and ↓ move highlight
                                          List will scroll if highlight
                                          moved beyond top or bottom
                                        GRAPH (F10) previews marked graph
```

Figure 48.4: PrintGraph Image-Select

17. Move the pointer to BARCHART, using the Down Arrow key if necessary. 1-2-3 allows you to view a graph on screen by using the GRAPH (F10) function key. Try this now with BARCHART. Press **GRAPH (F10)**. Then press any key to return to the menu.

18. Press the spacebar to select BARCHART. A number (#) sign appears. It is possible to select multiple graphs to print out by placing a # symbol next to them. Press Enter to return to the main PrintGraph menu.

19. Be sure that paper is aligned in your printer and your printer is turned on. Select **Align** to synchronize 1-2-3 with your printer.

20. Select **Go** to print the graph. It will take a few moments for the graph to start printing.

21. Select **Page** to advance the paper when the graph is finished printing.

To Change Type Fonts, Colors, and Graph Size

22. Select **Settings**.

23. Select **Image** (Figure 48.5).

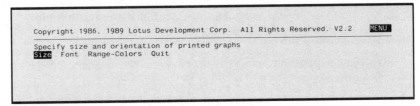

```
Copyright 1986, 1989 Lotus Development Corp.  All Rights Reserved. V2.2    MENU

Specify size and orientation of printed graphs
Size  Font  Range-Colors  Quit
```

Figure 48.5: PrintGraph Settings Image Menu

24. Select **Font**. At this point you have two choices to make for specifying type fonts. The font selected under Font 1 will be used for the main title of the graph. The font selected under Font 2 will be used for all other text and numbers on the graph. If you do not specify a font for Font 2, Font 1 will be used for the entire graph.

25. Select **1** to specify the font that will be used in the main title of the graph. 1-2-3 displays a list of fonts, each of which comes in two shades, one lighter, the other darker. Block1 is lighter than Block2, for example. Generally, Block, Bold, Forum, and Roman will work on most printers; you should normally choose the darker version. The Italic and Script fonts generally are better for plotters and may not produce high-quality graphs on ordinary printers.

26. Select a font by moving the pointer to one and pressing the Enter key.

27. Select **Size** (Figure 48.6).

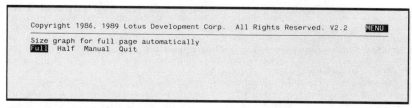

Figure 48.6: *The PrintGraph Size menu*

28. Select **Full**. This will rotate the graph ninety degrees. The default setting is Half. If you have a plotter you can use **Range-Colors** to change the pen color. Skip this step now.

29. Press **Quit** twice to return to the initial PrintGraph menu.

30. Print the graph BARCHART again by selecting **Go**.

31. Now experiment using the other graph STACKBAR. Select it with **Image-Select**, then change the type fonts and size using the Settings menu. You can Save any of these changes. To print a number of graphs sequentially, select **Image-Select** and press the spacebar next to each graph you want to print. They will be printed in the order selected. You can cause 1-2-3 to **Eject** a page after each graph. **Pause** will cause 1-2-3 to stop after each graph until you press a key. Both of these commands are accessed using the **Settings** command.

To Return to the Worksheet

32. Select **Exit**.

33. From the Access menu, select **123**. You will need to insert the System disk if you are using two floppy disks.

LESSON

49

Creating a Pie Chart

FEATURING

/Graph Type Pie
Shading and Coloring

1-2-3 (except for 1A) enables you to create pie charts with "exploded" sections—one or more sections that are set apart from the rest of the pie chart. In addition, each section can be distinctively shaded or colored, depending on the monitor and printer or plotter that you have.

A 1-2-3 pie chart requires only two ranges: the X-range and the A-range. The A-range identifies the values that will be represented by the wedges of the pie. The X-range is used to identify the labels for each wedge. Using the B-range for pie charts (except for 1-2-3 1A), you can shade and explode wedges of the pie.

The pie chart you are about to build will be shaded, and it will show how much of the annual expenses is represented by each individual expense.

How to Reset a Graph's Settings to Create a Pie Chart

1. Retrieve 91BUDGET and select /**Graph Reset** to clear the graph settings associated with the previous graph. This will *not* affect graph settings that you have named using Graph Name.

2. Select **Graph** to clear all settings. You also have the option here of resetting only specific ranges. In Release 2.2, you can reset the options settings separately.

3. Now set up the pie chart. Select **Type**.

4. Specify **Pie**.

5. Select range **A**.

6. Specify the A-range as the total expenses for each category: Overhead, Marketing, Salaries, Legal Fees. Use the range:

   F11..F14

7. Press Enter.

8. Select **X**.

9. Specify the X-range. Type in the range that contains the expense labels (Overhead, Marketing, Salaries, Legal Fees):

   A11..A14

10. Press Enter.

11. Select **View** to display the graph. See Figure 49.1. A basic pie chart, without shading or colors, is displayed. The percentage

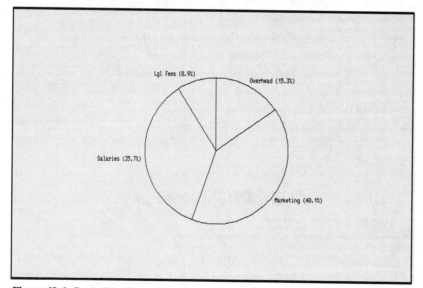

Figure 49.1: Basic Pie Chart

of the pie represented by each wedge is also calculated and displayed.

12. Press any key to return to the Graph menu.

How to Shade and Explode a Pie Chart

To instruct 1-2-3 to shade, color and explode sections of a pie chart, you need to type special codes into a range of cells and then specify those cells as the B-range. This range can be located anywhere on the worksheet and must be the same size as the A-range. Typing in a number from 1 to 7 indicates the type of shading or color for each section. Code 0 or 8 specifies an unshaded section, as does a blank cell. If you want one or more sections exploded, add 100 to the shading code. For example, if you want a wedge shaded using code 6 and you want it exploded, specify 106. Figure 49.2 displays the eight possible shadings.

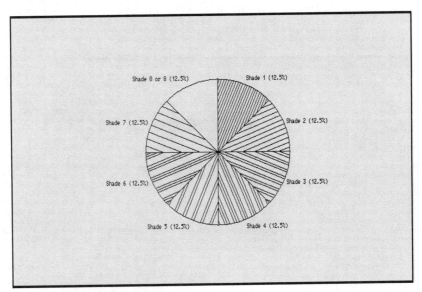

Figure 49.2: Sample Pie Chart

13. **Quit** the Graph menu to return to the READY mode.
    Type these codes in the following cells:

    In cell H11, type: **1**

    In cell H12, type: **102**

    (To separate out an "exploding" section)

    In cell H13, type: **3**

    In cell H14, type: **8**

    (To create a unshaded section).

    Typing 102 in H12 will explode the Marketing section.

14. Before viewing the graph, specify the B-range as the range with the codes. Select **/Graph B**.

15. Specify the range as **H11..H14** and press Enter.

16. Now **View** the graph. See Figure 49.3. The graph should be shaded if you have a graphics monitor, or colored if you have a color monitor, and the Marketing section should be set apart from the rest of the pie.

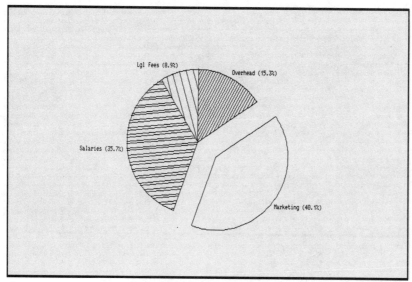

Figure 49.3: Pie Chart with Shading and Exploded Section

17. Press any key to return to the Graph menu.

18. **Quit** the Graph menu. Experiment with changing the codes. Again, use 1 through 7 to specify different types of shading, and add 100 to any code to explode that section. Use the GRAPH (F10) function key to display the graph again.

19. When you are satisfied with the pie chart, use the /**Graph Name Create** command to name it **PIE CHART**. Press Enter.

20. In the Graph menu, select **Save**.

21. Use **PIECHART** for the graph file name. Press Enter. (Remember, no spaces in file names.)

22. Press **Quit** to exit the Graph menu.

23. To print the graph, save the worksheet using /**File Save**.

24. **Quit** the worksheet.

25. Select the **PrintGraph** program.

26. Select the image **PIECHART**.

27. Use the **Settings Image Range-Colors** settings to determine the color of each pie section, if you are using a color printer or color plotter.

28. Press **Go** to print the graph.

29. **Exit** PrintGraph when through.

30. Select **1-2-3** to reenter the worksheet.

50

Using Quick Graph
(Release 2.2)

FEATURING

/Graph Group

Release 2.2 of 1-2-3 makes creating certain types of graphs easier with a new feature called Quick Graph. If the data to be graphed is grouped on neighboring rows and columns, you can specify the X-range and data ranges with one command: **/Graph Group**.

1. Retrieve the **91BUDGET** if necessary.

2. Clear any current graph settings: **/Graph Reset Graph**.

3. In the Graph menu, select **Group**.

4. When prompted for the range, highlight **A11..E14**. This range represents the expenses for the four quarters including the descriptions. Press Enter.

5. When prompted for Columnwise or Rowwise, answer **Columnwise**. Notice that the style sheet changed to reflect the new data ranges (Figure 50.1). The labels in column A are used as the X-range. The remaining columns are used as the A-D data ranges.

6. Change the graph type to bar. Select **Type Bar**.

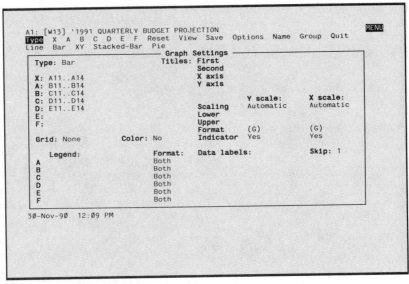

```
A1: [W13] '1991 QUARTERLY BUDGET PROJECTION                          MENU
Type  X  A  B  C  D  E  F  Reset  View  Save  Options  Name  Group  Quit
Line  Bar  XY  Stacked-Bar  Pie
                             Graph Settings
     Type: Bar                    Titles: First
                                          Second
     X: A11..A14                          X axis
     A: B11..B14                          Y axis
     B: C11..C14
     C: D11..D14                                  Y scale:      X scale:
     D: E11..E14                          Scaling  Automatic     Automatic
     E:                                   Lower
     F:                                   Upper
                                          Format   (G)           (G)
     Grid: None       Color: No           Indicator Yes          Yes

        Legend:              Format:      Data labels:         Skip: 1
     A                       Both
     B                       Both
     C                       Both
     D                       Both
     E                       Both
     F                       Both

     30-Nov-90  12:09 PM
```

Figure 50.1: */Graph Style Sheet*

7. Select **View**. Each of the four shaded bars for each expense represents a quarter.

8. Press any key to exit the graph.

9. Select **Options Legend**.

10. Select **Range**. This Release 2.2 command allows you to specify multiple legends at one time if they are in adjacent cells.

11. Specify **B3..E3** and press Enter.

12. **Quit** the Options menu.

13. Select **View**.

14. Name and save the graph, if desired.

15. Save the worksheet as **91BUDGET**.

_____ A

_____ C

_____ B

_____ 1

_____ 3

_____ 1

_____ 2

_____ 2

Part Five

Database Management

3

51

Creating a Database

FEATURING

/Data Fill

To build a database, you enter information—such as inventory, personnel, or client records—on the worksheet as text and numbers just as you previously entered data in your budget projection. All of the commands used with the worksheet are available for the database. Thus you will print the database, for example, the same way you printed the worksheet, using Print commands.

So what's new? **Data** commands. By using **Data** commands in the sections that follow, you will manipulate the data you've entered.

The database is organized into rows and columns that function as *fields* and *records*. A row in the database represents one record, such as one employee or one product. Data for the one record cannot extend to a second row.

Each data item in a record is entered into a separate column or field. Similar data must be entered in the same column. For example, you might put employee names in one column, addresses in another. And a column must consist of either labels or values. You cannot, for example, enter one zip code as a value and another as a label with a label prefix.

There are a maximum of 8,191 records in a 1-2-3 database. This number is one less than the total number of rows because one row must contain *field names* or column headings, each of which must be unique and occupy only one row. There should not be any blank rows between the column headings and the data. For each record, you can enter 256 data items—one in each column in the worksheet. Finally, if you like you can enter more than one database in a 1-2-3 worksheet. Figure 51.1 is a sample 1-2-3 database.

To get started, you will first build a small employee database. Next, you will assign a unique ID number to each employee. This will allow you to restore the database to its original order after you have sorted it.

You will use the **/Data Fill** command to add the ID numbers. **Data Fill** creates a sequence of numbers, dates, or times automatically. It requires that you specify a *fill range* in which to place the values, a *Start value* (number to start the sequence with), a *Step Value* (how much to increase the start value for the next number), and a *Stop Value* (the last number). If the end of the fill range occurs before the stop value has been reached, **/Data Fill** will stop there.

*H*ow to Enter Information

1. Be sure that the screen is blank and you are in the **READY** mode.

2. Enter the following information the same way you entered labels, numbers, and formulas. However, be sure that you do not add any blank spaces after the last character in each entry. Adding a space with the spacebar causes problems when 1-2-3 reorganizes the data. Columns A, B, and C should be left-aligned. Column headings for D and E will be right-aligned (with the ” label-prefix) to match the numbers that follow. Be sure not to use a label-prefix with the numbers. Enter this

information:

	A	B	C	D	E
1	INPUT RANGE (IR)				
2	EMPLOYEE	STORE	DEPT	"SALARY	"SALES
3	Gomez, F.	New York	Sales	42600	260000
4	Wong, C.	Atlanta	Admin	45400	
5	Stein, B.	Atlanta	Sales	43300	235000
6	Gupta, T.	Atlanta	Sales	39400	153000
7	Nash, A.	New York	Admin	40000	
8	Brand, F.	New York	Sales	42900	216000
9	Land, J.	New York	Sales	39400	187000

3. Select /**Worksheet Global Column** to widen the columns to **12**.

4. Select /**Worksheet Global Format ,(Comma) 0** to display the numbers as whole numbers with commas. The result should look like Figure 51.1.

5. Select /**File Save** and save the file under the name **EMPLOYEE**. In case of any problems, this step will prevent you from having to type the database again.

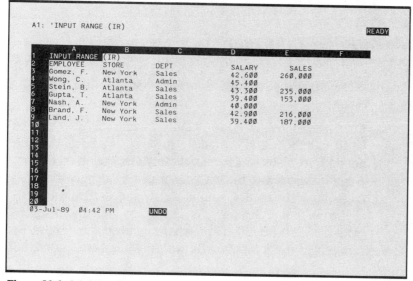

Figure 51.1: 1-2-3 Database

*H*ow to Add a Sequence of Numbers to the Database

6. Select **/Data** (see Figure 51.2). 1-2-3 prompts you to enter the fill range.

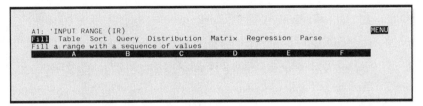

A1: 'INPUT RANGE (IR)   MENU
Fill Table Sort Query Distribution Matrix Regression Parse
Fill a range with a sequence of values

Figure 51.2: The Data menu

The Data Menu

- The **Fill** command automatically assigns a sequence of numbers to a range of cells.

- **Table** creates statistical tables.

- **Sort** reorganizes the information.

- **Query** finds and lists subsets of information.

- **Distribution** tallies the number of times an item occurs within a range.

- **Matrix** multiplies a row of numbers by a column of numbers and produce a table of the results. You can also invert a matrix, or table, of numbers.

- **Regression** creates statistical data based on variables.

- **Parse** converts a column of long labels into several columns of labels or values. Parse was introduced in Lesson 39 in the section on transferring data from other programs to 1-2-3. Refer to the 1-2-3 manual for further explanations of Matrix and Regression.

7. Select **Fill**.

8. Place the ID numbers in the column to the right of the numbers. Specify:

    F3..F9

    After pressing Enter, 1-2-3 prompts you to enter a start number.

9. The first employee will have ID number 1. Type:

    1

    After pressing Enter, 1-2-3 prompts you for the step number, or the amount of change from one number to the next. 1-2-3 suggests 1.

10. Press Enter since you want the numbers to increase by one. 1-2-3 prompts you to enter a stop number and suggests 8191 or the last record (or row) number.

11. Press Enter to leave this as is; the initial fill range of F3..F9 will stop the "fill" of numbers. After you press Enter, the database in Figure 51.3 appears on the screen.

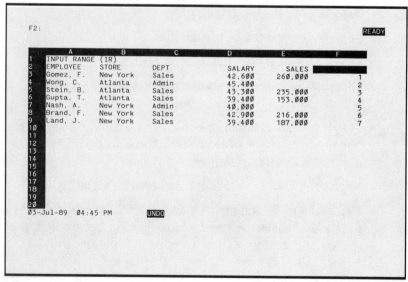

Figure 51.3: Database with ID Numbers

12. Enter a label at the top of column **F**. Type: **"ID#**.

13. Save the file.

LESSON

52

Sorting the Database

FEATURING

/Data Sort

At the moment, 1-2-3 isn't anything more than a space-saving filing cabinet. But, just as 1-2-3 distinguished itself as more than a ledger pad, it will distinguish itself as more than a filing cabinet with its ability to organize and reorganize information. With the **/Data Sort** command, you can change the order of the records to any order that you specify.

Continuing with the personnel list you entered in the previous lesson, you will use **/Data Sort** to sort the records in various ways. To sort records you must specify a *sort range* (what columns and rows are to be sorted?) and *keys* (what column or columns do you want to sort by?).

How to Sort the Database

To Sort Alphabetically

1. Select **/Data Sort**. 1-2-3 displays the Data Sort menu (Figure 52.1).

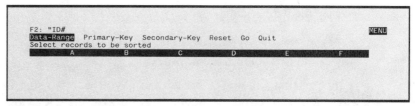

Figure: 52.1 / Data Sort Menu

Data Sort Menu

- **Data-Range** refers to the cells you will include in the sort.

- Using the **Primary-Key**, you specify the first field (formerly referred to as a column) that you will use to sort the data base by, such as by department.

- With the **Secondary-Key**, you can further sort the data using an additional field, such as salaries or sales.

- **Reset** cancels the Data-Range and key settings.

- **Go** tells 1-2-3 to sort.

- **Quit** exits the Sort menu.

Release 2.2 will also display a Sort Settings sheet. Press WINDOW (F6) to display the worksheet. Press WINDOW (F6) again to return the Settings sheet.

2. Since you must first tell 1-2-3 what you want to sort, select **Data-Range**. 1-2-3 prompts you to enter the range.

3. Specify all of the data except the labels at the top of each column: **A3..F9**. (Use the period and arrow keys to point.)
   Warning: Be sure to include all the columns in your database.

4. After pressing Enter, select **Primary-Key**. 1-2-3 prompts you to enter the primary sort key address.

5. Specify the name field:

   A1

   Any cell in this column would work.

6. After pressing Enter, 1-2-3 asks you if you want to sort in ascending or descending order. *Ascending* orders data from the lowest number to the highest and from the first letter of the alphabet to the last. *Descending* does the reverse.

7. Type:

   A

   Since this column consists of labels (names), 1-2-3 will sort it alphabetically. After pressing Enter, the Sort menu returns to the screen.

8. Select **Go**. The sorted database is shown in Figure 52.2.

To Sort by Department and Sales

9. Select **/Data Sort Primary-Key**. Since you want to sort alphabetically by department, specify any cell in column **C** as the Primary-Key cell.

10. After pressing Enter, select **Ascending** order. Type: **A** and press Enter.

11. Select **Secondary-Key**.

12. To sort each department by sales, specify any cell address in the sales column, column **E**.

13. After pressing Enter, 1-2-3 again asks you if you want the information sorted in ascending or descending order. This time, use descending order. Type:

    D

    Since this field is filled with sales, 1-2-3 will sort it by number, placing the highest sales first.

14. After pressing Enter, select **Go**. As shown in Figure 52.3, you now have a list of employees by department, with each department organized by sales amounts.

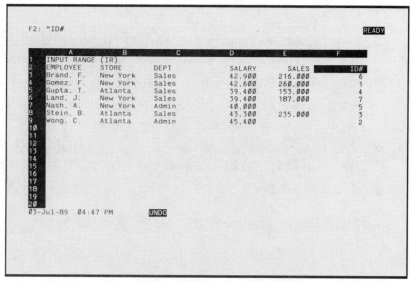

```
F2: "ID#                                                              READY

        A          B           C          D          E          F
 1  INPUT RANGE (IR)
 2  EMPLOYEE    STORE       DEPT        SALARY      SALES        ID#
 3  Brand, F.   New York    Sales       42,900     216,000        6
 4  Gomez, F.   New York    Sales       42,600     260,000        1
 5  Gupta, T.   Atlanta     Sales       39,400     153,000        4
 6  Land, J.    New York    Sales       39,400     187,000        7
 7  Nash, A.    New York    Admin       40,000                    5
 8  Stein, B.   Atlanta     Sales       43,300     235,000        3
 9  Wong, C.    Atlanta     Admin       45,400                    2
10
11
12
13
14
15
16
17
18
19
20
03-Jul-89   04:47 PM         UNDO
```

Figure 52.2: Database in Alphabetic Order

```
F1:                                                                 READY

        A          B           C          D          E          F
 1  INPUT RANGE (IR)
 2  EMPLOYEE    STORE       DEPT        SALARY      SALES        ID#
 3  Nash, A.    New York    Admin       40,000                    5
 4  Wong, C.    Atlanta     Admin       45,400                    2
 5  Gomez, F.   New York    Sales       42,600     260,000        1
 6  Stein, B.   Atlanta     Sales       43,300     235,000        3
 7  Brand, F.   New York    Sales       42,900     216,000        6
 8  Land, J.    New York    Sales       39,400     187,000        7
 9  Gupta, T.   Atlanta     Sales       39,400     153,000        4
10
11
12
13
14
15
16
17
18
19
20
04-Jul-89   04:26 PM         UNDO
```

Figure 52.3: Database in Department and Sales Order

To Restore the Database to Its Original Order

15. Select **/Data Sort Primary-Key**. Move the pointer to any cell in column F, the column with ID numbers.

16. After pressing Enter, type **A** to select **Ascending** order.

17. Select **Go**. 1-2-3 sorts the database using the ID numbers. The original order of the database has been restored.

18. If the results shown here do not match your own, retrieve the worksheet **EMPLOYEE** and start with step 1.

19. Save the worksheet.

LESSON

53

Querying the Database

FEATURING

/Data Query
QUERY (F7)

Once data is stored, either a single piece of information or a group of related data can be retrieved. With the employee list you have entered, you can use the /**Data Query** command to retrieve a list of all the salespeople in the Atlanta area or a list of the salespeople who have sold more than $200,000 in merchandise. Or, you could combine the two by querying for a list of the salespeople in Atlanta who have sold more than $200,000 worth of merchandise.

As with /**Data Sort,** you must specify a range of cells to query or search through—called the *input range.* An input range differs from a Data-Range in sorting; when you query, you specify the database *and* the column headings, or field names.

A second range is also specified in /**Data Query**: the *criteria range.* This range consists of field names and criteria, or the information 1-2-3 uses to determine what to select from the input range. When you query, 1-2-3 goes to the criteria range to get the criteria—actually a set of records consisting of labels, numbers, and formulas. Then 1-2-3 returns to the input range to find the records that match.

Finally, if you want 1-2-3 to make copies of the new list elsewhere on the worksheet, a third range must be specified: the *output range*. It tells 1-2-3 where to put the copy of the data it has selected. The output range must have the names of the fields you want copied in the top row.

All three ranges—input, criteria, and output—must have identical field names in the first row. This means that if one set of field names is capitalized, the others must be also.

How to Query for Subsets of Information

To Create Column Headings for the Criteria and Output Ranges

1. Using the **/Copy** command, copy the field names (column headings) twice: first, to row 12 to make a copy for the criteria range; then, to row 16 to make a copy for the output range. The database will look like the one in Figure 53.1.

```
A2:  'EMPLOYEE                                                          READY

           A          B          C          D           E          F
 1   INPUT RANGE (IR)
 2   EMPLOYEE      STORE      DEPT      SALARY      SALES      ID#
 3   Gomez, F.     New York   Sales     42,600      260,000        1
 4   Wong, C.      Atlanta    Admin     45,400                     2
 5   Stein, B.     Atlanta    Sales     43,300      235,000        3
 6   Gupta, T.     Atlanta    Sales     39,400      153,000        4
 7   Nash, A.      New York   Admin     40,000                     5
 8   Brand, F.     New York   Sales     42,900      216,000        6
 9   Land, J.      New York   Sales     39,400      187,000        7
10
11
12   EMPLOYEE      STORE      DEPT      SALARY      SALES      ID#
13
14
15
16   EMPLOYEE      STORE      DEPT      SALARY      SALES      ID#
17
18
19
20
03-Jul-89   04:53 PM              UNDO
```

Figure 53.1: Database with Copied Field Names

To Name the Input and Criteria Ranges

When working with the /**Data Query** commands, it is a good idea to assign range names to the input, criteria, and output ranges. This way you will not have to refer to specific cell addresses. (See Lesson 36, "Naming Parts of the Worksheet," for reference.)

2. Select /**Range Name Create**.

3. Type:

    IR

    This will be the range name for the input range (your database).

4. After pressing Enter, specify the range beginning with the field name EMPLOYEE and ending with the bottom right of the list. Type:

    A2..F9

5. Press Enter.

6. Select /**Range Name Create** again.

7. Type:

    CR

    This will be the range name for the criteria range.

8. After pressing Enter, specify the range beginning with the field names in row 12. Since the criteria range must include at least two rows, include the blank beneath, row 13. Be sure to extend the range to column F. Type:

    A12..F13

To Specify the Input and Criteria Ranges

9. Select /**Data Query**. 1-2-3 displays the menu, shown in Figure 53.2.

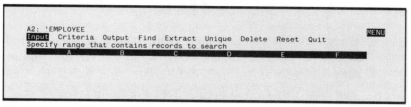

Figure 53.2: The Data Query Command Menu

The Query Menu

- **Input** identifies the cells contained in the database, including column headings.

- **Criteria** specifies where the data is to be stored that will be used to match against the database.

- **Output** specifies where copies of the matching records will be placed.

- **Find** highlights the records (one at a time) that match the selection criteria located in the criteria range.

- **Extract** copies records that match the selection criteria and places them in the output range.

- **Unique** eliminates duplicates while copying records to the output range.

- **Delete** erases records from the database that match the selection criteria in the criteria range and deletes the empty rows.

- **Reset** turns off the input, criteria and output range settings.

- **Quit** allows you to leave the Query menu.

With Release 2.2, a settings sheet will display the current query settings. Press **WINDOW (F6)** to display the worksheet. Press **WINDOW (F6)** again to return to the settings sheet.

10. Select **Input**. 1-2-3 asks for the input range. Instead of entering A2..F9 as the database range, you will enter the range name IR that you created above.

11. Press the **NAME (F3)** function key. A list of the range names is displayed.

12. Select **IR**. The Data Query menu returns.

13. Select **Criteria**.

14. Press the **NAME (F3)** key again.

15. Select **CR**. The criteria range is now specified, and the Data Query menu returns.

16. Select **Output**. 1-2-3 now asks for the output range.

17. Since you didn't assign a range name to the output range, specify the range beginning with the EMPLOYEE cell in the bottom group of field names and ending with the last field name in the row: **A16. .F16**. After pressing Enter, the output range is specified.

To Query Using the Extract Command

Once the input, criteria, and output ranges are specified, use the Extract command.

18. Select **Extract** to place a copy of the query data in the output range.

19. Select **Quit**.

The entire database is copied into the output range, as shown in Figure 53.3, because no criteria were specified in the criteria range. Leaving the criteria range blank pulls out the entire list of employees.

If the results shown here differ from your own, retrieve the worksheet **EMPLOYEE** and begin again with step 1.

To Query Using a Single Criterion

20. In B13, in the criteria range, type:

    Atlanta

    Remember: The criterion must be an exact match—the first letter only is capitalized.

21. After pressing Enter, try a quicker method of querying. Rather than returning to **/Data Query Extract** to copy the Atlanta records to the output range, press the **QUERY (F7)** function key.

QUERY (F7) tells 1-2-3 to perform the most recent Query operation—in this case, **Extract**—using the last input, criteria, and output ranges and any new criteria that are specified. All employees from Atlanta are now copied down to the output range, as shown in Figure 53.4.

To Query Using Multiple Criteria

To match against more than one criterion, type multiple criteria on the same row in the criteria range. A record in the database must match all criteria to be selected.

22. In E13, type the formula:

    +E3>200000

```
A24:                                                                    READY

        A            B            C            D          E           F
5   Stein, B.    Atlanta      Sales        43,300     235,000          3
6   Gupta, T.    Atlanta      Sales        39,400     153,000          4
7   Nash, A.     New York     Admin        40,000                      5
8   Brand, F.    New York     Sales        42,900     216,000          6
9   Land, J.     New York     Sales        39,400     187,000          7
10
11
12  EMPLOYEE     STORE        DEPT         SALARY     SALES          ID#
13
14
15
16  EMPLOYEE     STORE        DEPT         SALARY     SALES          ID#
17  Gomez, F.    New York     Sales        42,600     260,000          1
18  Wong, C.     Atlanta      Admin        45,400                      2
19  Stein, B.    Atlanta      Sales        43,300     235,000          3
20  Gupta, T.    Atlanta      Sales        39,400     153,000          4
21  Nash, A.     New York     Admin        40,000                      5
22  Brand, F.    New York     Sales        42,900     216,000          6
23  Land, J.     New York     Sales        39,400     187,000          7
24
03-Jul-89   04:59 PM      UNDO
```

Figure 53.3: All the Records in the Output Range

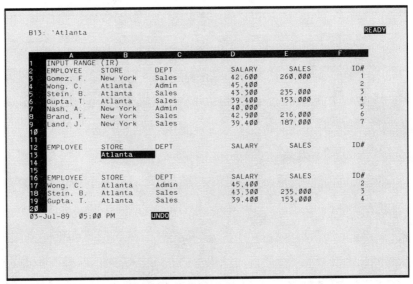

Figure 53.4: Extracting Using One Criterion

After you press Enter, a one is displayed. (The one means that the first record in the database does match; the first employee does have sales over $200,000. This is not important to the query.)

23. Press **QUERY (F7)**. All records must now match two criteria: Atlanta and sales greater than $200,000. One employee fits the criteria and is copied to the output range, as shown in Figure 53.5.

To Display Criteria Formulas

Instead of seeing 0 or 1 in the criteria range when you type in a formula, you can format the cell to display the formula.

24. Select **/Range Format Text**.

25. Specify the range as **D13..E13**, the two criteria cells that select number fields in the database. After you press Enter, the +E3>200000 is displayed. In the control panel, above the worksheet, (T) refers to the text format.

26. Select **/Range Name Labels Down**. You are prompted to enter a label range.

Lesson 53

```
E13:  +E3>200000                                                    READY

          A          B            C            D          E          F
1  INPUT RANGE (IR)
2  EMPLOYEE    STORE        DEPT         SALARY       SALES      ID#
3  Gomez, F.   New York     Sales        42,600      260,000       1
4  Wong, C.    Atlanta      Admin        45,400                    2
5  Stein, B.   Atlanta      Sales        43,300      235,000       3
6  Gupta, T.   Atlanta      Sales        39,400      153,000       4
7  Nash, A.    New York     Admin        40,000                    5
8  Brand, F.   New York     Sales        42,900      216,000       6
9  Land, J.    New York     Sales        39,400      187,000       7
10
11
12 EMPLOYEE    STORE        DEPT         SALARY       SALES      ID#
13             Atlanta                                    1
14
15
16 EMPLOYEE    STORE        DEPT         SALARY       SALES      ID#
17 Stein, B.   Atlanta      Sales        43,300      235,000       3
18
19
20
03-Jul-89   05:00 PM         UNDO
```

Figure 53.5: *Querying with Multiple Criteria*

27. Specify the range: **A2..F2**. After you press Enter, the control panel will display + SALES > 200000, instead of + E3 > 200000. You can now enter criteria formulas using the column headings as range names.

To Erase Data from the Criteria Range

Do not use the spacebar to delete criteria. Although the criterion disappears, a space character is entered in its place. The space character then becomes the selection criterion for the next query, and records with a space in the column would be considered as the match records. In this database, no records would match.

28. Select /**Range Erase** to erase Atlanta from B13. The next query will not select by store.

29. Press **QUERY (F7)**. All employees whose sales were greater than $200,000, regardless of their store, are copied to the output range.

To Query Using #AND# and #OR#

30. In E13, being sure not to add any blank spaces, enter the following formula:

    +SALES> = 175000#AND#SALES< = 200000

    The logical operator #AND# tells 1-2-3 to select those employees that satisfy *both* the first half of the formula *and* the second half: that have between 175,000 and 200,000 dollars in sales. (After you press Enter, only part of the formula is displayed because the formula is so long.)

31. Press **QUERY (F7)**. The employee who fulfills the criteria is copied to the output range, as shown in Figure 53.6.

```
E13: (T) +SALES>=175000#AND#SALES<=200000                          READY

         A          B          C          D          E           F
1  INPUT RANGE (IR)
2  EMPLOYEE   STORE      DEPT         SALARY       SALES        ID#
3  Gomez, F.  New York   Sales        42,600     260,000         1
4  Wong, C.   Atlanta    Admin        45,400                     2
5  Stein, B.  Atlanta    Sales        43,300     235,000         3
6  Gupta, T.  Atlanta    Sales        39,400     153,000         4
7  Nash, A.   New York   Admin        40,000                     5
8  Brand, F.  New York   Sales        42,900     216,000         6
9  Land, J.   New York   Sales        39,400     187,000         7
10
11
12 EMPLOYEE   STORE      DEPT         SALARY       SALES        ID#
13                                              +SALES>=175
14
15
16 EMPLOYEE   STORE      DEPT         SALARY       SALES        ID#
17 Land, J.   New York   Sales        39,400     187,000         7
18
19
20
03-Jul-89   05:03 PM        UNDO
```

Figure 53.6: Using the #AND# operator

32. Now change the formula to select employees who sold more than $200,000 or less than $150,000. Use **#OR#**.

    +SALES<150000#OR#SALES>200000

    The logical operator #OR# tells 1-2-3 to select those who satisfy *either* the first half *or* the last half of the formula.

33. Use **QUERY (F7)** to select employees. Five employees are selected. (One is shown on the next screen.) See Figure 53.7.

To Query Using Multiple Labels

If you want a list of employees from two cities, you must enter the labels in new rows beneath the appropriate column heading, one beneath the other. But first, new rows must be added to the criteria range.

34. Select **/Data Query Criteria**. The current criteria range is displayed.

35. Press the Down Arrow key to expand the range one row. After you press Enter, a blank row is added to the range.

36. **Quit** the Data Query menu.

37. Select **/Range Erase** to erase the formula beneath SALES.

38. In A13 type:

    Wong, C.

39. After pressing Enter, in A14 type:

    Nash, A.

```
E13: (T) +SALES<150000#OR#SALES>200000                          READY

        A            B            C            D            E            F
1   INPUT RANGE (IR)
2   EMPLOYEE     STORE        DEPT         SALARY       SALES        ID#
3   Gomez, F.    New York     Sales        42,600       260,000       1
4   Wong, C.     Atlanta      Admin        45,400                     2
5   Stein, B.    Atlanta      Sales        43,300       235,000       3
6   Gupta, T.    Atlanta      Sales        39,400       153,000       4
7   Nash, A.     New York     Admin        40,000                     5
8   Brand, F.    New York     Sales        42,900       216,000       6
9   Land, J.     New York     Sales        39,400       187,000       7
10
11
12  EMPLOYEE     STORE        DEPT         SALARY       SALES        ID#
13                                                     +SALES<1500
14
15
16  EMPLOYEE     STORE        DEPT         SALARY       SALES        ID#
17  Gomez, F.    New York     Sales        42,600       260,000       1
18  Wong, C.     Atlanta      Admin        45,400                     2
19  Stein, B.    Atlanta      Sales        43,300       235,000       3
20  Nash, A.     New York     Admin        40,000                     5
03-Jul-89   05:04 PM         UNDO
```

Figure 53.7: Using the #OR# operator

40. After pressing Enter, press **QUERY (F7)**. The two employees are copied to the output range (see Figure 53.8).

41. Select **/Data Query Criteria** to change the criteria range back to include only two rows: 12 and 13. Move the pointer up one row and press Enter.

42. Select **Quit** to exit the Data Query menu.

43. Select **/Range Erase** to erase the names from the criteria range in cells A13 and A14.

```
A14:  'Nash, A.                                                    READY

         A          B          C          D          E          F
1  INPUT RANGE (IR)
2  EMPLOYEE   STORE      DEPT       SALARY     SALES      ID#
3  Gomez, F.  New York   Sales      42,600     260,000       1
4  Wong, C.   Atlanta    Admin      45,400                    2
5  Stein, B.  Atlanta    Sales      43,300     235,000       3
6  Gupta, T.  Atlanta    Sales      39,400     153,000       4
7  Nash, A.   New York   Admin      40,000                    5
8  Brand, F.  New York   Sales      42,900     216,000       6
9  Land, J.   New York   Sales      39,400     187,000       7
10
11
12 EMPLOYEE   STORE      DEPT       SALARY     SALES      ID#
13 Wong, C.
14 Nash, A.
15
16 EMPLOYEE   STORE      DEPT       SALARY     SALES      ID#
17 Wong, C.   Atlanta    Admin      45,400                    2
18 Nash, A.   New York   Admin      40,000                    5
19
20
03-Jul-89   05:05 PM         UNDO
```

Figure 53.8: Adding Rows to the Criteria Range

Caution: It is easy to forget that there are multiple rows in a criteria range. If you erased Nash and forgot to change the criteria range to include only one row beneath the column headings, the following would happen:

- In Release 2.2, blank rows in a criteria range are ignored. In the above example, therefore, erasing Nash and presing **QUERY (F7)**, would list the other employee, Wong.

- In releases prior to 2.2, blank rows are not ignored. Erasing Nash and pressing **QUERY (F7)** would produce a list of *all* employees because 1-2-3 is looking for records that match either Wong or a blank criterion, and a blank criteria cell matches all records.

To Query Using Partial Matching

As mentioned earlier, if you type in a full label, it must match exactly, including uppercase and lowercase. However, to save keystrokes, or if you cannot remember the full spelling, you can type part of the criterion.

Three special characters act as wild cards with labels when using the Query command: *, ?, and ~ (tilde). The asterisk after a label matches all characters that follow the label, e.g., A* matches Atlanta. The question mark (?) matches single characters and can be used at the beginning, in the middle, or at the end of a label. For example, H?t selects Hot, Hat, Hit, and Hut, but not Halt or Hats. The tilde (~) before a label tells 1-2-3 to select all records except those matching that label. For example, ~New York would extract all employees except those in New York.

44. Since only one store starts with A, you can type A* instead of Altanta and achieve the same results. In cell B13 type:

    A*

45. Press **QUERY (F7)**. All people in Atlanta are selected.

46. Select **/Range Erase** to erase **A***. See Figure 53.9.

Use the ? wild card character to search for those having **nd** at the end of their last name.

47. Under EMPLOYEE, type: **??nd*** and press Enter.

48. Press **QUERY (F7)**. The employee Land, J. will be listed. The two question marks require that there be two characters in front.

49. Under EMPLOYEE, type: **???nd*** and press Enter. The employee Brand, F. will appear. The three question marks require three characters. See Figure 53.10.

```
 B13:  'A*                                                              READY

          A          B          C          D          E          F
 1   INPUT RANGE (IR)
 2   EMPLOYEE   STORE      DEPT           SALARY      SALES        ID#
 3   Gomez, F.  New York   Sales          42,600    260,000        1
 4   Wong, C.   Atlanta    Admin          45,400                   2
 5   Stein, B.  Atlanta    Sales          43,300    235,000        3
 6   Gupta, T.  Atlanta    Sales          39,400    153,000        4
 7   Nash, A.   New York   Admin          40,000                   5
 8   Brand, F.  New York   Sales          42,900    216,000        6
 9   Land, J.   New York   Sales          39,400    187,000        7
10
11
12   EMPLOYEE   STORE      DEPT           SALARY      SALES        ID#
13              A*
14
15
16   EMPLOYEE   STORE      DEPT           SALARY      SALES        ID#
17   Wong, C.   Atlanta    Admin          45,400                   2
18   Stein, B.  Atlanta    Sales          43,300    235,000        3
19   Gupta, T.  Atlanta    Sales          39,400    153,000        4
20
 03-Jul-89   05:33 PM              UNDO
```

Figure 53.9: Using Wild Cards in Queries

```
 A13:  '???nd*                                                          READY

          A          B          C          D          E          F
 1   INPUT RANGE (IR)
 2   EMPLOYEE   STORE      DEPT           SALARY      SALES        ID#
 3   Gomez, F.  New York   Sales          42,600    260,000        1
 4   Wong, C.   Atlanta    Admin          45,400                   2
 5   Stein, B.  Atlanta    Sales          43,300    235,000        3
 6   Gupta, T.  Atlanta    Sales          39,400    153,000        4
 7   Nash, A.   New York   Admin          40,000                   5
 8   Brand, F.  New York   Sales          42,900    216,000        6
 9   Land, J.   New York   Sales          39,400    187,000        7
10
11
12   EMPLOYEE   STORE      DEPT           SALARY      SALES        ID#
13   ???nd*
14
15
16   EMPLOYEE   STORE      DEPT           SALARY      SALES        ID#
17   Brand, F.  New York   Sales          42,900    216,000        6
18
19
20
 03-Jul-89   05:33 PM              UNDO
```

Figure 53.10: Querying Using the ? Wild Card

To Find and Change Records in the Database

Use **Find** to search through the database and point to matching records. This is useful when editing records. Find uses the current input and criteria ranges. There is no output range. The first record in the input range that matches is highlighted, and the mode indicator changes to **FIND**. When working in the **FIND** mode, the following keys are available:

- The pointer-movement keys move up and down the list and across the columns.

- The Home and End keys move to the top and the bottom of the list.

- The **EDIT (F2)** key edits a cell entry.

- Escape and Enter keys exit the **FIND** mode.

50. Change the criterion so that you can find those people who work in the Atlanta store. Select **/Range Erase** to erase the criterion under EMPLOYEE.

51. Enter **Atlanta** beneath STORE.

52. Select **/Data Query Find**. The first employee in the Atlanta store is highlighted.

53. Move the pointer down. 1-2-3 highlights the next employee in Atlanta.

54. Move across the record using the right and left pointer-movement keys. Watch the control panel in order to tell which column you are in.

55. Move to the record for Wong, C. in the EMPLOYEE column.

56. Press **EDIT (F2)** to change the spelling from Wong, C. to **Wing, C.** Press Enter.

57. Press **Escape** to leave the **FIND** mode.

58. Select **Quit** to exit the Query menu.

59. Now find New York employees. Move to the criteria range, cell **B13**.

60. Type: **New York** and press Enter.

61. Press **QUERY (F7)**. You are now in **FIND** mode. Pressing the **QUERY (F7)** key now instructs 1-2-3 to find, rather than extract, since it is the most recent query operation.

62. Move the pointer up and down the list to view the New York employees.

63. Press Escape to exit the **FIND** mode.

64. Save the worksheet.

54

Using Database @Functions to Derive Totals

FEATURING

@DSUM
@DCOUNT
@DAVG

So far you have been able to list employees based on certain criteria. However, it may be necessary to calculate totals from the database. For instance, it would be useful to determine the total number of employees per store and the total and average sales per store. To do this, use the database @functions.

Database @functions are different from the functions you have already used. With @SUM you were able to total a range of cells. With @DSUM you are not limited to totaling all cells in a range; you can total a subgroup of cells. For example, if you applied the @SUM function to the database @SUM(D3..D9), it would total the salaries of all employees. Using the database @function @DSUM instead, you could total the salaries for one store only.

The syntax for the @functions is:

@dfunction name(input range, column offset, criteria range)

where the input range is the location of the database, column offset is the column to be processed (added, averaged, counted, etc.), and criteria range is the location of the selection criteria. Input and criteria ranges are similar to those used by **/Data Query** in the last lesson. However, you do not specify them using **/Data Query Input** and **/Data Query Criteria**.

To total the salaries of all employees in one store, for example, the input range would be the database, including column headings; the column offset would be 3 (the SALARY column is offset three columns), and the criteria range would be the same criteria range as in the last lesson. Using the range names created in the last lesson, the formula is:

@DSUM(IR,3,CR)

The column offset, 3, is the number of columns to the right of the first column; column A equals 0, B equals 1, and so on.

In addition to using @DSUM, you will use @DCOUNT to count the number of employees for each store, and @DAVG to average the salaries and sales per store.

*H*ow to Use Database @Functions

You will set up formulas to count the total number of employees, and sum sales totals and averages for each store. You will use the existing database and criteria ranges. To make room for the database @functions, move down the existing output range.

To Set Up the Worksheet

1. Select **/Range Erase** to erase any data in the criteria range: **A13..F13**.

2. To create room for the @functions, insert rows above the output range. Select **/Worksheet Insert Row** and specify the range **A16..A20**. (The output range is moved to the next screen.)

3. Enter the following labels in the specified cells:

	B	C	D	E
15		"COUNT	"TOTAL	"AVERAGE
16	Per Store			
17				

To Enter @DCOUNT, @DSUM, and @DAVG

4. Move to cell **C16**, below COUNT.

5. Type:

   @DCOUNT(IR,0,CR)

   After pressing Enter, the total number of employees for the company is displayed. 1-2-3 selected all the records in the database because no criteria were specified in the criteria range. Make sure you enter a zero in the formula.

6. Move to **D16**, beneath TOTAL, and type:

   @DSUM(IR,4,CR)

   After pressing Enter, the total sales amount for the entire company will be displayed.

7. Move to **E16**, beneath AVERAGE, and type:

   @DAVG(IR,4,CR)

   After pressing Enter, the average sales amount for the company is displayed. 1-2-3 has selected all the records in the database because there are no criteria in the criteria range (see Figure 54.1).

8. Move to the criteria range, cell **B13**.

9. Type:

   Atlanta

   Remember that you can use wild cards; you could also type At*. In any case, make sure that the letters you type match those in the database exactly. After pressing Enter, the database @function totals reflect only the Atlanta store (see Figure 54.2).

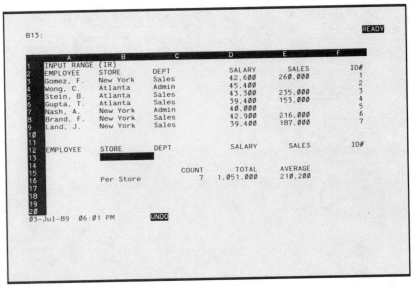

Figure 54.1: Totals for All Stores

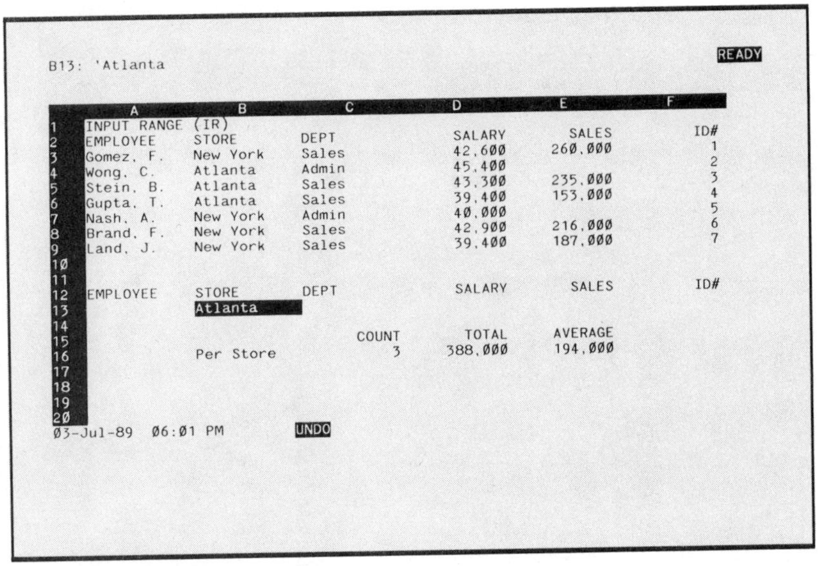

Figure 54.2: Totals for One Store

10. Now type **New*** directly over Atlanta. The total will change to reflect the different store.

11. Use **/Range Erase** to erase **New*** from the criteria range. The numbers now reflect totals for all stores.

12. Save the worksheet.

LESSON

55

Building Data Tables

FEATURING

/Data Table

Lesson 54 demonstrated how to calculate database totals, but you were limited to calculating totals for one store at a time. Using database @functions and /**Data Table**, you can produce a table, like the one in Figure 55.1, that contains the number of employees and the total and average sales for each store.

There are two types of data tables: Data Table 1 and Data Table 2. Several steps are involved in creating a data table using /**Data Table**.

1. Enter a list of stores in a column.

2. In the columns to the right, and on the row above the first store, enter the formulas, e.g., database @functions.

3. Select /**Data Table 1**.

4. Specify the table range with the list of stores in the left column and the formulas in the top row.

5. Specify where each store is to be temporarily stored while the calculations are being performed. This is the **input cell**.

The structure of the Data Table will be:

STORE

{input cell}	COUNT	TOTAL	AVERAGE
	Formula 1	Formula 2	Formula 3 ...
Store 1	{results}	{results}	{results}
Store 2	{results}	{results}	{results}
Store 3	{results}	{results}	{results}
...			

The formulas represent the database @functions (@DSUM, @DAVG, @DCOUNT). The database @functions use the criteria range: the column heading, STORE, and the blank cell beneath. Each store will be entered into the criteria range one at a time. The formulas will be calculated for each store, and the results will be displayed in the table, next to each store.

How to Build a Database Summary Table

To Calculate Totals Using /Data Table

Make sure cell B13 is blank before starting.

1. Type in the store names: **Atlanta** in B17 and **New York** in B18.

2. Select **/Data Table**. You have three choices: **1 2 Reset**. **1** represents Data Table 1, **2** represents Data Table 2, and **Reset** turns off any existing table range.

3. Select **1**. After you select 1, 1-2-3 asks for the **Data Table** range. In this case, the table range includes the list of stores in the first column, the formulas in the first row, and the blank area where the data is to be displayed.

4. Move to **B16** where the column of stores and the row of formulas intersect.

5. Type a period.

6. Move the pointer to the bottom right of the table, where SALES and the last row intersect: **E18**. After you press Enter, 1-2-3 asks you to enter the first input cell.

7. Specify **B13**, the cell in the criteria range where each store name will be entered successively. After pressing Enter, the Data Table results appear.

8. In cell **B16**, type **All Stores** directly over "Per Store." See Figure 55.1.

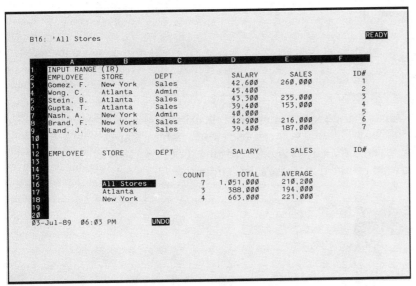

Figure 55.1: Totals by Store Using /Data Table 1

9. Save the worksheet.

While the database @functions are used in this section to demonstrate data tables, you can use other types of formulas. For example, the following table could be set up to calculate interest by multiplying a list of interest rates by a principal amount. Using /Data Table 1, the rates (Rate 1, Rate 2, etc.) would be entered into the input cell one at a time, with the formula multiplying each rate times the principal and entering it into the table. To build this you would need to type in the different rates and the principal, and indicate the cell address for the Input Cell. The table range would include the column of rates, the formula, and the area for results.

```
Principal    Input Cell
$100,000     {     }

             Principal * Input cell
Rate 1       {results}
Rate 2       {results}
Rate 3       {results}
Rate 4       {results}
```

How to Forecast Sales Amounts Using /Data Table 2

You used **/Data Table 1** to build a summary table using one variable: the store. With **/Data Table 2** you can use two variables. One common use is to do "what if" analysis and forecasting. For example, to forecast sales you might want to increase sales amounts by different rates. See Figure 55.2.

```
1st VARIABLE  2nd VARIABLE
(STORE)       (RATE)
{input cell 1}  {input cell 2}

SALES PROJECTION
Formula  Rate 1     Rate 2      Rate 3
Store 1  {results}  {results}   {results}
Store 2  {results}  {results}   {results}
Store 3  {results}  {results}   {results}
...
```

Another use of **/Data Table 2** is for creating "cross-tabulation" tables. For example, you could use **/Data Table 2** to calculate the totals for each department for each store.

```
STORE          DEPT
{input cell 1}   {input cell 2}

SALES TOTALS
Formula  Dept 1     Dept 2      Dept 3
Store 1  {results}  {results}   {results}
Store 2  {results}  {results}   {results}
Store 3  {results}  {results}   {results}
...
```

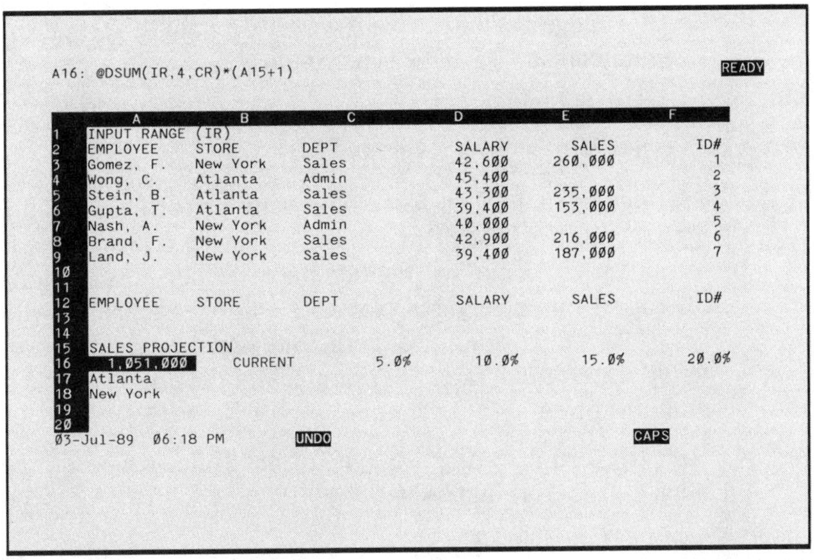

Figure 55.2: Setting Up for /Data Table 2

While /**Data Table 1** allows multiple formulas along the top of the table, /**Data Table 2** allows only one formula, located in the top left corner of the table. The first variable (the store, in our example) is listed along the left column and the second variable is listed along the top row.

For the table below, /**Data Table 2** will begin by calculating the total sales for the first store, then multiplying the sales by the first percentage number (.5). Then the process will repeat, using all the stores and all the percent numbers.

10. Select /**Worksheet Insert Row** to insert blank rows above the summary table. Specify the range as **A15..A20**. The last data table will be moved to the next screen.

11. Enter the following (the numbers will appear as zeros):

	A	B	C	D	E	F
15	SALES PROJECTION					
16		CURRENT	0.05	0.1	0.15	0.2
17	Atlanta					
18	New York					

The rates are entered as values.

12. Select /**Range Format Percent** with 1 decimal to format the rate numbers in **C16..F16** as percentages.

13. In cell **A16**, type:

    @**DSUM(IR,4,CR)** * **(A15 + 1)**

    See Figure 55.3. This formula is similar to the database @functions used for /**Data Table 1**. The cell A15 will be the second input cell and will contain the percentages listed along the top of the table. The total sales amount calculated with @DSUM will be multipled by the rate plus 1 to give the projected sales for that rate. For example, for the rate 5%, total is multiplied by 105% (0.05 + 1).

14. Hide the formula using /**Range Format Hidden**. Specify the range for the formula, **A16**.

15. Select /**Data Table 2**.

16. Press the Backspace key to undo the settings for /Data Table 1 used above and to return to **A16**.

17. Specify the table range as **A16..F18**.

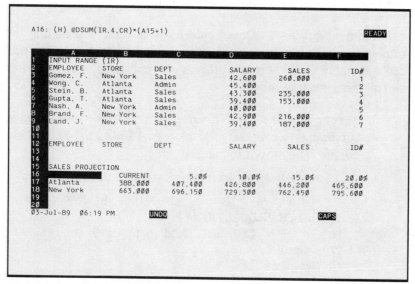

Figure 55.3: Projecting Sales with /Data Table 2

18. Input Cell 1 remains the same: the blank cell below the STORE heading in the criteria range (B13). Press Enter to select that cell.

19. Press Enter to specify **A15** as Input Cell 2. A15 can be used for an input cell even though it is already occupied the label SALES PROJECTION.

20. Press Enter and the new Data Table will be created. See Figure 55.3.

21. Save the worksheet.

LESSON

56

Playing "What If": Using the Data Table

FEATURING

TABLE (F8)

Frank Brand and Tom Gupta are ecstatic. Both just made new sales. Being a conscientious record keeper, you instantly record the increases in the sales log. You would also like to know how the sales affect your statistics.

To reflect changes in your data table, you only have to press the **TABLE (F8)** function key after you have revised the entries. 1-2-3 automatically recalculates the figures in the table.

How to Use the TABLE (F8) Key

1. Change the sales amount for T. Gupta to 175,000 and for F. Brand to 245,000.

2. Press the **TABLE (F8)** key. 1-2-3 recalculates the totals. Data tables must be recalculated with either the **TABLE (F8)** function key or the /**Data Table** command. They are not automatically recalculated in the same way that worksheets are.

57

*Building a Frequency
Distribution Table*

FEATURING

/Data Distribution

Suppose that you wanted to determine how many salespeople were high-sellers, how many were medium-sellers, and how many were low-sellers. One way would be to sort them using **/Data Sort**. Another way would be to use the database @function @DCOUNT with criteria ranges. Another way would be to use the **/Data Distribution** command.

/Data Distribution takes a range of values (the *values range*) and counts how many fit into various categories (the *bin range*). In the case of our salespeople, high-sellers might be those selling more than $250,000, medium-sellers would be those selling between $200,000 and $250,000, and low-sellers would be those selling below $200,000. Using **/Data Distribution**, you could easily count how many fit each category.

*H*ow to Use /Data Distribution

To Set Up the Table

1. Insert rows above the data tables you built in the last lessons. Select **/Worksheet Insert Row** and specify **A15..A20**. The Sales Projection data table will be moved to the next screen.

2. Enter the following:

    A
    15 **SALES FREQUENCY DISTRIBUTION**
    16 **Bin Range**
    17 **200000**
    18 **250000**

    The two numbers are the bin range. The sales numbers in the input range, or database, are the values range. When you run **/Data Distribution**, 1-2-3 will compare each sales amount to the two numbers in the bin range to see if the amount is smaller (or equal to) or larger than the number in the bin range.

3. Select **/Data Distribution**.

4. Specify the values range as the SALES column: **E3..E9**.

5. Specify the bin range as **A17..A18**. These values must be unique and in ascending order. See Figure 57.1. The results will be entered in the column to the right of the bin range. The first number (2) is the count of employees selling less than (or equal to) $200,000. The second number (2) is the count of employees selling more than $200,000 but less than or equal to $250,000. The third number (1) is the count of those over $250,000. This last number is below the last number in the bin range. Since labels and blank cells are ignored in the values range, five employees were included in the count.

6. Save the worksheet.

Do not use blank cells and labels in the bin range; they will produce incorrect results. Also, values in the bin range must be unique and in ascending order. To create a bin range with many values, use **/Data Fill**.

Lesson 57

```
A16: 'Bin Range                                                    READY

        A           B          C          D          E          F
1  INPUT RANGE (IR)
2  EMPLOYEE     STORE      DEPT          SALARY       SALES        ID#
3  Gomez, F.    New York   Sales         42,600     260,000         1
4  Wong, C.     Atlanta    Admin         45,400                     2
5  Stein, B.    Atlanta    Sales         43,300     235,000         3
6  Gupta, T.    Atlanta    Sales         39,400     175,000         4
7  Nash, A.     New York   Admin         40,000                     5
8  Brand, F.    New York   Sales         42,900     245,000         6
9  Land, J.     New York   Sales         39,400     187,000         7
10
11
12 EMPLOYEE     STORE      DEPT          SALARY       SALES        ID#
13
14
15 SALES FREQUENCY DISTRIBUTION
16 Bin Range
17     200,000                2
18     250,000                2
19                            1
20
03-Jul-89   06:28 PM      UNDO
```

Figure 57.1: *A Data Distribution Table*

_A

_C

_B

_1

_3

_1

_2

_2

Part Six

Macros

3

LESSON

58

Building a Simple Macro

FEATURING

Planning macros
The ~ key
/Range Name Label Right

Keyboard macros enable you to program 1-2-3 to accomplish tasks automatically. Simply defined, programming is writing a series of instructions that are automatically initiated one after the other. Once any of these instructions is stored in a macro, you can play it back at any time.

In 1-2-3, these instructions accomplish anything that you can accomplish by typing instructions at the keyboard. You might use a macro to copy ranges of cells, to erase numbers, or to save a file. Because they save keystrokes, macros are also called the *typing alternative*.

In addition to automatically performing tasks that are normally done manually, a macro can do special operations. For example, macros can make decisions based on whether or not certain criteria are fulfilled. Or you could create a macro that displays your own customized command menu, which would appear each time you retrieve a worksheet and would guide you and others in using the worksheet for specific needs, leaving no room for error. This menu might include entering data, viewing a graph, printing a report, and querying for information—and might look like the one in Figure 58.1.

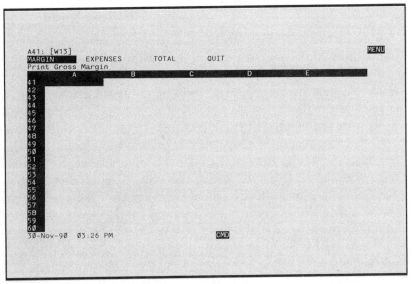

Figure 58.1: *Customized 1-2-3 Menu*

Whenever there is a series of frequently used instructions, you can create a macro. However, you might also want to create one if the instructions aren't frequently used, but are many and complicated.

Creating Macros

Five steps are necessary to set up and use a macro:

- Planning the macro
- Entering the macro as a label on the worksheet
- Documenting the macro
- Assigning a range name to the first cell of the macro
- Initiating the macro—that is, putting it into action

You may also need to *debug* or correct problems in the macro.

Planning Your Macros

With Release 2.2, if you are creating macros that you will want to use with multiple worksheets, you may want to enter them into a *macro library* that is saved separately from the worksheet and that is accessible from any worksheet. Creating and using macro libraries are covered in Lesson 65.

To store the macros in the worksheet, locate an out-of-the-way area. Because macros are stored in cells, you must be careful that deleting or inserting rows and columns of data elsewhere does not affect the macros. If you think that you might later have to insert or delete rows in your worksheet, place the macros above or below your work. If you will be inserting or deleting columns, place them on either side of the worksheet. However, if you think that you may insert and delete both columns and rows, enter the macros diagonally to one side and above or below your worksheet. This is the safest area.

It is a good idea to try your macros first manually.

Entering the Macro in the Worksheet

Macros are stored in one or more cells as labels. Each keystroke that you would type is recorded. For example, to create a macro that would erase one cell, you could enter the following on the worksheet:

'/RE ~

The label-prefix is necessary because the macro is a label beginning with the command key (/). A macro beginning with / or a number, to avoid bringing up the menus or entering a value, must be preceded by a label-prefix.

RE represents the **Range Erase** command. The tilde (~) represents the Enter key. Thus all of the characters after the label-prefix represent what you would type at the keyboard to erase a cell.

All the function and pointer-movement keys can be used when creating macros. All you have to do is enclose them in brackets. This is covered in Lesson 59.

Long macros are entered one instruction after the other down a column. Even if a macro is not long, you can break it up at any point and continue entering it in the next cell down. Blank cells signify the end of a macro. The preceding macro could also be entered as:

    '/R
    E ˜

Documenting the Macro

Once a macro is entered on the worksheet, it should be documented. This way, when you refer to the worksheet at a later date, you will know what the macro is called and what it accomplishes. One format for documenting macros is to place the macro name to the left of the macro and a description of the commands to the right. See the examples below.

Assigning a Name to the Macro

To assign a name, use **/Range Name Create**. For releases of 1-2-3 prior to 2.2, the name begins with a backslash (\) followed by a single letter, usually one that relates to the function, such as E for Erase. Using this method, there are 27 possible macro names on a worksheet: the letters of the alphabet, plus the zero. (The zero macro name will be covered later.)

For Release 2.2, you may use the backslash and a single letter as above, or any other name up to a maximum of 15 characters. These longer macros must be run using a different command. You do not need to precede these longer names with a backslash.

Only the first cell of the macro needs to be named, even if more than one cell is used.

Running the Macro

For releases prior to 2.2, run the macro by holding down the Alt key on the left side of the keyboard and tapping the macro's letter name. (The backslash (\) in the macro's name represents the Alt key.)

For Release 2.2, use the Alt-letter combination for macros named with \ followed by a single letter. Use RUN (Alt-F3) to run any other macros. RUN is explained in Lesson 59.

It is always a good idea to save your worksheet before running a macro. That way you can retrieve your original worksheet if the macro causes problems to your data when it's run. Also, for Release 2.2, if the undo feature is on, you can press UNDO (Alt-F4) to restore the worksheet to its prior condition.

How to Build a Macro

To Erase a Cell Using a Simple Macro

1. Retrieve the file **91BUDGET**. If you've forgotten what it looks like, refer to Lesson 6 for a complete picture of the worksheet.

2. Move to column AB, row 41. This is below and to the right of your worksheet.

3. In AB41, type:

   '/RE ~

4. Press Enter.

5. To name the macro, use **/Range Name Create**.

6. Specify the name as **\E**, press Enter, then the range as **AB41**.

7. To initiate the macro, move to any cell with information in it. (Not the cell with the macro in it!) Try **B5**.

8. Hold down the **Alt** key, and tap the letter **E**. The number in B5 is erased.

9. To document the macro move one cell to the left of the macro, cell AA41. Type in a name:

   '\E

   Include the apostrophe as a label-prefix. (You could center the name with the ^ key instead of the '.) See Figure 58.2.

Naming Several Macros at Once - /Range Name Label

10. Try a few more macros. Type in the list below, the names in column AA, the macros in column AB, and the descriptions in column AC.

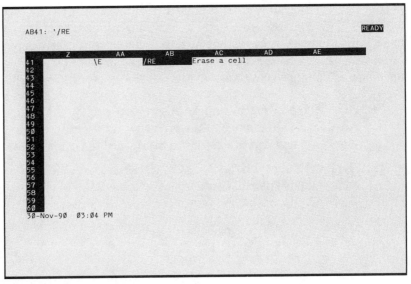

Figure 58.2: *Simple Macro*

To create a macro to erase a cell:

Assign this name	To this macro	Description
\E	'/RE ~	Erase a cell

To create a macro to format a cell in Currency format:

\F	'/RFC0 ~	Currency cell format
	1500 ~	Enter a number

To create a macro that will change a column width:

\C	'/WCS15 ~	Widen column to 15

To create a macro that will enter a company name:

\N	'General American Consolidated, Inc. ~

Remember to precede macros that start with a slash with a label-prefix character and to separate each macro with a blank line.

By entering the name of the macro in the column to the left (columns AA), you can save steps in assigning range names to the macros in column AB. Instead of having to name each macro separately with **/Range Name Create**, you can instead instruct 1-2-3 to use the names in column AA and assign them to the macros on the right.

11. Use **/Range Name Labels Right** to specify the range **AA41..AA49** (the range of macro names) as the range names. This command names each cell to the right of the macro name.

12. Use the **Alt** key with the **E**, **F**, **C**, or **N** keys to run the macros once you have named them.

LESSON

59

Using Key Names

FEATURING

Key Names
@NOW
RUN (Alt-F3) (Release 2.2)

Certain keys, such as the function keys and the pointer-movement keys, require a special syntax when used in macros. These keys (shown in Figure 59.1) are included in brackets when used in a macro. The macro that follows makes use of some of these.

How To Build a Date-Stamp Macro

With a macro you can set up an automatic date-stamp for your worksheets. A date-stamp is useful for keeping a history of changes to a worksheet. For instance, you can automate a daily log of transactions (phone calls, sales) by creating a macro to automatically stamp today's date next to each transaction entry.

For this lesson you will use the date function **@NOW**. (If you are using 1-2-3 1A, use **@TODAY**.) Date functions allow you to perform calculations based on dates and times. With them you can subtract one date or time from another or average among dates or times, for instance.

Lesson 59

Type Macro	For Key	Type Macro	For Key
~	Enter	{ESC}	Escape
{DOWN}	Down Arrow	{EDIT}	F2
{UP}	Up Arrow	{NAME}	F3
{LEFT}	Left Arrow	{ABS}	F4
{RIGHT}	Right Arrow	{GOTO}	F5
{PGDN}	Page Down	{WINDOW}	F6
{PGUP}	Page Up	{QUERY}	F7
{END}	End	{TABLE}	F8
{HOME}	Home	{CALC}	F9
{DEL}	Delete	{GRAPH}	F10
{BIGRIGHT}	Ctrl-Right Arrow	{BIGLEFT}	Ctrl-Left Arrow
{BS}	Backspace		

Figure 59.1: Key Names for Macros

Date functions generate numbers based on the number of days since the turn of the century (January 1, 1900), and time functions generate numbers based on the fraction of the day since midnight. For example, 31697 represents October 12, 1986, and 31697.5 represents noon on that day. Since these numbers are not easily decipherable, you can change them, using the Global or Range Format commands, to display in one of several date or time formats. The date function, **@NOW,** in this exercise produces a number that always reflects the current date and time.

The following macro will record the current date in your worksheet. Then, when the worksheet is retrieved next, this date will serve as a record of when it was last modified.

1. When building macros it is best to try it manually first. So... in the worksheet 91BUDGET, move the pointer to cell E1 and type: **@NOW**. Do not press the Enter key yet.
   Note: If you are using Lotus Release 1A, type **@TODAY**.

2. Press the **CALC (F9)** key. The function changes into a number that represents the current date and time.

3. Press Enter to enter the number into E1.

4. Format the number so it will display as today's date. Use:

   /Range Format Date 1

5. Press Enter to accept the range.

6. If asterisks appear, the column is too narrow. If this happens, select:

   /Worksheet Column Set-width 12

7. Move to column AB, below the other macros. Type:

   {HOME} {RIGHT 4}
   '@NOW
   {CALC} ˜
   '/RFD1 ˜
   '/WCS12 ˜

Make sure that you include a space between RIGHT and 4. **{HOME}** and **{RIGHT 4}** will move the pointer first to A1 (with the Home key), then right 4 cells. This will guarantee that the date is always entered in the same cell each time.

Note: Lotus Release 1A does not allow you to specify how many times a pointer-movement command is to repeat, as in: {RIGHT 4}. To repeat a macro in 1A, you must type it in the exact number of times you want, for instance, {RIGHT}{RIGHT}{RIGHT}{RIGHT}.

The @NOW function calculates the current date. {CALC} changes @NOW into a fixed number that won't change. A ˜ enters the number into E1. **/Range Format Date** displays the number as a date. Finally, the column is widened using **/Worksheet Column**.

8. Move the pointer to the cell with {HOME}{RIGHT 4}. Select
   /Range Name Create.
   For releases 1A, 2.0, and 2.01 of 1-2-3, type **\D**.
   For Release 2.2, type **DATE**. Release 2.2 of 1-2-3 now
   allows you to create macro names of up to 15 characters.

   - Press Enter.

   - Press Enter again to specify the range as the first cell in
     the macro.

9. Go to cell E1 and erase the date you entered before. You can
   use your erase macro with **Alt E**.

10. Save your worksheet before running the macro in case it
    doesn't work correctly.

11. To run the macro in Release 2.2, use **RUN (Alt-F3)**: hold
    down **Alt**, then tap **F3**. At the list of macro names, move the
    pointer to **DATE** and press Enter.

12. To run the macro in releases 1A, 2.0, and 2.01, hold down the
    Alt key and tap **D**.

13. If the macro doesn't work, 1-2-3 may beep and display an
    error message. Press Escape.

14. If you need to correct the macro, press **GOTO (F5)** then **NAME
    (F3)** to display a list of macro names. Select **DATE** or **\D**.

15. Correct the macro, if necessary, then run it again.

In Lesson 65 you will learn to add this macro to the Macro Library
Manager (Release 2.2).

LESSON

60

Debugging Macros

FEATURING

STEP mode (Alt-F2)

You will quickly find that macros often don't work the first time that you run them. Misspellings, forgotten commands, faulty logic— these are some of the problems that you will run into. Here is a list of some of the common problems:

- The macro was not assigned a name.
- A tilde is missing (for the Enter key), such as /RE instead of /RE ˜ .
- A command was left out, such as /PG instead of /PPG (/Print Printer Go).
- Incorrect or nonexistent cell addresses or range names were specified.
- A key name was mispelled, such as {DWN}.
- Incorrect brackets were used, e.g., [instead of {.
- Spaces were put in formulas or between commands where they do not belong.

Sometimes the results of the macro make it obvious what went wrong. In that case, going back to the macro and editing it will work.

However, at other times it is not apparent why a macro is not working. Instead, it is necessary to look at each step of the macro as it runs. The STEP mode accomplishes this.

The STEP mode allows you to run a macro one step or instruction at a time, until you locate an error. In Release 2.2, while you are running a macro in STEP mode, each instruction and its cell address will appear at the bottom of the screen. At each instruction, 1-2-3 will wait to run the next one until you press a key (normally use the spacebar).

Debugging the Date-Stamp Macro

Let's run the date-stamp macro while in the STEP mode, even though it may be correct.

1. Press the Home key.

2. Press **STEP (Alt-F2)**. STEP appears at the bottom of the screen.

3. Start the macro. For 1-2-3 Release 2.2, press **RUN (Alt-F3)** and select **DATE**. For earlier versions, press **Alt-D**.

4. Press the spacebar to execute the first step, or command, of the macro. Release 2.2 will display the step at the bottom of the screen.

5. Continue pressing the spacebar, looking at each step until the macro is finished or you find the error. To stop the macro prematurely, press Ctrl-Break.

6. When you find an error, stop running the macro and correct it. Run it again if desired. Stay in STEP mode until the macro is corrected.

7. When the macro is corrected, turn off the STEP mode **(Alt-F2)**.

LESSON

61

Using the Learn Feature (Release 2.2)

FEATURING

LEARN (Alt-F5)

You might be thinking, "How can I remember all the keystrokes that are necessary to create a macro?" "Will I always have to tediously record all the keystrokes on paper so that I can remember them?" Thankfully, Release 2.2 now makes it possible to record keystrokes while you type and have them entered automatically into cells in the worksheet using the *LEARN* feature.

There are five steps to creating a macro using the learn feature:

- Specify a *learn range* for the macro.
- Turn on the learn feature with Alt-F5.
- Type the keystrokes that you want to record.
- Turn off the learn feature with Alt-F5.
- Name the macro.

You may edit the macro, as necessary, afterwards. Run the macro as before.

In this lesson you will build the same date-stamp macro as in the last lesson, but in a different way.

Using the Learn Feature

1. Specify a Learn Range. This is a single-column range where the macro will be stored. Select /**Worksheet Learn Range**.

The Learn Menu

- The learn **Range** is where 1-2-3 stores the macro that will be generated.

- **Erase** will erase a macro from the learn range.

- **Cancel** will cancel the learn range.

---

2. Specify the range as **AB60..AB70**. Press Enter when through.
   The range must extend far enough down the column to be able to include all the macro keystrokes. If the learn range is too short, 1-2-3 will notify you that the learn range is full and turn off the learn feature. It is better to specify a learn range that is too large. If you specify more than one column, 1-2-3 will use only the first in the range.
   Any data in the learn range will be erased when the macros are recorded.

3. To turn on the learn feature, hold down the **Alt** key and press **F5**. LEARN appears at the bottom of the screen. Anything you type from now until you turn off the learn feature will be recorded as part of the macro. If you make a mistake, you will be able to edit the macro later.

4. Now start typing the keystrokes that you want to record: press the Home key.

5. Using the right arrow key, move the pointer to E1.

6. Type: @**NOW**. Do not press the Enter key yet.

7. Press **CALC (F9)**. @NOW changes into a number that represents the current date and time.

8. Press Enter to place the number on the worksheet.

9. Format the number so it will display as today's date. Select:

     /Range Format Date 1

10. Press Enter to accept the range.

11. Widen the column with the following:

     /Worksheet Column Set-width 12

12. Press Enter to accept the column width of 12.

13. Turn off the learn feature with **Alt-F5**.

14. Use **GOTO (F5)** to move the pointer to cell **AB60** to examine the recorded keystrokes. Compare the date macro there with the one you built in the last lesson. You will find that instead of {RIGHT 4}, the learn feature used four instances of {R}. This is an alternate notation new to Release 2.2. You could also use {R 4}. If you made mistakes while recording the macro, correct them here.

Naming the Macro

15. Move to the first cell of the new macro, if necessary. Use **/Range Name Create**.

16. Name the macro as **DATE2**. Press Enter.

17. Press Enter to accept the range.

18. Move to cell E1 and erase any data.

19. Run the macro using **RUN (Alt-F3)**.

20. From the list of macro names, select **DATE2**.

62

Using Advanced Macro Commands

FEATURING

Stop Macro (Ctrl-Break)
Interactive macros {?}
Looping Macros {BRANCH}

Lotus 1-2-3's advanced macro commands work similarly to commands in programming languages such as Pascal, BASIC, and C. In the following lessons you will use some of the more common advanced macro commands listed in Figure 62.1.

How to Build a "Numeric Keyboard" Macro Using Macro Commands

The macro that follows is useful when entering a lot of numbers in a column or row. After each number is entered, the macro will advance the pointer to the next cell, ready for the next number. It is especially useful when using a PC that has an old-style keyboard with a combined numeric and cursor movement keypad.

This macro is a repeating macro, a common procedure in programming. It makes use of the {**BRANCH**} command to jump to the beginning and to repeat. Use Ctrl-Break to stop it at any time.

Macro	Function
{?}	Waits for input from the keyboard before continuing.
{BRANCH}	Causes a macro to jump to a new location and continue running. (/XG in 1-2-3 1A.)
{INDICATE}	Controls the mode indicator in the right corner.
{MENUBRANCH}	Causes a macro to call up a custom menu located at the specified location. (/XM in 1-2-3 1A.)
{PANELOFF} {PANELON}	Freezes the control panel and worksheet area to speed up the macro and not cause the screen to flash.
{QUIT}	Quits the macro or menu. (/XQ in 1-2-3 1A.)
{WINDOWSOFF} {WINDOWSON}	Unfreezes the control panel and worksheet area.

Figure 62.1: Some Advanced Macro Commands

1. Move below the macros you have already created in column AB. Make sure you leave a blank cell between any existing macros. Type the following macro:

    ```
    {?}
    {DOWN}
    {BRANCH \K}
    ```

    When you execute the macro, the first thing it will do with {?} is allow you to enter the first number. After you enter the number, the macro will take over by moving down one cell. At that point, the macro loops or starts over with the {BRANCH} command, allowing you to type in the next number. The {BRANCH} command instructs the macro to continue at location \K. Since this is the starting cell of the macro, it repeats.

Note: For Lotus 1A, type:

'/XG\K ˜ instead of {BRANCH   \K}

2. Name the macro. Move to the first cell (containing {?}) and select /**Range Name Create**. Name it as **\K**.

3. Document the macro by typing the macro name in a cell to the left of the first cell. Precede the macro name with a label-prefix. Type '**\K**.

4. To use the macro, move to a blank range of cells in order to type in a column of numbers starting at the position of the pointer.

5. Turn on the numeric keypad by pressing the Num Lock key once. NUM will be displayed at the bottom of the screen. You can now use the numeric keypad rather than the numbers along the top of the keyboard.

6. Execute the macro by typing **Alt-K**. The only visible change is the **CMD** displayed on the screen. The macro is in execution waiting for you to type in the first number.

7. Type in **123**, and press Enter. The pointer moves down to the next cell, ready for the next number. You can see that the macro is still in execution by the **CMD** on the screen. Enter several more numbers.

8. To end the macro, hold down the Ctrl key and press Break on the top right of the keyboard.

9. Turn off the Num Lock key. Then press Escape to return to READY mode.

Whenever you are ready to enter a column of numbers, turn on the Num Lock key and execute this macro. To build a macro for filling in a row, instead of a column of numbers substitute {RIGHT} for {DOWN} in the macro.

Creating a Date-Entry Macro

Use the following macro to expedite entering dates into a work-sheet. (See Lesson 66 for an explanation of dates.)

10. Move down two cells beneath the last macro. Enter:

    '@date(90,{?},{?})~
    '/RFD1

11. Use **/Range Name Create** to name the macro as **\A** (for all 1-2-3 versions).

12. Move to a blank cell and run the macro. Press **Alt A**.

13. The macro will stop and wait for the month. Type **11** and press Enter.

14. The macro will stop and wait for the day. Type **30** and press Enter. This macro will enter the date and format the cell for date format. Press Enter to accept the range to be formatted.

LESSON

63

Creating Customized Menus with Macros

FEATURING

Menus {MENUBRANCH}
Controlling the Screen
    {INDICATE}
    {WINDOWSON}

Lotus macros allow you to create your own custom menus. Custom menus work similarly to the 1-2-3 menus: They are displayed above the worksheet, and you select choices by moving the pointer or by typing in the first letter of the choice. With your own menus you can further automate your worksheet. For a customized menu built with macros, refer to Figure 58.1.

How to Create a Print Menu

You will be creating a menu that allows you to print different parts of the **91BUDGET** worksheet without changing the print range manually. The following steps will also demonstrate the use of Range Names in macros.

Make sure you are in the **91BUDGET** file. In order to print out different areas of this worksheet, it is best first to assign names to each print range.

1. Select **/Range Name Create**.

2. Name the range **MARGIN**. Press Enter.

3. Highlight, or type, cells **A5..F8**.

4. Press Enter to complete the process.

5. Repeat steps 1–4, but this time use the name **EXPENSES** to name the range **A10..F16**.

6. Repeat steps 1–4 again, naming the cell range **A1..G18** as **TOTAL**.

7. Move the pointer to cell **AB80**, below any macros created previously. Type in the following macro in a single cell:

    {MENUBRANCH menu}

    Note: With Lotus 1A, type: '/XMmenu ˜ .

    {MENUBRANCH menu} instructs 1-2-3 to go to the menu named "menu" and display it above the worksheet. You can then move the pointer to a selection or press the first letter of a selection.

8. In the cell to the left, type in '**\P** to document the macro name.

Customized menus are composed of up to eight selections. Each is entered in a separate cell, and all are entered in the same row. It is a good idea to start each selection in a menu with a different letter in order to be able to select a choice using the first letter. Refer to Figure 63.1.

Below each menu selection is a description. Below the description are the actual commands that are executed when that menu selection is chosen.

9. Move the pointer two cells down, to cell AB82, in order to leave at least one blank cell between the {MENUBRANCH} command above and the menu you will create. The blank cell marks the end of the preceding macro. Type the macro in columns, as shown in Figure 63.1.

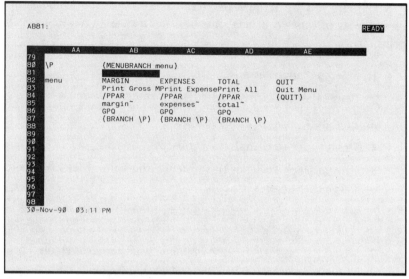

```
AB81:                                                                    READY

              A A          AB            AC           AD           AE
79
80    \P            {MENUBRANCH menu}
81
82    menu          MARGIN         EXPENSES      TOTAL        QUIT
83                  Print Gross MPrint ExpensePrint All      Quit Menu
84                  /PPAR          /PPAR         /PPAR        {QUIT}
85                  margin~        expenses~     total~
86                  GPQ            GPQ           GPQ
87                  {BRANCH \P}    {BRANCH \P}   {BRANCH \P}
88
89
90
91
92
93
94
95
96
97
98
30-Nov-90   03:11 PM
```

Figure 63.1: A Print Menu Macro

Note: With Lotus 1A, type:

'/XG\P ~ instead of {BRANCH \P}
'/XQ& ~ instead of {QUIT}

10. Move to the cell with \P.

11. Select **/Range Name Labels Right**.

12. Enter the range **AA80..AA82**. This will assign the names \P and MENU to the cell to the right of each one.

    When the {MENUBRANCH} macro is executed by typing Alt-P, it will, in turn, call up the menu called MENU. After a selection is made, the menu will display itself again; the {BRANCH \P} causes it to loop. Selecting Quit from the menu will end it. (Ctrl-Break will also end a macro.)

13. Turn on your printer before executing the macro. Then hold down **Alt** and press **P**. The menu is displayed in the Control Panel above the worksheet.

14. Select one of the reports to print. To stop the report before it has finished printing, press Ctrl-Break. After the report prints, the menu will be displayed again.

15. To exit the macro, select **Quit**.

16. Save the worksheet under **91BUDGET**.

Enhancing the Menu Macro

The Advanced Macro command {**INDICATE**} allows you to change the mode indicator in the top right of the screen. In Release 2.2 the mode indicator now can be as long as the width of the screen. In prior versions, it can be five characters maximum. Use the {**INDI-CATE**} command to display PRINT when the macro is running.

In addition, use the {**WINDOWSOFF**} command to freeze the screen. The print ranges will not flash on the screen as the macro runs.

17. Move to cell **AB80**, the cell containing {MENUBRANCH menu}.

18. Use **EDIT (F2)** to change the cell contents to:

    {**WINDOWSOFF**} {**INDICATE "PRINT"**} {**MENUBRANCH menu**}

19. When through, press Enter.

20. Edit the cell that contains {QUIT} as:

    {**WINDOWSON**} {**INDICATE**} {**QUIT**}

    This will reset the mode indicator to display READY when you exit the custom menu by selecting Quit.

21. Run the macro with **Alt-P**. PRINT will be displayed in the top right corner of the screen.

22. Either select a report to print or press **Quit** to exit the macro.

64

Creating an Automatic Macro

FEATURING

AUTO123
\0 macros
/Worksheet Global Default
   Autoexec

It is possible to create a macro that will execute automatically whenever you retrieve a worksheet—you don't have to press the Alt key with a letter or use RUN (Alt-F3). For example, in the last exercise you created a macro for a print menu. It might be useful to have this print menu displayed automatically whenever the **91BUDGET** worksheet is retrieved. A special macro name is used for this: **\0**.

It is also possible to instruct Lotus to retrieve an entire worksheet automatically. Then, when you start 1-2-3, this worksheet would be retrieved without using the /**File Retrieve** command. This is done by naming a worksheet with a special file name: **AUTO123**. Normally this procedure is most useful in setting up "turnkey" or "foolproof" systems in Lotus that direct computer users to perform various tasks without the need for extensive knowledge of how to use the program as a whole. These turnkey systems usually consist of extensive custom menus created with macro commands.

In the following steps, you will use both the automatically executed macro (**\0**) and the automatically retrieved worksheet (**AUTO123**).

1. Move the pointer to the cell containing {**WINDOWSON**} {**INDICATE "PRINT"**}{**MENUBRANCH menu**}.

2. Use /**Range Name Create** to name the print macro as **0**. This is the number zero, not the letter O. This creates the automatically executed macro. The macro has already been named as **P**, but it is possible to assign two or more range names to the same macro, or cells. Whenever this worksheet is retrieved, the print macro will execute.

3. Use /**File Save** to save the worksheet under a new name: **AUTO123**.

    Whenever you start Lotus 1-2-3, this worksheet will be retrieved automatically. In addition, the print macro will be executed automatically because of the **0** macro name.

4. Try this by selecting /**Quit** to return to the Access menu.

5. From the Access menu, return to the worksheet by selecting **1-2-3**. AUTO123 will be retrieved and the print menu will be displayed.

6. When you have completed the previous steps and are satisfied with your knowledge of automating Lotus 1-2-3 macros, erase AUTO123 using /**File Erase Worksheet**. This will prevent it from being retrieved automatically the next time you start up Lotus 1-2-3. (Don't worry, the worksheet is still saved as **91BUDGET**.)

Warning: When building an automatically executing \\0 macro that cannot be disabled (using the macro command {**BREAKOFF**}), make sure you have a choice on one of your custom menus that will allow you to break out of it. If you cannot break out, you will not be able to modify the worksheet and may be locked in to your macro (except in Release 2.2).

Release 2.2 of 1-2-3 now allows you to turn off the automatic executing of \\0 macros. If you find that a worksheet always executes a macro and you cannot break out of it, use /**Worksheet Global Default Autoexec** before retrieving it to **disable** the autoexecuting. Then when you retrieve your worksheet, the \\0 macro will not be executed. Use /**Worksheet Global Default Update** to change the autoexec setting permanently.

LESSON

65

Using the Macro Library Manager (Release 2.2)

FEATURING

/ Add-in

Let's suppose you've created a new worksheet and you want to quickly stamp it with today's date. You've previously created a date-stamp macro that will do this, but it is located in another worksheet. How can you get it into the new one? One way is to copy the macro into the worksheet using **/File Combine**. (/File Combine was covered in Lesson 37, "Transferring Data from One Worksheet to Another.") An easier way is to use the Macro Library Manager.

The Macro Library Manager is a separate program, called an *add-in*, that is included with Release 2.2 of 1-2-3. This program will take a range of macros, formulas, and data, called a *macro library*, from a worksheet and store them in a special *library file* on your disk and in memory apart from your worksheet. You may have multiple macro libraries available.

To use the Macro Library Manager you must first *attach* it to 1-2-3 using the Add-In commands. This needs to be done each time you use 1-2-3, although it can be automated. You may have multiple add-ins attached to 1-2-3—for instance, the Allways "spreadsheet publisher" and the Macro Libary Manager. However, for each add-in that is attached, less memory is available for your worksheet. (Use **/Worksheet Status** to determine how much memory is available.) Once you have attached the Macro Library Manager, or any add-in, you must *invoke* it to use it. The Macro Library Manager has its own commands to use when creating macro libraries.

After attaching the Macro Library Manager, to create a macro library, you must first enter the macros (or data) as you would normally into a range of cells. Then invoke the Macro Library Manager to *save* the macros to a macro library. The macros are removed from the worksheet. The new library is stored separately from the worksheet in memory and in a special file with .MLB as an extension. You run library macros and worksheet macros the same way, with the RUN (Alt-F3) key.

Erasing the worksheet or retrieving another worksheet will not erase the macros, formulas, or data in the library. A library can be used with any worksheet. If you have multiple libraries you can *load* the one that contains the macros, data, or formulas that you need.

In this lesson you will use the Macro Library Manager to create a macro library that contains the date-stamp macro created in Lesson 59.

A ttaching the Macro Library Manager

To attach the Macro Library Manager, the file named **MACRO-MGR.ADN** must be located in the same directory as the 1-2-3 program files. (If you have a two-diskette system you will need to insert the Install disk in one of the disk drives to attach it.)

When you attach the Library Manager to 1-2-3, you will be asked whether you want to assign a function key combination that will be used to invoke, or start, the program. If you do not select a function key combination, you will have to use the Add-In commands in 1-2-3 each time you want to invoke the Macro Library Manager. Otherwise, you may assign Alt-F7, Alt-F8, Alt-F9, or Alt-F10 to invoke the program.

1. If you are not running 1-2-3 on a hard-disk system, place the Install disk in one of the floppy drives.

2. In Lotus 1-2-3, select **/Add-In Attach** (see Figure 65.1).

Lesson 65

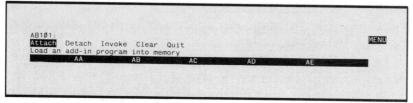

Figure 65.1: *The Add-In Menu*

The Add-In Menu

- **Attach** brings an add-in into memory and makes it available to be used with 1-2-3.

- **Detach** erases an add-in program from memory.

- **Invoke** activates one of the attached add-ins.

- **Clear** erases all add-ins from memory.

- **Quit** returns to the READY mode.

You will see a list of add-in programs ending in **.ADN**. If you don't see a **MACROMGR.ADN**, specify the disk or directory that contains this file. Press Esc to clear the current file names and edit the disk or directory name. Press Enter.

3. Select **MACROMGR.ADN** as the add-in.

4. Select which function key combination you want to use to invoke the Macro Library Manager. In this case select **7**. This will select Alt-F7 to invoke the add-in.

5. Select **Quit** to return to the READY mode.

Invoking the Macro Library Manager and Saving a Macro

Before invoking the Manager, it is necessary to build the macros that are to be *saved* in the macro library. The macros should be as close together as possible because blank cells take up space in the macro library. Since you have already created the date-stamp macro in an earlier lesson, you do not need to create a macro at this point. Instead, invoke the Manager and save the macro.

6. From the Add-In menu you could have invoked the Macro Library Manager, but since you assigned Alt-F7 as a function key combination, press **Alt-F7** in the READY mode. (See Figure 65.2.)

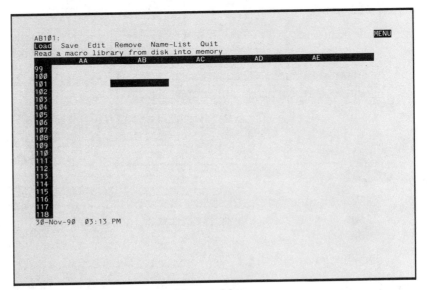

Figure 65.2: The Macro Library Manager Menu

7. Select **Save**.

8. When prompted for a library name, type: **AUTOLOAD**. This is a special library that will be loaded whenever the Macro Library Manager is attached. Other libraries will have to be loaded manually using the Manager. Keep your most used macros in this library. It will be saved as **AUTOLOAD.MLB** on disk. Press Enter to enter the name.

    Note: \0 macros will not be executed automatically from this library, however.

Macro Library Manager Menu

- **Load** copies a library file from the disk into memory so you can use it.

- **Save** moves the macro, including its range name, into the library in memory and into a library file (**.MLB**) on disk.

- **Edit** copies the contents of a macro library to a range in the current worksheet so that you can make changes to the library.

- **Remove** erases a macro library from memory (but not from the disk).

- **Name-List** enters a list on the current worksheet of the range names of the macros and data in a macro library.

- **Quit** leaves the Macro Library Manager menu and returns to 1-2-3.

9. When prompted for the range in the current worksheet that contains the macro, specify the range that contains the first date-stamp macro.

10. When prompted for a password, select **No**.

The date-stamp macro along with its range name has disappeared from the **91BUDGET** worksheet.

Using a Macro Library

While the macro has disappeared from the worksheet, it is still available.

11. Move to E1 and erase the date.

12. Press **RUN (Alt-F3)**.

13. Select **DATE** and press Enter.

Note: Since you created the macro library in the steps above, you did not have to load it before using it. Normally, after starting 1-2-3 and attaching the Macro Library Manager, you will need to load a macro library in order to use it.

To Edit a Macro in the Macro Library Manager

You can use the Edit command in the Macro Library Manager to change the contents of a macro library. The Edit command will copy the entire contents of the library into the current worksheet so that you can make changes and add or delete macros or data. When through, use the Save command to move the edited macros back to the library.

14. Move to a new area of the worksheet. Use **GOTO (F5)** to move to AB100.

15. Press **Alt-F7** to invoke the Macro Library Manager.

16. Select **Edit**. A list of library files will be displayed.
    Note: In some situations you may first have to load a library before editing.

17. Select **AUTOLOAD**. You will be asked whether to Ignore or Overwrite existing range names. If macros in the worksheet have the same range names as macros in the library, Ignore will maintain the ones in the worksheet, and Overwrite will replace those in the worksheet with those in the library. It is best not to use the same macro (range) name in both places.

18. Select **Ignore**.

19. Press Enter to accept the range of AB100. Be careful when specifying an edit range. If the range you specify contains data, it will be erased by the incoming macros. The date-stamp macro appears. You could now either edit this macro or enter more macros to add to the library.

20. After editing, save it back to the library. Press **Alt-F7** to invoke the Manager.

21. Select **Save**.

22. Specify the same library name: **AUTOLOAD**. You will be notified that the file already exists and asked whether you want to overwrite it.

23. Select **Yes**. The date-stamp macro will be moved from the worksheet into the library.

*L*oading the Macro Library Manager Automatically

You may want to attach the Macro Library Manager automatically whenever you start 1-2-3. Use the following steps.

24. Select **/Worksheet Global Default Other Add-In**.

25. Select **Set**. If the Macro Library Manager was not already attached, it would be attached at this point.

26. Select a number to assign to this add-in. Select **1** if it has not been used.

27. Select **MACROMGR.ADN** from the list of add-in files listed.

28. Select the key to use to invoke the add-in. Select **Alt-F7**.

29. The next prompt asks whether you want the add-in to be automatically invoked whenever you start 1-2-3. Select **No**. Selecting Yes at this point would cause the Macro Library Manager menu to appear whenever you got into 1-2-3. While multiple add-ins can be automatically *attached*, only one can be automatically *invoked*.

30. Save these new global settings, if desired. Remain in the /Worksheet Global Default menu and select **Update**.

A

C

B

1

3

1

2

2

Part Seven

Functions

3

LESSON

66

Applying Commonly Used Functions

FEATURING

@SUM
@AVG
@HLOOKUP
@IF
@DATE
@COUNT
@MAX
@MIN

The function @SUM was introduced earlier. Using @SUM, you were able to save keystrokes by entering @SUM(A1..A6) rather than the entire range of numbers: +A1+A2+A3+A4+A5+A6. However, @SUM is only one of many 1-2-3 formulas that perform specialized calculations.

Lotus 1-2-3 functions provide shortcuts when calculating numbers and manipulating labels. In addition to the @SUM function, you can average ranges of numbers with @AVG, do statistics such as standard deviation with @STD, do mathematical functions with @SIN, and make decisions with @IF. With Release 2.2, you can now perform "string" manipulation of labels as well. For instance, you can find a label from a list, and you can join two labels from different cells into a third cell.

Below is a list of some of the most commonly used functions: @SUM, @AVG, @HLOOKUP, @IF, and @DATE. In this chapter you will use them to build a worksheet.

@SUM	adds a range of numbers
@AVG	averages a range of numbers
@HLOOKUP	finds a label or value from a table
@IF	makes a choice between two options
@DATE	translates a date to a five-digit number for use in calculations

To learn about other 1-2-3 functions, refer to the Lotus User Manual or the Help screens [F1].

How to Use the @HLOOKUP and @AVG Functions

1. Save the current worksheet. Then clear the screen with /Worksheet Erase. Enter the Monthly Salary Report shown in Figure 66.1.

   The BONUS TABLE is necessary in order to calculate the BONUS amounts later. The Bonus Pct figures should be typed in either as .05 or as 5%. To display these figures with percent signs, use **Range Format Percent** with 2 decimal places.

2. In cell C15, type the following formula for total salaries:

   @SUM(C9..C13)

3. In cell D15, calculate the average of all LEVELS using the following formula:

   @AVG(D9..D13)

4. In the following formula you will use the @HLOOKUP function to search through a table and find the correct Bonus Pct value based on an employee's base salary. The format of this function is:

   @HLOOKUP(search value,table range,table row)

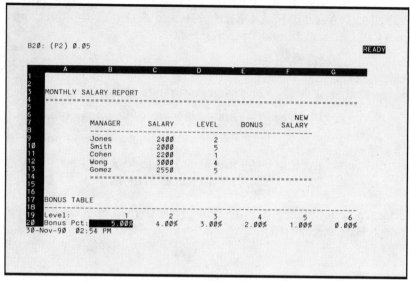

Figure 66.1: The Monthly Salary Report

where the *search value* is a manager's salary, the *table range* is the Bonus Table below, and the *table row* is the number of rows to search down in the Bonus Table. The formula will take the search value (number or label) and scan along the numbers in the first row of the lookup table. When it finds a match, it drops down the designated number of rows and selects the correct value or label. The value or label selected is then used in further calculations above or displayed in the cell of the @HLOOKUP formula.

In cell E9, type:

@HLOOKUP(D9,$B$19..$G$20,1)∗C9

In this formula, @HLOOKUP compares the level located in cell D9 with the levels in the first row of the Bonus Table located in B19 through G20. When it finds a match, it drops down one row and selects the Bonus Percent for that rating. The Bonus Percent is then multiplied by the base Salary to produce the Bonus amount.

The dollar signs in the table range in the formula make the cell addresses absolute. This is necessary in order to copy them down the column into the other Bonus amount cells without the table range changing. (See Lesson 25, "Entering Absolute Formulas.")

The @VLOOKUP function is used for vertical tables.

5. Use the Copy command to copy the @HLOOKUP formula into the other four BONUS cells, once for each manager. Check to see that the Level cell address and the base SALARY cell address were adjusted, but the Bonus Table range was not.

6. In column F for the first manager, enter a formula that will add the base SALARY with the newly calculated BONUS amount.

   + C9 + E9

7. Copy the formula down for each manager as well.

8. Use @SUM to build two formulas that will add Bonuses together and New Salaries together. Refer to Figure 66.2.

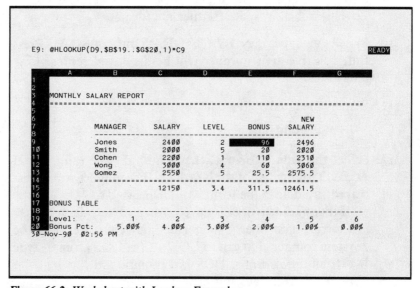

Figure 66.2: Worksheet with Lookup Formula

*H*ow to Use the @DATE and @NOW Functions

Date and time functions were explained in Lesson 59. They allow you to perform calculations based on dates and times. With date and time functions you can subtract one date from another, average among dates, add dates, and so on.

To use the @DATE function, follow it with the year, month, and day: @DATE(90,1,10). To use the @TIME function, follow it with the hour, minute, and second: @TIME(10:10:10). @NOW does not require any date or time elements; it generates the current date and time: @NOW.

In the following steps you will enter the date-of-hire for each manager, then use it to determine whether a manager is eligible for a bonus. Assuming that a manager must work for two months, or 60 days, before becoming eligible for a bonus, the formula must subtract the hire date from today's date. If a manager has worked more than 60 days, he is included in the lookup operation to calculate his bonus.

9. Move to column A and widen it with **Worksheet Column** to 12. This will allow space for the date format.

10. In cell A5, type: @NOW (@TODAY for Lotus 1A). Press Enter. A five-digit number will be displayed representing today's date.

11. Display the number in a date format. Type:

    /Range Format Date

12. Select the 1 date format, then highlight the range from A5..A13 for the rest of the hire dates. The number will be displayed as a date in the format of DD-MM-YY.

    (If today's date is not displayed, you probably did not enter the correct date when you started your computer. Use the **/System** command to exit to DOS. At the DOS prompt, type **DATE** and press Enter. DOS will prompt you for the date. Type the correct date and press Enter. At the DOS prompt type **EXIT** followed by the Enter key to return to 1-2-3.)

13. Now that the column is formatted for dates, enter the hire dates for each manager.

in A9   **@DATE(84,7,12)**

in A10   **@DATE(84,2,11)**

in A11   use the **@DATE** function to type in the date for one month ago, using the format above

in A12   type in the date for one week ago

in A13   type in the date for yesterday

Refer to Figure 66.3.

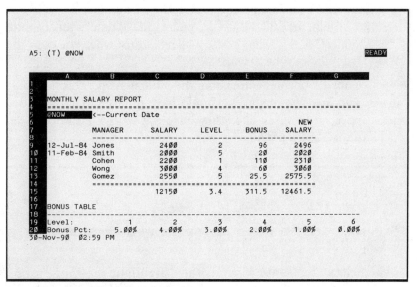

```
A5: (T) @NOW                                                              READY

        A          B          C          D          E          F         G
1
2
3   MONTHLY SALARY REPORT
4   ================================================================
5   @NOW      <--Current Date
6                                                              NEW
7             MANAGER    SALARY     LEVEL      BONUS      SALARY
8             ---------------------------------------------------
9   12-Jul-84 Jones      2400       2          96         2496
10  11-Feb-84 Smith      2000       5          20         2020
11            Cohen      2200       1          110        2310
12            Wong       3000       4          60         3060
13            Gomez      2550       5          25.5       2575.5
14            ================================================================
15                       12150      3.4        311.5      12461.5
16
17  BONUS TABLE
18  ---------------------------------------------------------------
19  Level:            1          2          3          4          5          6
20  Bonus Pct:    5.00%      4.00%      3.00%      2.00%      1.00%      0.00%
    30-Nov-90  02:59 PM
```

Figure 66.3: Worksheet with Dates

How to Use the @IF Function

The @IF function allows you to make decisions within formulas. If a condition is true, then do option 1; otherwise do option 2. The format of the @IF function is:

@IF(condition, option 1, option 2)

Lesson 66

Use the @IF function in this worksheet to determine whether a manager is eligible for a bonus based on whether his date of hire is 60 days or more from today's date. If a manager's date of hire is fewer than 60 days from today, then there is no bonus; otherwise use the @HLOOKUP function to calculate the bonus, as earlier.

14. Use the Edit key, F2, to edit the formula in E9, the first Bonus formula, to read as follows:

    @IF($A$5-A9<60,0,@HLOOKUP(D9,$B$19..$G$20,1)*C9)

    There are no spaces in the formula. This formula states: If today's date (A5) minus the hire date (A9) is less than 60 days, then the bonus amount is 0, otherwise calculate the Bonus amount by using the @HLOOKUP formula.

    Again, the dollar signs designate today's date as an absolute value. Cell A5, today's date, will not adjust when you copy the formula into the cells below.

15. Copy the formula down into the other managers' bonus cells. The first two managers should have bonuses. The last three have no bonuses since they have not worked more than 60 days. See Figure 66.4.

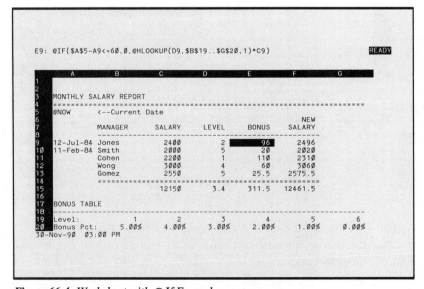

Figure 66.4: Worksheet with @If Formula

16. Experiment with several other functions in column G.
    Calculate the number of employees with @COUNT(range)
    Calculate the highest paid employee with @MAX(range)
    Calculate the lowest paid employee with @MIN(range)
    Calculate the average salary with @AVG(range)
    These functions are entered like @SUM(range).

A

C

B

3

1

1

2

2

Part
Eight

The Allways
Spreadsheet Publisher

3

LESSON

67

Allways Spreadsheet Publishing

FEATURING

/ Add-In
Allways commands
Allways GRAPH (F10) key
Allways WINDOW (F6) key

1-2-3 Release 2.2 includes Allways, a spreadsheet-publishing add-in program designed to enhance 1-2-3 reports. Some of the things you can do with Allways are:

- Combine a worksheet with mulitiple graphs in one report

- Use up to eight different fonts (typefaces) in a report

- Draw lines and boxes

- Shade areas of the worksheet

- Print the worksheet in different colors if you have a color printer or plotter

An example of an Allways report is in Figure 67.1.

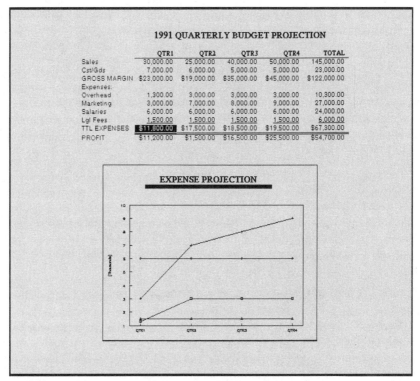

1991 QUARTERLY BUDGET PROJECTION

	QTR1	QTR2	QTR3	QTR4	TOTAL
Sales	30,000.00	25,000.00	40,000.00	50,000.00	145,000.00
Cst/Gds	7,000.00	6,000.00	5,000.00	5,000.00	23,000.00
GROSS MARGIN	$23,000.00	$19,000.00	$35,000.00	$45,000.00	$122,000.00
Expenses:					
Overhead	1,300.00	3,000.00	3,000.00	3,000.00	10,300.00
Marketing	3,000.00	7,000.00	8,000.00	9,000.00	27,000.00
Salaries	6,000.00	6,000.00	6,000.00	6,000.00	24,000.00
Lgl Fees	1,500.00	1,500.00	1,500.00	1,500.00	6,000.00
TTL EXPENSES	$11,800.00	$17,500.00	$18,500.00	$19,500.00	$67,300.00
PROFIT	$11,200.00	$1,500.00	$16,500.00	$25,500.00	$54,700.00

EXPENSE PROJECTION

Figure 67.1: An Allways Report

Allways is one of several add-in programs that come with 1-2-3
Release 2.2. Add-in programs allow you to accomplish tasks that
1-2-3 itself is not able to do. Add-ins are run from within 1-2-3 and
usually have similar commands. Additional add-ins are available
from Lotus Development Corporation and other software vendors.
Some of these programs allow you to do word processing, build rela-
tional databases, create three-dimensional graphs, and print a 1-2-3
worksheet sideways. Add-in programs are *attached* to 1-2-3 using the
/Add-In command.

Allways formats a 1-2-3 worksheet only. You do not enter text,
numbers, or formulas using Allways. For this reason, you must first
create your worksheet and graphs in 1-2-3, then use Allways to complete them.

In order to display worksheets and graphs in Allways the same way as they will print out, you must have a monochrome graphics or color graphics monitor. If you do not, Allways worksheets will look like 1-2-3 on the screen, without showing formatting and fonts and without showing worksheets and graphs combined. If you have a color monitor, you can use Allways to display your work in different colors.

In addition to the standard 1-2-3 cell formats, such as currency and percentage, Allways provides additional formats. They include: different fonts (Allways includes Courier, Times, and Triumvirate—similar to Helvetica), boldface, underlining, coloring, shading, and lines around cells.

It is important that you keep Allways attached to 1-2-3 when you are working with worksheets that you have set up using Allways because changes you make using Allways are saved in a separate file with the extension .ALL, not in your worksheet file (.WK1). If you use 1-2-3 to modify your worksheet when Allways is not attached, this special file will not be updated, and formatting that you have done with Allways will be disrupted or lost.

Because Allways settings are stored in a separate file from the worksheet, UNDO (F4) is not available for certain operations in 1-2-3 when Allways is attached. These include /Move, /Worksheet Insert and Delete, and /File Save and Retrieve.

In order to print graphs using Allways, you must first create and save them using 1-2-3's /Graph commands. Then use Allways to add titles or shading, change fonts, change the format of text and numbers, or combine a graph with a worksheet.

In order to complete this lesson, you should be familiar with Part 2, "Building a Worksheet," and Part 4, "Graphing the Worksheet."

*H*ow to Use Allways

To Attach and Invoke Allways

1. If you are not running 1-2-3 on a hard-disk system, place the Install disk in one of the floppy drives.

2. In Lotus 1-2-3, select /**Add-In Attach**. See Figure 67.2.

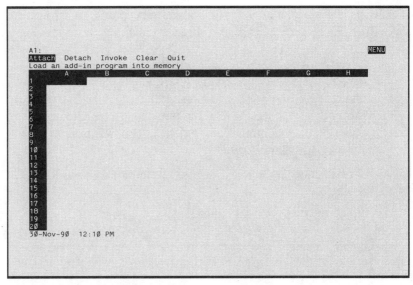

Figure 67.2: */Add-In Menu*

The Add-In Menu

- **Attach** brings an add-in into memory and makes it available to be used with 1-2-3.

- **Detach** erases an add-in program from memory.

- **Invoke** activates one of the attached add-ins.

- **Clear** erases all add-ins from memory.

- **Quit** returns to the READY mode.

You will see a list of add-in programs ending in .ADN. If you don't see the ALLWAYS.ADN, specify the disk and/or directory that contains the .ADN file. Press Escape, if necessary, to clear the current file names and type the disk and/or directory name. Then press Enter.

If the Allways files do not exist on your disk, refer to Lesson 5 to install Allways.

3. Select **ALLWAYS.ADN**.

If Allways is already attached, you will get a beep and an error message. Press Escape in that case and skip steps 4 and 5.

4. Specify which function key combination you want to use to invoke the add-in program. There are a maximum of five choices: No-Key, 7 (Alt-F7), 8 (Alt-F8), 9 (Alt-F9), 10 (Alt-F10). (You will have to use the /Add-in menu to invoke Allways if you choose no key-combination.) Select **8**. This will reserve Alt-F8 for use with Allways.

5. When Allways is attached, select **Quit** to return to the READY mode.

6. Press **Alt-F8** to invoke Allways. See Figure 67.3.

```
FONT(1) Triumvirate 10 pt                                    ALLWAYS
A2:

            A          B          C          D          E          F
1  1991 QUARTERLY BUDGET PROJECTION
2
3                   QTR1       QTR2       QTR3       QTR4       TOTAL
4  ******************************************************************
5  Sales        30,000.00  25,000.00  40,000.00  50,000.00  145,000.00
6  Cst/Gds       7,000.00   6,000.00   5,000.00   5,000.00   23,000.00
7
8  GROSS MARGIN $23,000.00 $19,000.00 $35,000.00 $45,000.00 $122,000.00
9
10 Expenses:
11 Overhead      1,300.00   3,000.00   3,000.00   3,000.00   10,300.00
12 Marketing     3,000.00   7,000.00   8,000.00   9,000.00   27,000.00
13 Salaries      6,000.00   6,000.00   6,000.00   6,000.00   24,000.00
14 Lgl Fees      1,500.00   1,500.00   1,500.00   1,500.00    6,000.00
15
16 TTL EXPENSES $11,800.00 $17,500.00 $18,500.00 $19,500.00  $67,300.00
17
18 PROFIT       $11,200.00  $1,500.00 $16,500.00 $25,500.00  $54,700.00
19
20
30-Nov-90  12:40 PM
```

Figure 67.3: Allways Worksheet in Text Mode

Note that instead of READY, the mode indicator in the right corner of the screen now displays ALLWAYS. In the top left of the screen, the format of the current cell is displayed, including some or all of the following: font, text color, boldface, underline, shade, or lines. The default setting for each cell is: *FONT (1) Triumvirate 10 pt*.

7. Return to 1-2-3 by pressing the Escape key (or Alt-F8 again). READY will reappear.

8. Invoke Allways again with **Alt-F8**.

9. There are two way of viewing worksheets in Allways: in text mode and in graphics mode. Graphics mode is most like the final printout will be. Graphics mode has a light background with darker text. See Figure 67.4 for a graphics mode sample. Text mode resembles 1-2-3 and is used when you do not have a graphics monitor. Text mode has a black background and light text. See Figure 67.3 for a text mode sample.

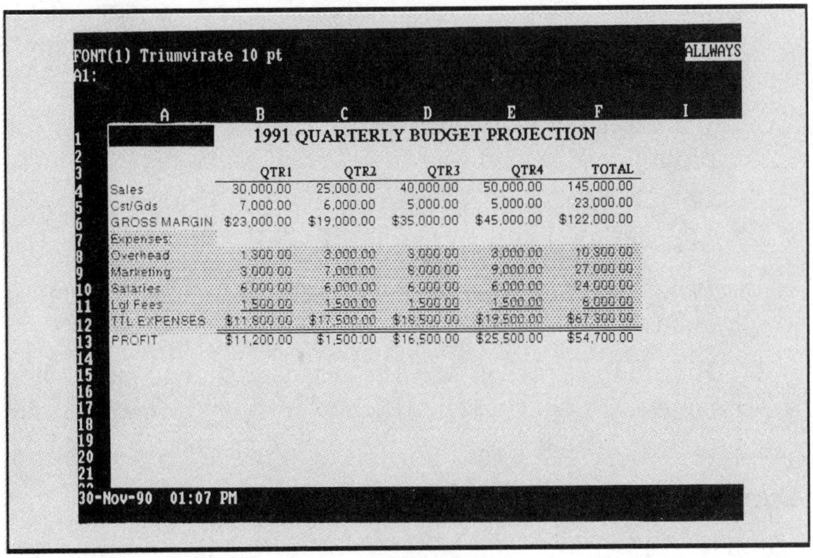

Figure 67.4: Allways Worksheet in Graphics Mode

Press **WINDOW (F6)** to toggle between text and graphics mode. Notice that the text mode resembles 1-2-3 except that instead of READY, ALLWAYS is displayed as the mode indicator. (*Note:* /**Display Mode Graphics** and /**Display Mode Text** will also toggle between the two modes.) If possible, stay in graphics mode.

10. Return to 1-2-3 by pressing Escape.

To attach Allways automatically each time you start 1-2-3, refer to the end of this lesson.

Preparing the Worksheet

Because Allways displays the worksheet differently than 1-2-3, it is often useful to make some minor changes before working with Allways. The sample worksheet used in Lesson 6, **91BUDGET,** has blank rows to separate the detail from the totals. You will delete them and use lines instead in Allways. In addition, you will also move the worksheet title in order to center it.

11. Use **/Worksheet Delete Row** to delete the blank rows below the Cst/Gds, GROSS MARGIN, Lgl Fees, and TTL EXPENSES. Also delete the row beneath the QTR headings, with the asterisks.

12. Use **/Range Erase** to erase any other numbers below the profit line, if needed.

13. Move the title from A1 to D1. Go to A1 and select **/Move**. This will allow Allways to center it later.

14. Use **/Range Label Center** to change the format of the title cell in D1.

15. Hide the column with the percentage figures and pie shading numbers, columns G and H. Use **/Worksheet Column Hide**. Press the Home key when you are through. See Figure 67.5.

Creating a Graph

Graphs are created in 1-2-3 before formatting them in Allways. Create a line graph of the expenses for the four quarters. Each Expenses category will be a separate line on the graph.

16. Select **/Graph Reset Graph** to clear any current graph settings.

17. In the Graph menu, select **Group**. This allows you to specify multiple graph ranges at one time.

18. Specify the range B7..E11. When you use **/Graph Group** the first row of the range is always the X-range. The first row consists of blank cells now, but you will correct it later. The remaining rows or columns (up to a total of six) are assigned A through E graph ranges.

19. Select **Rowwise**. This will cause the rows to be plotted as the data ranges. The data ranges are displayed in the settings sheet.

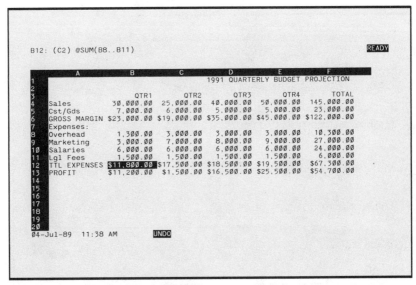

Figure 67.5: Altered Budget Worksheet

20. Select **X** to correct the X-range for the graph.

21. Instead of B7..E7, specify the cells with QTR: **B3..E3**.

22. Select **View**. Two Expenses should be increasing and two should be "flat" (see Figure 67.6). /**Graph Group** chooses the line graph type by default.

23. Press any key to return to the Graph menu.

Next set up legends, and x- and y-titles for the graph.

24. In the Graph menu, use **Options Legend Range** to set the legend range to **A8..A11**. The settings sheet will reflect the four legends. **A8** instructs 1-2-3 to use the cell contents of A8 for the legend.

25. **Quit** the Options menu.

26. In the Graph menu, use **Save** to save the graph as a .PIC file. Give it the name **EXPENSES**.

27. Leave the Graph menu with Escape or **Quit** and save the file with /**File Save Replace** or **Backup**.

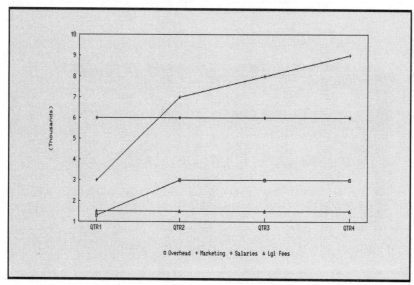

Figure 67.6: Line Graph of Expenses

To Format a Worksheet with Allways

Now that the basic graph has been built in 1-2-3, you can add formatting to it using Allways.

28. Invoke Allways with **Alt-F8**.

29. Press the / (slash) key. Allways uses the same command key as 1-2-3. You may also use < (Shift comma). Figure 67.7 shows the Allways main menu.

Use the Allways menus the same way as 1-2-3 menus; that is, either press the first letter of the command or move the pointer to the command and press Enter.

To Widen a Column

Because Allways displays the worksheet differently than 1-2-3, one of the labels is cut off in column A. Use **/Worksheet Column** to widen the column.

30. Select **/Worksheet**.

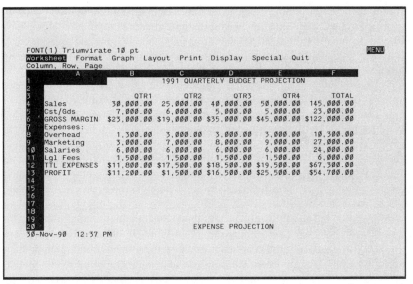

Figure 67.7: Allways Main Menu

The Allways Menu

- **Worksheet** allows you to alter the width of columns and the height of rows by fractions of a character or row. In addition, it allows you to place a page break at a row or column.

- **Format** allows you to assign fonts, boldface, underlining, shading, and lines around cells.

- **Graph** adds or deletes 1-2-3 graphs from the Allways worksheet and alters graph settings.

- **Layout** sets the page size, margins, headers and footers.

- **Print** sets the print range, changes print settings, and prints the worksheet.

- **Display** controls how worksheets and graphs display on the screen.

- **Special** allows you to copy, move, and import Allways cell formats. You can also justify labels.

- **Quit** exits the Allways menu.

The Worksheet Menu

- **Column** adjusts the width of a column or columns. Unlike 1-2-3, you can adjust widths by a fraction of a character.

- **Row** adjusts the height of a row or rows by fractions of a row. These two commands allow you to adjust horizontally and vertically for different character fonts.

- **Page** inserts a page break at either a row or column.

31. In column A, select **Column Set-width 14**.

To Format a Cell

32. Move to D1 to format the title of the worksheet. Notice how centered labels are displayed in Allways. They do not align on the left as in 1-2-3.

33. Select /**Format**. See Figure 67.8.

34. Select /**Font**. See Figure 67.9.

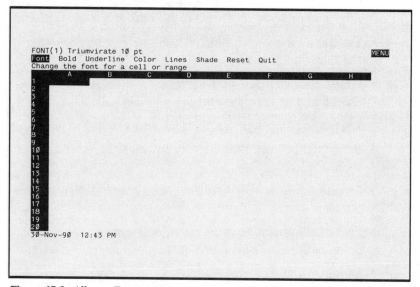

Figure 67.8: Allways Format Menu

The Format Menu

- **Font** changes the typeface and size of the text and numbers on your worksheet.

- **Bold** allows you to darken cell entries.

- **Underline** will place single or double underlines beneath a range of cells.

- **Lines** surrounds a range of cells with an outline or creates lines on the top, bottom, or sides of a cell.

- **Color** prints your worksheet in different colors if you have a color printer.

- **Shade** will shade cells in light or dark shadings, or create a solid black box or line.

- **Reset** removes all formatting from a range, setting it back to Font 1.

- **Quit** exits the menu.

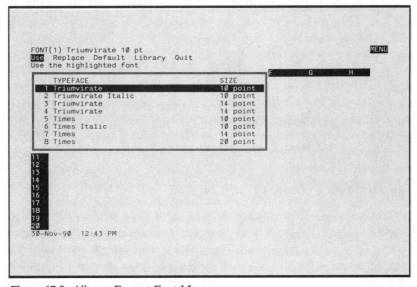

Figure 67.9: Allways Format Font Menu

The /Format Font Menu

- **/Format Font** displays a pulldown menu of eight fonts. These eight fonts make up the default *font set*. You can change any of these fonts, or replace the entire font set with another that you have previously created. The first font, Font 1, is the default format for all cells in the worksheet. To change the default font, replace the font in Font 1 (Triumviate—similar to Helvetica) with another font. Additional fonts are available with Allways and built into your printer. Multiple font sets are stored in a font set library.

- **Use** allows you to pick one of the eight fonts to format a cell or cells.

- **Replace** displays another menu of *soft fonts* that come with Allways and the fonts that come with your printer. You can use the soft fonts or the printer fonts to replace one of the eight fonts in the font set.

- **Default** makes the current font set the default set, or vice versa.

- **Library** saves a font set to or retrieves a font set from the font set library.

- **Quit** exits the Format Font menu.

35. Move the pointer down the font set menu to **Times 14 point**. Press Enter twice to change the font for the title in D1.

36. Select **/Format Bold Set** and press Enter.

To Highlight a Range in Allways

Unlike 1-2-3, Allways allows you to highlight a range *before* selecting a command. This allows you to perform several operations without specifying the range each time. When you are through with the command press Escape, or move the cursor, to get rid of the highlight.

The next steps will change the font, underline, and darken the column headings.

37. Move the pointer to B3 (Qtr1).

38. Press the period key to anchor the cell, then move to **F3**. The cells will be highlighted. Do not move the cursor at this point.

39. Select **/Format Font**. You can select commands while a range is highlighted.

40. Move down to **Times 10 point** and press Enter to change the headings from Triumvirate to Times typeface. The range remains highlighted.

41. Without moving the pointer, select **/Format Bold Set** to make the heading darker. The range remains highlighted.

42. Select **/Format Lines Bottom** to underline the headings. The range remains highlighted.

43. Move to **B11** to highlight a new range. Moving to B11 causes the prior highlighting to disappear so that you can highlight a new range.

44. Press the period key and move to **F11** to highlight the range.

45. Select **/Format Underline Single** to underline the Expenses rows.

46. Move to **B12**. The highlight at B11..F11 disappears.

47. Press a period and move to **F12** to highlight a new range.

48. Select **/Format Underline Double** to underline the TTL EXPENSES row. See Figure 67.10.

To Shade a Portion of the Worksheet

Shading allows you to emphasize part of a worksheet in either light or dark shading. In addition, you can use shading to draw solid black lines and bars. The next steps will shade the Expenses section of the worksheet.

49. Move to **A7** to change the cell shading there. The highlighting will disappear.

Lesson 67

FONT(1) Triumvirate 10 pt Dbl-Underline   ALLWAYS
B12: @SUM(B8..B11)

	A	B	C	D	E	F	I
1		1991 QUARTERLY BUDGET PROJECTION					
2							
3		QTR1	QTR2	QTR3	QTR4	TOTAL	
4	Sales	30,000.00	25,000.00	40,000.00	50,000.00	145,000.00	
5	Cst/Gds	7,000.00	6,000.00	5,000.00	5,000.00	23,000.00	
6	GROSS MARGIN	$23,000.00	$19,000.00	$35,000.00	$45,000.00	$122,000.00	
7	Expenses:						
8	Overhead	1,300.00	3,000.00	3,000.00	3,000.00	10,300.00	
9	Marketing	3,000.00	7,000.00	8,000.00	9,000.00	27,000.00	
10	Salaries	6,000.00	6,000.00	6,000.00	6,000.00	24,000.00	
11	Lgl Fees	1,500.00	1,500.00	1,500.00	1,500.00	6,000.00	
12	TTL EXPENSES	$11,800.00	$17,500.00	$18,500.00	$19,500.00	$67,300.00	
13	PROFIT	$11,200.00	$1,500.00	$16,500.00	$25,500.00	$54,700.00	
14							
15							
16							
17							
18							
19							
20							
21							

30-Nov-90 01:09 PM

Figure 67.10: Formatted Budget

50. Select **/Format Shade Light**. Press Enter to shade A7.

51. Move to **A8**.

52. Press the period key to anchor at A8.

53. Move to **F12** to highlight the Expenses labels and numbers.

54. Select **/Format Shade Light** to shade the worksheet. Move the pointer to view the shading.

To Add a Graph to the Worksheet

Allways allows you to combine worksheets and graphs. You can add up to 20 graphs to a worksheet. (Before adding a graph in Allways, you must have created one in 1-2-3. You have already created and saved a graph called **EXPENSES**.)

55. At any location, select **/Graph**. See Figure 67.11.

56. Select **Add**. A list of all .PIC files in the directory is displayed. To look at another directory or drive, press Escape to clear the current file names and type the disk and/or directory name. Press Enter.

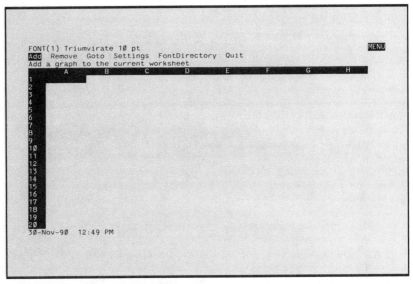

Figure 67.11: *Allways Graph Menu*

The Graph Menu

- **Add** adds a graph to the Allways worksheet.

- **Remove** deletes a graph from the worksheet. It does not remove it from 1-2-3 or from the disk.

- **Goto** moves the pointer to a graph on the worksheet.

- **Settings** designates the range, fonts, colors, scaling, and margins of the graph.

- **FontDirectory** allows you to specify the directory that contains the graph font files.

- **Quit** exits the Graph menu.

57. Select **EXPENSES.PIC** to select a graph file.

58. Specify the range on the worksheet in which to display the graph. Type in or highlight: **B22..F40**.

59. **Quit** the Graph menu.

60. Press the Page Down key. Allways will display crosshatching where the graph is located. Press **GRAPH (F10)** to view the graph. See Figure 67.12.

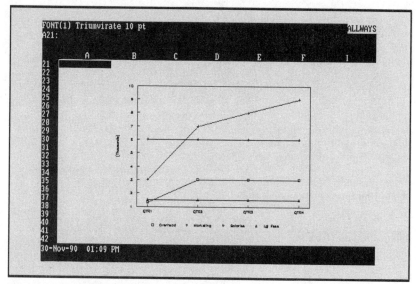

Figure 67.12: Allways Worksheet with Graph

To Format the Graph

While graph titles can be created using the **/Graph Title** command in 1-2-3, Allways provides more options for fonts. In the next steps you will enter a graph title in 1-2-3 and then format it using Allways. Entering text and numbers is always done in 1-2-3.

61. Move the pointer to **D20**. You will place a title for the graph here.

62. Press Escape (or **Alt-F8**) to return to 1-2-3.

63. Enter **^EXPENSE PROJECTION** to create a graph title.

64. Return to Allways: **Alt-F8**.

65. Press the period key to anchor the cell D20.

66. Use **/Format Font** to set the font to **Times 14 point**.

67. Make the graph title bold with **/Format Bold Set**.

68. Move to cell **C21**. This undoes the highlight.

To Create a Solid Black Bar

By varying the height of a row, you can alter the thickness of a line.

69. Create the solid bar with **/Format Shade Solid**.

70. Specify the range as **C21..E21**.

71. Make the height of row 21 smaller. Use **/Worksheet Row Set-height**.

72. Move the pointer up until the point size is **5**, then press Enter.

To Create a Box

73. Use **/Format Lines Outline**.

74. Set the range to **B19..F41** to specify the range to create a box around. See Figure 67.13.

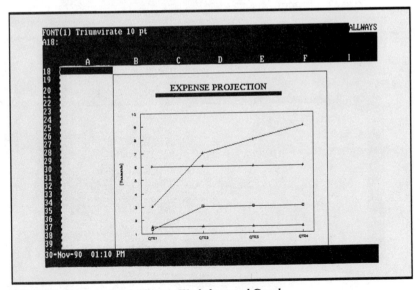

Figure 67.13: *Formatted Allways Worksheet and Graph*

To Save the Allways Settings

75. Press Escape to exit Allways and return to 1-2-3.

76. Select /**File Save** to save the worksheet and the Allways settings.

If you make changes to the **EXPENSES** graph in 1-2-3, you will have to save them with /Graph Save before the graph in Allways will change.

To Print the Worksheet and Graph in Allways

77. Select /**Print**. See Figure 67.14.

78. Select **Configuration**.

79. Select **Printer**. A list of installed printers is displayed.

80. Move the pointer to select the printer that you are using. If the correct printer is not listed, leave Allways, save this file, and refer to the Allways installation instructions for adding printers in the manual.

81. When the printer is selected, press Escape to return to the initial Print menu.

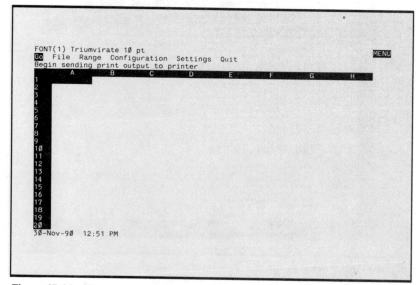

Figure 67.14: *Allways Print Menu*

The Print Menu

- **Go** instructs Allways to print the range specified.
- **File** prints the worksheet and graph to a file for later printing.
- **Range** specifies which cells to print.
- **Configuration** contains the commands for selecting which printer to use and changing the settings on that printer.
- **Settings** controls the page numbering, number of copies, and printer pause.
- **Quit** exits the Print menu.

82. Select **Range Set**.

83. Specify a print range of: **A1..F41**.

84. Select **Go** to print the worksheet and graph.

To Attach Allways Permanently

85. In the 1-2-3 READY mode, select /**Worksheet Global Default Other Add-in**. See Figure 67.15.

86. Select **Set**.

87. Select **1** if it is not in use already. Otherwise select another number. If there are ∗.ADN files in the current directory they will be displayed.

88. Select **ALLWAYS.ADN**.

89. Choose the key to use to invoke Allways. Select **8** or one of the other numbers.

90. Select **No**. Do not automatically invoke Allways at this point. Otherwise, each time you started 1-2-3, the Allways menu would appear first.

91. To save the settings permanently, in the **Worksheet Global Default** menu, select **Update**.

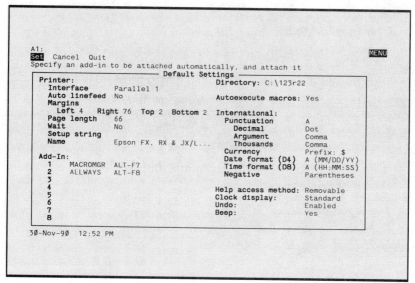

Figure 67.15: 1-2-3 Global Default Menu

Index

Selections from The SYBEX Library

SPREADSHEETS AND INTEGRATED SOFTWARE

The ABC's of 1-2-3 (Second Edition)
Chris Gilbert/Laurie Williams
245pp. Ref. 355-4

Online Today recommends it as "an easy and comfortable way to get started with the program." An essential tutorial for novices, it will remain on your desk as a valuable source of ongoing reference and support. For Release 2.

Mastering 1-2-3 (Second Edition)
Carolyn Jorgensen
702pp. Ref. 528-X

Get the most from 1-2-3 Release 2 with this step-by-step guide emphasizing advanced features and practical uses. Topics include data sharing, macros, spreadsheet security, expanded memory, and graphics enhancements.

Lotus 1-2-3 Desktop Companion (SYBEX Ready Reference Series)
Greg Harvey
976pp. Ref. 501-8

A full-time consultant, right on your desk. Hundreds of self-contained entries cover every 1-2-3 feature, organized by topic, indexed and cross-referenced, and supplemented by tips, macros and working examples. For Release 2.

Advanced Techniques in Lotus 1-2-3
Peter Antoniak/E. Michael Lunsford
367pp. Ref. 556-5

This guide for experienced users focuses on advanced functions, and techniques for designing menu-driven applications using macros and the Release 2 command language. Interfacing techniques and add-on products are also considered.

Lotus 1-2-3 Tips and Tricks
Gene Weisskopf
396pp. Ref. 454-2

A rare collection of timesavers and tricks for longtime Lotus users. Topics include macros, range names, spreadsheet design, hardware considerations, DOS operations, efficient data analysis, printing, data interchange, applications development, and more.

Lotus 1-2-3 Instant Reference SYBEX Prompter Series
Greg Harvey/Kay Yarborough Nelson
296pp. Ref. 475-5; 4 3/4x8

Organized information at a glance. When you don't have time to hunt through hundreds of pages of manuals, turn here for a quick reminder: the right key sequence, a brief explanation of a command, or the correct syntax for a specialized function.

Mastering Symphony (Fourth Edition)
Douglas Cobb
857pp. Ref. 494-1

Thoroughly revised to cover all aspects of the major upgrade of Symphony Version 2, this Fourth Edition of Doug Cobb's classic is still "the Symphony bible" to this complex but even more powerful package. All the new features are discussed and placed in context with prior versions so that both new and previous users will benefit from Cobb's insights.

SYBEX Computer Books
are different.

Here is why . . .

At SYBEX, each book is designed with you in mind. Every manuscript is carefully selected and supervised by our editors, who are themselves computer experts. We publish the best authors, whose technical expertise is matched by an ability to write clearly and to communicate effectively. Programs are thoroughly tested for accuracy by our technical staff. Our computerized production department goes to great lengths to make sure that each book is well-designed.

In the pursuit of timeliness, SYBEX has achieved many publishing firsts. SYBEX was among the first to integrate personal computers used by authors and staff into the publishing process. SYBEX was the first to publish books on the CP/M operating system, microprocessor interfacing techniques, word processing, and many more topics.

Expertise in computers and dedication to the highest quality product have made SYBEX a world leader in computer book publishing. Translated into fourteen languages, SYBEX books have helped millions of people around the world to get the most from their computers. We hope we have helped you, too.

For a complete catalog of our publications:

SYBEX, Inc. 2021 Challenger Drive, #100, Alameda, CA 94501
Tel: (415) 523-8233/(800) 227-2346   Telex: 336311
Fax: (415) 523-2373

*L*otus 1-2-3 Function Keys

Key	Function
F1 (HELP)	Provides on-line help.
F2 (EDIT)	Used to edit the current cell.
F3 (NAME)	In POINT mode, displays a listing of range names
F4 (ABS)	In POINT or EDIT mode, changes relative cell reference to mixed or absolute references.
F5 (GOTO)	Moves cell pointer to a specified cell.
F6 (WINDOW)	Moves cell pointer between the two screen windows. In MENU mode, turns Settings sheet on and off.
F7 (QUERY)	Repeats last data query operation. In FIND mode, switches between FIND and READY modes.
F8 (TABLE)	Repeats last data table operation.
F9 (CALC)	Recalculates all formulas in worksheet.
F10 (GRAPH)	Displays the current graph.
Alt-F1 (COMPOSE)	When used with alphanumeric keys in READY, EDIT, and LABEL modes, creates characters that cannot be direcly entered from keyboard.
Alt-F2 (STEP)	Activates STEP mode, which executes macros step-by-step for debugging purposes.
Alt-F3 (RUN)	In READY mode, displays range names from which to select name of macro to be run.
Alt-F4 (UNDO)	In READY mode, cancels alterations in worksheet made since 1-2-3 was last in READY mode. Pressing UNDO again will restore changes.
Alt-F5 (LEARN)	Activates Learn feature.
Alt-F7	
Alt-F8	In READY mode, activates add-in program if one has been assigned to the the key.
Alt-F9	
Alt-F10	In READY mode, displays Add-In menu or activates add-in program assigned to key.